Links to Our Legacy

Insights into Hebrew, History, and Liturgy

Mitchell First

KODESH PRESS

LINKS TO OUR LEGACY:
Insights into Hebrew, History, and Liturgy

Hardcover ISBN: 978-1-947857-65-0
Paperback ISBN: 978-1-947857-66-7

PUBLISHED AND DISTRIBUTED EXCLUSIVELY BY
Kodesh Press LLC
New York, NY
www.kodeshpress.com
kodeshpress@gmail.com

Set in Minion Pro by Raphaël Freeman MISTD, Renana Typesetting

Printed in the United States of America

Sponsors

The author would like to express his appreciation to the following individuals for their generous donations which helped fund the publication of this book:

Dr. Atara Breliner, in memory of her parents
Rabbi Albert Berliner and Marilyn Berliner, *z"l*,
who devoted their lives to Torah education

Patty and Sam Borodach, in memory of Patty's parents,
Seymour and Pauline Madow, *z"l*

Arielle and Chanan Cohen,
in memory of Chanan's father
Michael R. Cohen, *z"l*

Michele and Dr. Ben Cooper

Dean Rachel and Allen Friedman

Roz and Ira Friedman, in loving memory of their parents,
David J. & Rose Anne Friedman, *z"l*,
and Abraham & Charlotte Remer, *z"l*

Ellen and Dr. Richard Gertler

Dr. Elliot Goldofsky

Amy and Ziggy Hirsch

Altie Karper

Rabbi Avrohom Lieberman

Pearl Neuman and David Schachter,
in honor of their children and grandchildren:
Ariel, Chana, Eitan and Livvy

Aliza and Kal Staiman

Drs. Dora and Zalman Suldan,
in honor of our friend Mitch First
and the light he shines on Torah and Jewish scholarship

Rabbi Simcha Weinberg,
in memory of his sister
Dr. Aviva Weisbord, *z"l*

Dr. Barry Weissman, in honor of his grandchildren:
Ezra, Jakob, and Elan Landa, and Ayla Jaffee

Freya and Richard Wigler, in memory of their parents
Philip & Mollie Wigler, *z"l*,
and Marvin and Naomi Caplan, *z"l*

Barbara and Neal Yaros,
in honor of their grandchildren:
Gavi, Tzvi, Tamar, Liana, Shani, Caleb, and Aiden

The Zell Family

Rabbi Yishmael ben Elisha said: Once I entered the innermost sanctum on Yom Kippur to offer incense, and in a vision I saw the Lord of Hosts seated upon a high and exalted throne. He said to me: Yishmael, My son, bless Me. I said to Him "May it be Your will that Your mercy overcome Your anger… The Holy One, Blessed be He, nodded His head, accepting the blessing. (Berakhot 7a.)

Rebecca and Josh Teplow,
in honor of our dear children
Joe, Avery and Tamara;
in honor of our mother, Miriam Teplow;
and in memory of our parents,
Elaine and Leonard Wacholder, *z"l*,
and Josef Teplow, *z"l*

Preface

I started writing columns for the *Jewish Link* newspaper in 2014. When I began to write my first book collecting sixty-two columns (*Roots and Rituals*, published in 2018), I took a vacation from writing columns for about two months, so I could concentrate on the book.

I always imagined that I would write another book to include columns composed after that. But I thought that I would not be able to do it until I retired from my day job as an attorney. But then I got far ahead in columns. (I was over 40 weeks ahead.) Then came the Covid-19 pandemic which began in March 2020. It was a trying time for the world and of course for the New Jersey-New York area as well.

As a result I could not commute to work in Manhattan and had time to write more *Jewish Link* articles. But I realized that if I got 70 weeks ahead, it would not benefit me. So I took advantage of the additional time that I was unfortunately granted to collect my more recent columns and turn them into a book. (It is not that simple to turn my columns into a book. I improve the weekly columns with additional material, and add more Hebrew and some footnotes.) I am very grateful that I was able to stay in good health throughout.

* * *

As I did in the introduction to *Roots and Rituals*, I would again like to thank Moshe Kinderlehrer, co-founder and co-publisher of the *Jewish Link*, for giving me the opportunity to write regularly for this paper. When I started, I had no idea that I would learn so much from writing these columns and that they would end up as my third and fourth books. These books are the direct result of his faith in me as a writer.

A few months after I started writing for the paper, I realized that I had to write my columns a few weeks in advance. This way, there was no rush each week. There was time to think out each topic carefully, and do the additional research that may be necessary, and to consult with others when necessary. My goal was always not only to produce interesting columns but to produce accurate ones as well.

Writing for the *Jewish Link* was the third time that I was fortunate enough to find a regular place for my writings. My first two opportunities came with the founding of the print journal *Ḥakirah*, and the online site seforimblog.com. With each of these, I had the opportunity to publish relatively long scholarly articles, and these articles ended up forming the basis for my second book, *Esther Unmasked: Solving Eleven Mysteries of the Jewish Holidays and Liturgy* (Kodesh Press, 2015).[1] Then, just when I needed it, along came the *Jewish Link* newspaper, giving me the opportunity to write shorter articles on a wider variety of topics.

---

1. My first book, *Jewish History in Conflict: A Study of the Major Discrepancy Between Rabbinic and Conventional Chronology*, published in 1997, was based on my M.A. paper at the Bernard Revel Graduate School of Yeshiva University.

Acknowledgements

I would like to thank the following individuals who reviewed this book and greatly improved it with their criticisms and suggestions (in alphabetical order): Sam Borodach, Michoel Chalk, Allen Friedman, Ira Friedman, Daniel Klein, and Rabbi Avrohom Lieberman.

In the introductions to my two previous books, I particularly thanked Sam Borodach, Rabbi Ezra Frazer, Allen Friedman, Rabbi Avrohom Lieberman, Meylekh Viswanath and Rabbi Moshe Yasgur for their many years of extensive discussions and sharing of sources with me.

Also very important is my *chavruta* for two decades, Josh Teplow, with whom I have been learning Neviim and Ketuvim. He has provided many ideas and much encouragement.

I have gained much over the years from the *shiurim* and guidance of Rabbi Ephraim Kanarfogel and Rabbi Laurence Rothwachs.

I would also like to acknowledge some of the many others who contributed over the years towards my efforts, either by sharing and discussing particular ideas and sources, or by encouraging me in my research: Joey Adler, Michael Alweis, Ze'ev Atlas, David Barach, Leonard Berkowitz, Lazer Borgen, Menachem Butler, Avi-Gil Chaitovsky, Myron Chaitovsky, Joel Chudow, Chanan Cohen, Ben Cooper, Mollie Fisch, David Fisher, Howard Friedman, Ira Friedman, Rabbi Mordy Friedman, Rachel Friedman, Aharon Gal, David Gertler, Richard Gertler, Jeff Glazer, Rabbi Jay Goldmintz, Elliot Goldofsky, Binyamin Goldstein, Azriel Haimowitz, Shulamis Hes, Dick Harris (of blessed memory), Ziggy Hirsch, Rabbi Aryeh Kaplan, Daniel Klein, Heshie Klein, Rabbi Reuven Chaim Klein,

Rabbi Stephen Knapp, Rabbi Ariel Kopitnikoff, Steve and Abby Leichman, Ari Leifer, Arvin Levine, Josh Levy, Yehiel Levy, Moshe Markovitz, Yaakov Metzger, Yehuda Miller, Jeff Neugroschl, Efraim Palvanov, Rabbi Michael Pariser, Lenny Presby, Rabbi Baruch Price, Michael Rapoport, Moshe Rosenberg, Chanani Sandler, Eli Schaap, David Schachter, Steve Schaffer, Richie Schiffmiller, Fred Schulman, Menachem Shapiro, Mark Siletski, Rob Sperber, Kal Staiman, Zalman Suldan, Nati Sulimanoff, Rabbi Chaim Sunitsky, Josh Waxman, Rabbi Simcha Weinberg, Zvi Weissler, Barry Weissman, Rabbi Richard Wolpoe, Rabbi Benjamin Yablok, Neal Yaros, Joshua Zakheim, Heshey Zelcer, Rabbi Alan Zelenetz, and Ariel Zell.

I would like to thank Rabbi Reuven Chaim Klein of Beitar Illit for his continuing "What's in a Word?" posts, and David Curwin of Efrat for his continuing posts at his site balashon.com. Both of them continually provide me with ideas and material for columns. (In the case of the latter, I would often begin my search on his site for a post on one topic and then accidentally find a post on a completely different topic that was of even more interest, leading me to switch topics!)

I would particularly like to thank Rabbi Simcha Weinberg and Michael Rapoport for their exceptional feedback and encouragement to me on my weekly columns. Also, Leonard Berkowitz, Mollie Fisch, Aharon Gal, Abby Leichman, Jesse Schwartzman, and Kal Staiman provide regular encouragement and feedback.

Over the past several years, Rabbi Moshe Schapiro, Mary Ann Linahan, and Rebekah Shoemake have saved me hundreds of trips to the Yeshiva University library by graciously responding to my requests for sources. I could not have written my weekly columns without their assistance, especially that of Rabbi Schapiro.

I would also like to thank Daniel A. Klein whose 1998 edition of S.D. Luzzatto's commentary on Genesis introduced me to the world of close analysis of the meanings and subtleties of Hebrew roots.

Special thanks to Rabbi Alec Goldstein of Kodesh Press for his third tremendous job of publishing for me. Alec has always been a pleasure to work with. Moreover, he knows ancient languages (better than I do) and has contributed many insights.

I would like to thank my beloved wife Sharon for allowing me to live this additional life as a scholar, outside my legal career, and pursue my research and writing interests.

My previous book was dedicated to my father Harry First who passed away in 2017.

I would like to dedicate this book to my mother, Judge Lee Blech First. At age 92 (or "three times 30," as she likes to say) she is still making parties, arranging *shidduchim* and *shidduch* events, and attending *shiurim*. (Of course, in our recent period, much of this is done over Zoom.) She also regularly posts Instagrams for her many followers. She is an inspiration to us all!

* * *

Please feel free to contact me with comments on any of the topics that I have addressed. I can be reached at MFirstAtty@aol.com. (I still use AOL as it helps me relate to the ancient world!)

Mitchell First
Teaneck, NJ
February 2021

Contents

Hebrew Roots

History

Liturgy

Hebrew Roots

1. אהב: The Meaning of Love

Surely you realize I am not going to write some deep psychological article or catchy saying here.[1] Rather, I am going to discuss the etymology of the Hebrew word אהב.

אהב, with the translation "love," sounds somewhat abstract. Can we find a more concrete meaning that underlay this verb? The relevant article in *Theological Dictionary of the Old Testament* states that there is "insufficient information as to the original meaning of this root," but it then offers some suggestions. One suggestion notes that in Arabic there is a word *habba* that means "breathe heavily, be excited" and theorizes that this was the original meaning of אהב. Another suggestion notes that in Arabic there is a word *ihab* that means "skin, leather." Based on this, the suggestion is made that אהב may have originally had to do with some positive feeling that you felt in your skin and that was then applied to the emotional stimulation that produced it.

There is an interesting use of the word אהבה at Song of Songs 3:9–10. We are told that Solomon made himself an *aperion* (=canopy) of various materials and that it was *ratzuf ahavah*, e.g., inlaid with *ahavah* (from *benot Yerushalayim*). Many have suggested that *ahavah* has a concrete meaning here and that it was perhaps that "leather" meaning.

Surprisingly, the Koehler-Baumgartner lexicon gives prominence to the "breathe heavily, be excited" suggestion as the etymology of

1. For example, in my generation, there was a saying: "Love means never having to say you're sorry."

אהב.[2] It does not mention any other. It could easily have said that the etymology was "uncertain," as it does many times. In general, evidence from Arabic is only from the time of the Quran (early 7th century CE) and later. It is not that probative on meanings of words in *Tanakh*.[3]

Now, I have a further question. Can we find a more concrete meaning for the verb שׂנא =hate? Perhaps if we cannot find one there, this might indicate that our search for a more concrete meaning in the case of אהב is unnecessary.

* * *

A common *devar Torah* that is given at wedding celebrations is that the word אהב is related to the word הב =give. I.e., the foundation of "love" is giving to one another.[4] Is there a legitimate etymological basis for this beautiful idea?

It is generally agreed that the root of הב, הבה,הבו and הבי with their "give" meaning is יהב.[5] All these are just command forms.[6] In Hebrew, the first root letter sometimes drops in the command form. This is what happened here.[7] יהב is of course different from אהב. Since the words for "love" and "give" have two different three-letter roots, they are probably not related.[8]

---

2. It also surprisingly agrees that the *ahavah* of Song of Songs 3:10 means "leather."

3. Evidence from South Arabian inscriptions would be more convincing. They at least come from the (late) biblical period.

4. Rav S.R. Hirsch is one who makes this connection. See his comm. to Gen. 37:4. He also connects שׂנא to thorn (סנה). With regard to אהב, I should also mention that *Sifrei* 89 seems to assume that it is related to אבה=desire. This is followed by Rashi on Deut. 13:9. (I would like to thank Rabbi David Dombrowski for the *Sifrei* and Rashi references.)

5. In the Hebrew sections of *Tanakh*, הב, הבה, הבו, and הבי appear over 30 times, yet a form with the initial root letter *yod* only appears once, at Ps. 55:23: יהבך. In contrast, in the Aramaic sections of *Tanakh* (portions of Daniel and Ezra), יהב appears twenty-seven times in forms with initial *yod*.

6. Several biblical verses with הבו (=ascribe/give!, plural command form) are recited regularly in our prayers. Most prominent is Deut. 32:3 which is recited at the beginning of every *Amidah* for *Minḥah*.

7. Another example is the command קח =take, from לקח.

8. I am hesitant to definitively reject the connection between אהב and יהב because in essay #14, I was willing to relate words with those same initial letters

(But note that when the **first two** letters of a root are the same, there is more of a basis to argue that the roots are related. This is because many scholars believe that Semitic languages originally had two letters as their root and the third letter just expressed a variant or modification that was still related to the original root.[9])

* * *

Although I have not found the meaning of "love," I can provide an explanation for the modern Hebrew word עגבניה=tomato. You will see the connection shortly.

The tomato was first brought to Europe from its native South America in the sixteenth century. Initially most Europeans were afraid to eat it and believed it was poisonous, so it was used mainly for decorative purposes. The Italians were the first Europeans to eat it extensively.

For whatever reason, one of the tomato's affects was thought to be as an aphrodisiac. Already in the sixteenth century, we find it referred to in English as a "love apple," and in French as a *pomme d'amour.*

So what was it going to be called in Modern Hebrew? This is how the language columnist Philologos summarizes what happened:[10]

> As Hebrew was being revived as a spoken language in the late 19th century, an argument broke out between two of its great champions and rival word-coiners, Eliezer Ben-Yehuda and Yechiel Michel Pines. Ben-Yehuda wanted to call the tomato a "badura" from Arabic "bandura," which itself is from Italian

(*aleph* and *yod*). I argued for the relationship between ארח and ירח. Of course there the "wander" factor in both words strongly suggested the relationship. At Hos. 4:18 the words אהבו and הבו are found next to one another. But this is probably mere wordplay.

Sometimes it is morally justified to give a *devar Torah* that is not technically true but has an uplifting message. I leave that decision to your discretion.

9. See Eduard Yechezkel Kutscher, *A History of the Hebrew Language* (1984), p. 6. He gives the example of the initial root letters פר. They seem to have an underlying meaning of "divide, break" because many three letter words that begin with פר have this meaning.

10. See his column in the *Forward*, 2/25/09.

> "pomodoro."[11] Pines rejected that as non-Hebraic and came back with "tapu'ah agavim" =love apple, which he then shortened to "agvaniya." To this, Ben-Yehuda countered, correctly arguing that the Hebrew verb "agav" meant to lust, not to love, and suggesting "ahaviya"... For whatever reason... "agvaniya" won out, and generations of Israelis have eaten lust apples ever since."[12]

If you are not familiar with the biblical verb עגב for "lust," this is not surprising. The verb only appears a few times: ten times in the book of Ezekiel and once at Jeremiah 4:30.

However we all should be familiar with the noun עוגב or עגב, a kind of musical instrument. It is perhaps a flute, or pipe, the exact meaning in the *Tanakh* is unclear.[13] This word for a musical instrument appears four times in *Tanakh* and two of these times are well-known to us: Gen. 4:21 (regarding Yuval) and Ps. 150:4 ("praise Him with *minim ve-ugav*"). According to some scholars, the name for this instrument may derive from עגב=lust, due to the sensuous tunes that come from it![14]

But admittedly many do not agree with this etymology for the musical instrument. S.D. Luzzatto (comm. to Gen. 4:21), for example, thinks that עוגב is a shortening from על גב =on the back, related to the position of the musical instrument. The Koehler-Baumgartner lexicon views it as a "flute" and does not mention any connection to "lust." Similar is *Daat Mikra*, comm. to Ps. 150:4.

* * *

---

11. Arabic lacks a letter for the sound "P."

12. There is voluminous interesting material online about the history of tomatoes. For more on the background to the Hebrew word עגבניה, see the post at balashon.com of April 16 2010.

13. In modern Hebrew, it means "organ." *Daat Mikra* explains that this is based on the Greek translation of the word *ugav* at Ps. 150:4.

14. See, e.g., Brown-Driver-Briggs: "possibly... because of sensuous or appealing tones." S. Mandelkern points out that the name for the other instrument, *minim*, also has a sexual connotation! This name for a musical instrument appears only here. For various possible interpretations, see *Daat Mikra* to Ps. 150:4. *Daat Mikra* does not give either *minim* or *ugav* any sexual connotation.

Since I am an attorney, I am going to end this column on a legal note. The tomato, although botanically a fruit (a type of berry), has many of the qualities of a vegetable. This led to a major legal dispute in the U.S. at the end of the nineteenth century. As summarized on Wikipedia (entry "tomato"): "In 1887, U.S. tariff laws imposed a duty on vegetables but not on fruits, causing the tomato's status to become a matter of legal importance. The U.S. Supreme Court settled this controversy on May 10, 1893, by declaring that the tomato is a vegetable, based on the popular definition that classifies vegetables by use – they are generally served with dinner and not dessert. *Nix v. Hedden*, 149 U.S. 304. The holding of this case applies only to the interpretation of the [above tariff]...and the court did not purport to reclassify the tomato for botanical or other purposes." (Of course, we recite *borei pri ha-adamah* on tomatoes, regardless of whether they are botanically considered a "fruit" or a "vegetable." For our purposes, all that matters is that they grow from the ground.)

* * *

Mitchell First is a personal injury attorney and Jewish history scholar. While lustily eating tomatoes, he searches for the meaning of אהב=love.

2. אילת השחר: What is *Ayelet Ha-Shaḥar*? (Psalms 22:1)

Psalms 22:1 reads: "*la-menatzeaḥ al* ***ayelet ha-shaḥar*** *mizmor le-David*." What is the meaning of *ayelet ha-shaḥar*? The phrase is so unclear that Rashi has to offer four interpretations, and Radak suggests five.

Literally, אילת השחר means: "doe of the dawn." A doe is a female deer. A male deer would be an *ayal*. A female deer is an *ayalah*. *Ayelet* is the construct state of *ayalah*. It means "*ayalah* of the..."

There are two times in *Tanakh* where the root איל mean "strength." See Psalms 22:20 and 88:5.[15] Accordingly, some suggest that that the meaning in our verse is something like "strength of the morning."

15. Accordingly, the Targum gives *ayelet* the "strength" meaning at 22:1, translating it as תקוף.

Then we could interpret this with a meaning like "sunrise."[16] But our *ayelet* has a *dagesh* in the *yod*. With the *dagesh*, the meaning is always the "deer/doe" meaning.

An Amora in the Jerusalem Talmud (*Berakhot* 1:1) explains *ayelet ha-shaḥar* by taking the position that the light of morning first appears like two horns on the horizon and then illuminates the entire horizon. He probably means that there is a similarity to the antlers of a deer which branch out in different directions. In this interpretation, the verse is referring to the morning light.[17] But the word used in Psalms 22:1 is *ayelet*, not *ayal*, and female deer, 99% of the time, have no antlers![18] (Of course, a response could be that the verse is speaking about male deer and for some poetic reason chose to use the female form.)

The above Amora also mentions an alternative view that *ayelet* means כוכבתא. כוכבתא literally means "star," but is commonly translated as a reference to the planet Venus.

Could *ayelet ha-shaḥar* have implied "morning star," a common understanding of the term today, based on the Jerusalem Talmud? If a star appears in the morning it is going to look like a dot, not a deer or doe. If we suggest the alternative approach that *ayelet* itself meant "star" here, this is farfetched. Nowhere else in *Tanakh* do *ayal*, *ayalah*, or *ayelet* have such a meaning.

Many interpret *ayelet ha-shaḥar* as a musical instrument. Note for example that Psalms chapter twelve begins as follows: *la-menatzeaḥ al ha-sheminit mizmor le-David*. Most likely, *ha-sheminit* is a musical instrument, one of eight strings. The format of our verse, 22:1, perfectly parallels the format of verse 12:1. But try as I might, I cannot imagine a musical instrument with a name like "doe of the dawn."[19]

---

16. This is the view of R. Saadia Gaon.

17. This statement in the Jerusalem Talmud is best understood in light of a statement at *Yoma* 29a.

18. Female deer only have antlers when they have excess testosterone. This is very rare. Rashi (*Yoma* 29a) points out that *ein karnayim le-nekeivah*.

19. My son Shaya jokingly suggested that it could be a musical instrument that looked like a doe and was used to wake people in the morning!

Rashi and Radak mention a view that the doe symbolizes *Bnei Yisrael* who seek the redemption symbolized by the word *shaḥar*.[20]

The key to solving our problem is the introductory sentence of psalm 56: *la-menatzeaḥ al yonat eilem reḥokim*. There are several possible interpretations of the words *yonat eilem reḥokim*, but most likely the reference is to a dove that is far away and the only issue is the meaning of *eilem* (אלם).[21] A "dove that is far away" cannot possibly be a reference to a musical instrument. The Soncino commentary writes here that it "is doubtless the title of a song to whose melody the Psalm was sung."

This must be the approach we should take to verse 22:1. The introductory sentence is pointing to a well-known song called *ayelet ha-shaḥar* and telling the conductor to use the tune of this song.[22] This approach is taken in the *Encyclopaedia Judaica* (13:1321)[23] and in the Soncino commentary on our verse: "In all probability, the name of a melody to the accompaniment of which the Psalm was to be rendered."[24] Among our Rishonim, Ibn Ezra takes this approach as well, on both verses, 22:1[25] and 56:1.

Although this "tune instruction" approach does not fit the word על perfectly, I can live with it. The entry in the *Encyclopaedia Judaica* takes the position that ***al*** *ayelet ha-shaḥar* may have been the name of the song, but this is unlikely. It is too coincidental that the song at 56:1 would begin with *al* as well. Rather, על is a common word used

20. See further Song of Songs 6:10.

21. As to *eilem*, perhaps it means "silent" or is a reference to a tree. Accordingly, the *EJ* entry suggests "speechless dove far-off" and "dove of the far-off terebinths."

22. As Dr. Richard Gertler suggested to me, in our times it would be as if the instruction said: "to the tune of Mary Had a Little Lamb"!

23. This entry was authored by Nahum Sarna.

24. Robert Alter, *The Book of Psalms* (2007), p. 71, writes that the reference is to "a musical instrument of some sort, or alternately, to a melody." Koehler-Baumgartner, p. 40, has: "beginning of a song?" *Daat Mikra* follows the "tune instruction" interpretation in its main commentary (and suggests that the song is about the morning star) and then offers many other suggestions in the footnote.

25. He thinks that the allusion is to a love song, since that word *ayelet* is used in the expression *ayelet ahavim* at Prov. 5:19.

in those first line instructions in the book of Psalms. Sometimes it is an instruction regarding the specific musical instrument to be used and other times, like here, it can be an instruction with regard to the tune. (For examples of other times where the introductory verse likely refer to a tune, see the introductory verses to chapters 45, 57–59, 60, 69,75, and 80, and the Soncino commentary on each.)

* * *

Here are the four approaches that Rashi had mentioned: (1) the name of a musical instrument, (2) a way of referring to the Israelites, (3) the Sages' homiletical approach that it refers to Esther (see *Yoma* 29a) and (4) strength, citing Menachem Ibn Saruk.

Here are the five approaches that Radak had mentioned: (1) the name of a musical instrument, (2) strength of the morning, implying "sunrise," (3) the name of a morning star, (4) an allusion to David fleeing from Saul, and (5) a way of referring to the Israelites. He preferred the last approach.

Uriel Simon[26] points out that Ibn Ezra wrote two poems based on the theme that Israel is an *ayelet*. But as a commentator, he does not even mention this view in his standard commentary, since it is not at all a plain sense approach.[27]

* * *

Mitchell First is a personal injury attorney and Jewish history scholar. He recalls hearing the line "Doe a deer, a female deer" in the film *The Sound of Music* when he was a little child. That line finally came in handy!

3. אישון: The Little Man in the Eye

The word אישון appears five times in *Tanakh*: at Deuteronomy 32:10, Psalms 17:8, and Proverbs 7:2, 7:9, and 20:20.

Let us look at the first of these occasions. Deut. 32:10 reads: "He

26. *Four Approaches to the Book of Psalms* (1991), p. 240.
27. But Simon points out that he does mention and reject it in an earlier recension of his Psalms commentary.

found him (=the Israelites) in a desert land, in a waste, a howling wilderness. He encompassed him. He gave him understanding. He guarded him like *ishon eino*."

From the context here and in two of the other times *ishon* appears (Ps. 17:8 and Prov. 7:2), it seems to mean "pupil." The pupil of the eye is something that must be guarded carefully, as one's sense of sight depends on it. But why does *ishon* have this meaning? Most likely, it is because if one looks at an eyeball, one sees one's own reflection in a small image in the pupil. There is in effect "a little man" (איש) in the pupil. One can find this explanation in the *Sefer Ha-Shorashim* of Ibn Janaḥ and in the slightly later work with the identical title by Radak.[28] (See also Radak's commentary to Psalms 17:8.)

This interesting etymology is accepted in the scholarly Koehler-Baumgartner lexicon (p. 44).[29] One reason it is accepted is because Arabic too has the image of the "man in the eye." The Arabic word for pupil is: "*insaan-al-ayn*=man of the eye.[30]

What about our English word "pupil"? Same thing! It derives from a Latin word *pupilla* which originally meant "little girl" (from *pupa*= girl). *Pupilla* expanded to its "pupil" meaning because of the tiny image one sees when looking in the eye.[31]

Finally, what is the source of that phrase "apple of the eye"? It turns out that it comes from *Tanakh*, but it is not in the Hebrew of the *Tanakh*. Rather, it is how the King James Bible of 1611 and the earlier English translations translated three of the references to *ishon*,

---

28. Radak also writes that the ון added at the end indicates the smallness of the image seen. But *Daat Mikra* to Psalms 17:8 disagrees on this detail.

Rashi and Ibn Ezra have a different approach to *ishon*. They note that it means "darkness" in two of the five verses. They both agree that it means "pupil" in the other three verses but believe that the "pupil" meaning derived from the "darkness" meaning. As to Rashbam (comm. to Deut. 32:10), he believes that *ishon* refers to the eyelids, because they cover the eyes and make things look dark.

29. See similarly, E. Klein, p. 26, and M.Z. Kaddari, p. 36.

30. See E. Klein, p. 26 and Koehler-Baumgartner, p. 44. The first word is the Arabic cognate for the Hebrew איש. As is evident, our Hebrew word איש once had a *nun*.

31. I learned this from the post of balashon.com of Feb. 3, 2015.

and the בבת of Zech. 2:12. As early as the 9th century, and continuing through the 17th century, the word "apple" was used in English, for whatever reason, to mean "pupil."

* * *

Mitchell First is a personal injury attorney and Jewish history scholar. He wants to share with you his favorite mistranslation in the King James Bible, but he can't decide which to share with you because there are just too many![32]

4. גזר: The Connection Between Cut and Decree

I have always been fascinated by this root. גזר in *Tanakh* has a meaning like "cut" or "separate." But at Esther 2:1, it has the meaning "decree": Achashverosh remembers Vashti and what was נגזר עליה (=decreed against her). The verb also has the meaning "decree" at Job 22:28 and at two places in the book of Daniel, in its Aramaic section (4:14 and 4:21).

Of course, it has meanings like "decree" and "decide" in Hebrew thereafter. But what is going on here? How did a verb that originally meant "cut" develop meanings like "decree" and "decide"?[33]

Maybe we can explain all the biblical meanings of גזר with an idea related to "carrots"? Please cut that thought out! *Gezer* as "carrot" is a

32. For an interesting and light-hearted book on this topic, see Aviya Kushner, *The Grammar of God* (2015). The author writes that when she first read these translations of the Bible into English, she was "often in shock, mouth literally open." This is because these translations were so different in meaning from the Hebrew. I would like to thank Zal Suldan for telling me about this writer.

33. It is generally agreed that such verbs are later developments that arise from concrete verbs. This is a phenomenon that occurs in all languages. As linguist Guy Deutscher has written: "The only way we have of expanding our expressive range to encompass abstract concepts is to draw on concrete terms… [I]f not from the physical world, where else could terms for abstract concepts come from?… The mind cannot just manufacture words for abstract concepts out of thin air – all it can do is adapt what is already available." See his *The Unfolding of Language* (2006), cited in *Shadal on Exodus*, ed. Daniel Klein (2015), p. 209.

later, medieval development, entering Hebrew from another language, perhaps Arabic or Persian.[34]

An early verdict in *Tanakh* was one by Solomon when he ordered that a baby be divided (*gizru et ha-yeled*, 1 Kings 3:25). It has been suggested that, based on this paradigm, גזר became a verb for "to decide" in general! [35] This is obviously farfetched. Moreover, there is a connection between "cutting" and words like "decide" and "decree" in many languages.[36] So there must be something deeper going on.

One suggestion is that a decree divides the past from the present. Another suggestion is that a decree divides what is permitted from what is forbidden. A more concrete suggestion is that the cutting referred to is the cutting of the parchment that the decree needed to be written on.

I saw the first of the above ideas in the Radak, *Sefer Ha-Shorashim*, entry גזר. When he discusses Esther 2:1, he explains that the meaning of *nigzar* is: *neḥtakh ha-davar she-lo yashuv od aḥor*=the matter is decided so it will not go back to the previous way. (Regarding the word נחתך, see my discussion below.)

In English, when we make a decision, we often say that "we are drawing a line," i.e., making a separation. This would be consistent with either of the first two approaches I just mentioned. We also have an expression "cut a check." This would be consistent with the more concrete suggestion.

Finally, a cut is a form of a stroke. I have seen the suggestion that a decree can be viewed as a decision that resolves a difficulty in a single stroke.

* * *

To finish up our discussion of גזר in *Tanakh*, let us talk about the nouns:

---

34. Alternatively, perhaps from Pashto, one of the two official languages of Afghanistan.

35. See, e.g., the article in *TDOT* that suggests this approach and does not mention any others.

36. See *Shadal on Exodus*, ed. Klein, p. 209, citing linguist Guy Deutscher. For example, the English words "decide" and "decree" both derive from Latin words that mean "cut" or "separate."

- *Gezarim* means "parts." The plural form only appears in two passages in *Tanakh* but they are important ones. At Genesis 15:17, a symbolic representation of God walks through the parts of cut animals (*bein ha-gezarim*). At Psalms 136:13, we are reminded of God's dividing the sea into parts: *le-gozer Yam Suf le-gezarim*. At Leviticus 16:22, as part of the Yom Kippur ritual, the goat that bears all of Israel's sins goes to *eretz gezerah*, a far off, separated area, so that it cannot return.
- The book of Ezekiel (chapters 41 and 42) uses the word *gizrah* several times. Many interpret the meaning to be a "separate section" of the Temple.
- The book of Daniel mentions *gazrin* and *gazraya* four times. These words are usually understood as deriving from our root and as meaning people who decide/determine the future by looking at the stars, i.e., astrologers.[37]
- A *magzerah* is a cutting instrument. This word is found at 2 Sam. 12:31 (in the plural).
- At Lamentations 4:7, the word *gizratam* means "their form." A "form" is related to a "cutting," even if only a figurative one.
- The *Tanakh* also refers to city in ancient Israel named "Gezer." It has been suggested that its name reflects that it was separated off in some way. But this is only conjecture. (This city is very old. It was first settled in the fourth millennium BCE. We are not sure when it began to be called "Gezer." In 1908, an important inscription in old Hebrew from the tenth century BCE was found there, the "Gezer calendar." It describes an annual cycle of agricultural activities.)

Moving on to Arabic,[38] in this language *jazira* means "island." It is called this because it is cut off from the land.

Also, the country Algeria gets its name from this word. The country is known in Arabic as *Al Djazair*. There are a number of small islands nearby which gave this name to the city Algiers. Later, the country took its name from the city.

37. *Daat Mikra* also suggests *shoterim*, since they are *gozrei ha-din*. But "astrologers" fits the context better.

38. I learned all of these insights into Arabic from the post of Jan. 25, 2007 at balashon.com.

The Arabic television network *Al Jazeera* means "the island." Here it means the peninsula of Qatar, which is surrounded by water on three sides and desert on the other.

* * *

There is one more important aspect of the root גזר. In modern Hebrew, גזרון (=*gizron*) means "etymology," the study of the derivation of a word. Even in medieval Hebrew the root גזר was being used in connection with the derivation of words. I wish someone would write an article about the *gizron* of the word *gizron*![39]

Additional Note

In *Tanakh*, both גזר and חרץ mean "cut" and "decide, decree." Also, there is the root חתך, which appears only one time in *Tanakh*, at Daniel 9:24. There it means "decree" and we know this root well from post-Biblical Hebrew with the meaning "cut."

Finally, what is perhaps the most important Hebrew or Aramaic word that we know today for "decide"? That would be *pesak*. What is the origin of this word? We all know this word from the phrase *pesik reisha*=cut off its head. So פסק initially meant "cut" and then expanded to mean "decision, decree."[40]

* * *

Mitchell First is a personal injury attorney and Jewish history scholar. He is now eating a carrot, with his replica of the Gezer Calendar in full view, separating out his source sheets and deciding what etymological article to write next.

39. That would be like a coffee table book about coffee tables! (I hope some of you understand my allusion!)

40. פסק is not in *Tanakh*. But it is related to פשק which is in *Tanakh* (at Prov. 13:3 and Ezek. 16:25) with the related meaning "open."

5. דבר: Insights into the Plague of *Dever*

We are all used to this word as the fifth plague. But it only appears one time in that plague. It has a life of its own elsewhere in Torah and *Nakh*.

1. In the fifth plague, it is only mentioned one time, at Exodus 9:3. But it is mentioned at 5:3 (pre-plagues), and at 9:15 (plague of hail). In the seven sentences that tell the story of the *dever* plague, the words *davar* and *ha-davar* with standard meanings are mentioned three times. This is an obvious word play.[41]
2. *Dever* is mentioned once each in Leviticus, Numbers, and Deuteronomy. In Lev. 26:25 and Deut. 28:21, the context is the curses. In Num. 14:12, the context is God threatening to destroy the Israelites (after their reaction to hearing the report of the spies): *akkenu va-dever ve-orishenu.*[42] God then offers to make a new nation for Moses.
3. In *Nakh*, *dever* is mentioned **43 times**. Only one of these times, Ps. 78:50, is it in connection with the Exodus plagues.
4. In the description of the Exodus plague, it is a plague on animals only. But once we look at the rest of *Tanakh*, we see that it in all the other places it is not limited to animals.

   For example, in a story at 2 Samuel chapter 24 about God punishing David for ordering a census, we are told that 70,000 Israelites perished in the ensuing *dever*. Throughout *Nakh*, *dever* is constantly used to threaten the Israelites (and other nations), along with items like famine and death by sword. Nowhere else is the threat or result limited to the death of animals. By focusing only on Exodus chapter 9, where *dever* affected the animals only, we had a very skewed perspective of *dever*!
5. It is evident from many places in *Tanakh* that *dever* is typically fatal. If one looks through all the *dever* verses, we see it often used in the contexts of מות and חרב (where the latter implies "death by sword"). *Dever* is used as a parallel to death at Ps. 78:50.

---

41. There is also a *ve-dibbarta* at 9:1 which may or may not be unusual.
42. Translation: I will destroy the people via *dever*.

Targum Onkelos always translates *dever* as מותא (=death). The Septuagint always renders it by *thanatos*, the Greek word for "death."

Dever is not a broad word like מגפה. The latter can include a war. *Dever* is a specific disease, just that there is not enough data in *Tanakh* to specify which one.[43] *Theological Dictionary of the Old Testament* explains it simply as a "fatal pestilence… which comes upon men and domestic animals."

6. Psalms 78:50 refers to *dever* and the next verse refers to the smiting of the first-borns. Many read these two verses together as implying that the first born were killed through *dever*. See, e.g., Ibn Ezra, Radak, and *Daat Mikra*.[44]
7. The Latin Vulgate always translates *dever* as *pestilentia*. But in the early sixteenth century William Tyndale, in his English translation, decided to use the term "murrain" for the *dever* in the ninth chapter of Exodus and to use the term "pestilence" everywhere else. This distinction was retained by the King James translation.

   With regard to "murrain," it entered English in the 13th century from a French word *morine*, which was a plague on cattle. Ultimately, it derives from the Latin *mors*. This Latin word is the source for our English words "mortality" and "mortal" (=someone who will die someday, as opposed to the gods).
8. Some connect our *dever* plague word with a Ugaritic word, *dbr*, that means "death."[45] Others suggest a relation to the Akkadian word *dibiru* which means "calamity."[46]
9. Our initial goal should be to see if we can find a relationship between Hebrew words that have the same three-letter root. But in a case where this seems difficult, like this one, we do not have to make weak arguments to support such a relationship.

---

43. See *TDOT*, vol. 3, p. 126.
44. See also Nahum Sarna, *Exploring Exodus* (1986), p. 75 (chart). For a different view, see Rashi to Ps. 136:10 and the midrash *Yalkut Ha-Makhiri* cited in the *Daat Mikra* there.
45. See *TDOT*, vol. 3, p. 126.
46. Ibid. Akkadian is also a Semitic language, but it is not as closely related to Hebrew as is Ugaritic. The Akkadian word *dibiru* may have originated in Sumerian, an older non-Semitic language that influenced Akkadian.

Nevertheless, I always find it interesting to collect the proposals of those who suggest word relationships in challenging situations like this one. In the next paragraph, I will summarize three of the suggestions that have been made.

The root דבר has two other main meanings in Hebrew: one is "speak," and the other is "lead" (probably by pushing from behind[47]). Regarding the first meaning, one source I saw theorized that the root דבר fundamentally has the meaning of "combining separate items into one." "Speech" is of course a collection of words. Then this source used the word "epidemic" as its definition of *dever.* Alternatively, Rav S.R. Hirsch saw the *dever* of Exodus 9:3 as a fulfillment of the "Word" of God. Perhaps he would expand that to all the references to *dever* in *Tanakh.* Finally, another view focused on the "lead" meaning and points out that, in a plague, the illness of one person causes illness to another person. (I mention all these suggestions only because they are creative. I am in no way advocating them.)

* * *

I wish to acknowledge the Philologos column of April 22, 2020: "The Plague-Words of the Bible" for some of the above material.

* * *

Mitchell First is a personal injury attorney and Jewish history scholar. (Unfortunately, he sees nothing to joke about in connection with that deathly plague, *dever.*)

6. הסתכל: What is the Original Meaning of הסתכל?

We all know the word הסתכל and we assume it means "to look at." But wait a minute, let us analyze this word and see what it meant originally.

First, we have to realize that when we analyze this word, we have to pretend it is spelled: H-T-S-C-L. We have a word here in the *hitpael* stem. Sometimes, the second and third letters get switched in this stem. So we have to pretend that we are looking at הת plus סכל.

---

47. See my article on the word מדבר in *Roots and Rituals* and in this work.

But wait a minute, סכל is a root that means "foolish." It is found, for example, at Genesis 31:28 and many times in Ecclesiastes (and elsewhere in *Tanakh*). The *hitpael* often means doing something to yourself. What is going on here? Does הסתכל mean "being foolish to oneself"?

Obviously, we are on the wrong track and there is something that we are missing. The trick here is to realize that שׂ in biblical roots often evolved into ס in Rabbinic Hebrew. Our word הסתכל is a word that is not found in Biblical Hebrew. It is a word from Rabbinic Hebrew. A classic example of this change in spelling between Biblical and Rabbinic Hebrew is the case of the word *erusin*. In *Tanakh*, it is always spelled with a שׂ. In Rabbinic Hebrew it is spelled with a ס.[48] (If *histacel* were in *Tanakh*, it would have been spelled השׂתכל and I would not have had to write this column!)

So the word we are really trying to analyze is התשׂכל (after we have re-arranged the first two letters.) What does the root שׂכל mean? It means things like "to act wisely, to consider." So our word should be understood as the *hitpael* of שׂכל. It originally meant something like: **to self-reflect**.

All of a sudden we understand! So, for example, at *Avot* 3:1, when one of the Sages says הסתכל בשלשה דברים and you will not come into the grip of sin: know from where you came, where you are going and before whom you will in the future give *din ve-ḥeshbon*," these are abstract matters and הסתכל ב- does not mean "look at." It means "self-reflect about, think to yourself about." The *Complete ArtScroll Siddur* (p. 557) properly translates הסתכל as "consider" here.

I am not denying that the meaning evolved from "self-reflect" to "look." Surely we can find the "look" meaning in Rabbinic Hebrew. I am just trying to show what the original meaning of this word was.

* * *

There is a different root in *Tanakh*, סכל, that means "foolishness." This root appears most often in Ecclesiastes, nine times elsewhere in *Nakh*,

48. The curious can investigate the spelling in the Hebrew portions of Ben Sira that have survived and in the Dead Sea scrolls. I have not done so.

and one time in the Torah, at Gen. 31:28.[49] It has no relation to the biblical root שׂכל.[50]

An interesting use of the verb שׂכל is found at Gen. 48:14. We are told that Jacob was שׂכל (*sikel*) his hands when he put his right hand on Ephraim, who was the younger. Rashi and most of the commentaries see the word "wisdom" in this root. They understand the meaning as Jacob purposely put his hands on the one who was younger. But there are commentaries who translate this word as if it were סכל. For example, S D. Luzzatto suggests that the meaning is Yaakov seemingly erred in the way he placed his hands. [51]

* * *

Mitchell First is a personal injury attorney and Jewish history scholar. When not doing either of the above, he is busy self-reflecting.

7. חידה: The Riddle of the Word חידה

The word חידה appears 17 times in *Tanakh*, in various forms. Its basic meaning seems to be a question that is a riddle. (But sometimes, the word is used with a broader meaning.)

The earliest example of a riddle in *Tanakh* is at Judges 14:12–14 where Samson challenged the Philistines. The phrase used by Samson in his challenge was אחודה נא לכם חידה (=let me now put forth a riddle to you). The riddle itself was a cryptic six-word statement alluding to food. The last three words were: ומעז יצא מתוק (=out of the strong, came forth sweetness). The Philistines were supposed to guess what Samson was alluding to. (He was alluding to his having recently eaten honey from bees that were in the carcass of a lion.) He gave them seven days to figure out what he was alluding to and specified a reward to them if they could. After a few days, they threaten Samson's wife

49. At Eccles. 1:17, for whatever reason, it is spelled with a שׂ.
50. Many have suggested a relation to כסיל, via metathesis.
51. S.D. Luzzatto summarizes the various views and prefers the "seemingly erred" approach. I.e., the hands were placed in a way that a viewer would think they made no sense.

and have her get the answer from Samson. She gets the answer and secretly reveals it to them.

The riddle of today's column is: what is the origin and meaning of the verb חוד and the noun חידה? Surely these words have their origin in something more concrete than a "riddle."

To review, we all know of a verb חדה that means "rejoice." (E.g., the word *ḥedvah.*) We also all know of a verb חדד that has a "sharpness" meaning. (On *va-yiḥad Yitro*, Ex. 18:9, Rashi mentions both of these as possible interpretations.) But nowhere in *Tanakh*, outside of this riddle context, are there verbs חוד or חיד.

A widespread explanation is as follows. Parts of the book of Daniel are in Aramaic. There the word for "riddles" (at Dan. 5:12) has an *aleph* in front of it: אחידן. (The *nun* at the end reflects that the word is in the plural.) The suggestion is that perhaps the original word for riddle in Hebrew had that initial *aleph*. The root would be אחד. The next step is to realize that *dalet* and *zayin* are related letters in Semitic languages.[52] So אחד could have a meaning like אחז. We all know that this root means "seize." But sometimes in *Tanakh* it seems to have a meaning like "shut, close up." See Nech. 7:3 and the *Daat Mikra* commentary there.[53] So the suggestion is that a riddle comes from a "shut, close up" meaning of the root אחד, since a riddle is something whose meaning is "shut" and "closed up."[54]

Of course, not everyone agrees with this multi-step solution. We just took a word in Hebrew and assumed that there was once an initial *aleph* there that got lost. Maybe that assumption was not justified. Maybe Aramaic **added** the initial aleph, as it often does. [55]

What are our other choices to explain חוד and חידה?[56]

The Brown-Driver-Briggs lexicon noted an Arabic word *ḥada* that

52. For example, זהב means "gold" in Hebrew and דהב has this meaning in Aramaic.

53. This commentary also sees this meaning in the אחז at Ps. 77:5.

54. This explanation is set forth in *TDOT*, vol. 4, p. 320, with the remark that this is the "commonly assumed" explanation. But *TDOT* rejects it.

55. This point is made in *TDOT*.H. Tawil (pp. 101 and 104–05) cites some Akkadian cognates which may (or may not) mean "riddle" and they have no initial *aleph*.

56. A related issue is which of these two came first.

meant "turn side, avoid" and suggested that it was perhaps connected to the Hebrew word because of the "obscure" nature of a riddle.

The more recent work, the Koehler-Baumgartner lexicon, related it to an Aramaic root חוד that means "to join together." This etymology is implicit in the dictionary of Marcus Jastrow as well.[57]

Another suggestion notes that there is an Arabic word that means "tie in a knot" with a root similar to the Hebrew חד. See, e.g., the Soncino commentary to Judges 14:9: "The word *chidah* is derived from a root 'to tie in a knot'..."[58]

A riddle can be viewed as a knotty problem that needs to be solved. But it can also be viewed as one that ties together and joins two disparate ideas.

According to Ernest Klein (p. 455), the etymology of the word ספק (*safek*, "doubt") remains "uncertain"! Perhaps we should conclude that the etymology of the word חידה remains a "riddle"![59]

P.S. I cannot leave this topic without mentioning Solomon Mandelkern's comment that every riddle has a "sharp sting" to it.[60] Thus he also suggests a relation to the verb חדד!

* * *

Mitchell First is a personal injury attorney and Jewish history scholar. A riddle for my readers: Which Jewish author has a (distant) relative named "Last"? That would be me!

8. חלה: What is the Meaning of... ויחל משה את פני (Ex. 32:11)

We all know the above phrase. It is the beginning of the Torah reading on fast days. The context is that the Israelites had sinned with the Golden Calf. At verse 32:10, God offers the plan that He will destroy

---

57. See similarly, M. Jastrow, p. 430.

58. This is one of the suggestions mentioned in *TDOT*. At Dan. 5:12, after it refers to Daniel as a declarer (=solver) of riddles, it calls him a משרא קטרין =a loosener of knots. See similarly S. Mandelkern, who cites this verse and the above evidence from Arabic.

59. Perhaps we should ask Adam West to ask Frank Gorshin for the solution!

60. עוקץ חד.

the Israelites and turn Moses and his descendants into a great nation. Verse 32:11 is the prelude to Moses' response: *Va-yeḥal Moshe et pnei Adoshem Elokav*. After Moses made his arguments (e.g., remember the promises to the forefathers, and why should the Egyptians say that God took the Israelites out only to destroy them), God was convinced to change his mind.

From the context, ויחל משה את פני describes a petition to God. The 1917 Jewish Publication Society translation (included at the top in the Pentateuch of Rabbi Dr. J.H. Hertz) translates it as "besought." The ArtScroll Stone edition translates it as "pleaded."

But how do we get this from the Hebrew? After all, the widespread meaning of the root חלה is "to be weak, ill."

Let us review some possibilities:

1. He prayed so hard he made himself sick. I did see this suggestion, but it does not fit the balance of the phrase.
2. *Va-yeḥal* is related to "beginning." For example, in *The Living Torah* (1981), Rabbi Aryeh Kaplan translates: "Moses began to plead. . . . " But if *va-yeḥal* means "began to," then the Torah did not use any word for what Moses actually did.
3. The root is יחל. This root means "wait, hope." Accordingly, we could translate: "he hoped [for a response]." But anyone who knows Hebrew grammar realizes that the *yod* in ויחל is not part of the root. [61]

After that warm-up, it is now time to provide the solution.

The root חלה followed by some form of the word *panim* (=face) appears sixteen times in *Tanakh*. (Exodus 32:11 is the only time it appears in the Torah.) The idiom occurs both in the context of petitions to God and in the context of petitions to fellow men.

The solution is based on the root חלה meaning "to be weak, ill." That is what the root means in the *kal*. But in our sixteen expressions, it is in the *piel*. The suggestion is that in the *piel* it means "to cause

---

61. There is an oft-recited phrase in the High Holiday liturgy: אוחילה לא-ל אחלה פניו. The first word here is based on the root יחל and it is followed by an expression similar to our phrase. But this is just wordplay, not evidence of word relation.

someone else to be weak."[62] Moreover, as to *panim*, although it means "face," it often has the connotation of an "angry face." See, e.g., Lev. 26:17 and Ps.34:17. **Therefore, the entire expression means: "to weaken the angry face."** I.e., Moses was trying to weaken God's angry face.

Rav S.R. Hirsch mentions this suggestion but disagrees with it since our expression "חלה + face" also occurs in passages where no anger is involved. For example, it occurs in a general context of attempting to gain someone's favor. He cites Ps. 45:13, Prov. 19:6 and Job 11:19 as examples.

Nevertheless, we can easily suggest that the idiom arose in the context of "weakening an angry face" and then expanded into other contexts where no anger was involved. Some who propose the above solution are: Solomon Mandelkern, Umberto Cassuto, and *Daat Mikra*.[63]

(Also supporting our interpretation is that *Tanakh* has an expression for a "hard face." See Deut. 28:50, Dan. 8:23, Ecc. 8:1, and Prov. 7:13 and 21:29.)

There is one other solution that is sometimes proposed.[64] This interpretation observes that there is an Arabic root that sounds like חלה and means "to be sweet, pleasing." Perhaps this Arabic root existed as early as the time of *Tanakh* and the meaning of our ויחל would be "to appease someone with sweet words." (Most interestingly, as mentioned in the *Daat Mikra*, the name for the candy *halva* probably derives from this "sweet" word!)

But the assumption that this Arabic root existed as early as the time of *Tanakh* is speculative.[65]

---

62. There is probably only one other instance of the *piel* in *Tanakh*. It is at Deut. 29:21. There the meaning is "cause the land to be sick."

63. See their n. 12 on Ex. 32:11. This is the first interpretation they mention and seems to be their preferred interpretation, even though they mention others in n. 13.

64. See, e.g., Brown-Driver-Briggs. This interpretation is mentioned in *Daat Mikra*, n.13. See also Soncino comm. to 1 Kings 13:6. M.Z. Kaddari, p. 303, mentions both interpretations without choosing. See also *Ex. Rabbah* 43:3 (מתוק).

65. A weak argument has been made based on certain words for jewelry in *Tanakh*. See *TDOT*, vol. 7, p. 400.

Interestingly, S.D. Luzzatto sees the "sweetness" meaning in *Tanakh* in the

Theological Dictionary of the Old Testament is a source that prefers the "sweet, pleasing" solution. Their article makes the following argument. The "חלה + face" expression "designates a gesture of respect, of worship, and of submission, performed with the purpose of seeking favor. It appears very dubious, therefore, that the usage of the phrase carries overtones associated with the semantic field of *chalah*, 'be weak, sick.'"[66] But I do not find this argument compelling.

The above article also mentions the possibility that the root of our ויחל is חלל with the meaning "be free, empty." I.e., Moses was trying to make God's face free and empty of anger. An example of a word in *Tanakh* from this root is חלון. In *Tanakh*, this meant something like an open area for ventilation and illumination. But the root חלל in *Tanakh* is more of a word for "opening" than a word for "emptiness."

Finally, the Talmud (*Berakhot* 32a) provides many interpretations of our ויחל. But they are not plain sense ones.[67]

* * *

Mitchell First is a personal injury attorney and Jewish history scholar. He tries to stay strong and avoid weakness, while eating his sweet *halva*.

9. חמד: What Is the Difference Between לא תחמד and לא תתאוה?

The Ten Commandments are found in *Parshat Yitro* and again in *Parshat Va-Etḥannan*. But there are differences. One major difference is that in *Parshat Yitro*, the tenth commandment uses לא תחמד twice, while in *Parshat Va-Etḥannan*, we have לא תחמד regarding the wife, but לא תתאוה on the rest (house, field, etc.).

What is the difference between *lo taḥmod* and *lo titavveh*? Long ago, already in the *Mekhilta*, there was a suggestion that תאוה is

---

name מחלת. See his comm. to Gen. 36:3. He points out that she also has the name בשמת. Both her names can be viewed as the same if we give מחלת this "sweetness" meaning. I thank Daniel Klein for this reference. (Luzzatto is not writing about our "חלה + face" expression here.)

66. *TDOT*, vol. 7, p. 409. See also p. 407.

67. See also *Berakhot* 30a.

be-lev (=with the heart), while חימוד is *be-maaseh* (=with deed). This distinction is adopted by Rambam. See his discussion at *Sefer Ha-Mitzvot*, Negative Precept 365: "This means therefore that once you let yourself covet in your mind a desirable object that you have seen in your friend's house you have violated the precept of '*lo tit'aveh*.' If your passion for the object becomes so intense that you take steps to acquire possession of it, pressing him to sell it and exchange it for something better or more valuable – once you have bought out the unwilling purchaser, you have violated both prohibitions."[68] See also Rambam, *Gezeilah ve-Aveidah* 1:9–10.

Others view no deed required for חימוד and view both prohibitions as equivalent. See, e.g., *Sefer Mitzvot Gadol*, Negative Precept 158.

But as Nehama Leibovitz writes (*Yitro*, section 6),[69] it is difficult to accept the view that the two roots are synonymous: "Surely language has no absolute synonyms." What then is the difference between the two roots?

Nehama then cites Malbim, Solomon Wertheimer, and the scholar Benno Jacob and explains it all.[70] Malbim, Wertheimer, and Jacob all take the same approach.

First she quotes Malbim: "*ḥemdah* refers to a physical experience, the actual impact of something that is pleasant to the eye, usually collocating with "eyes".... *Ta'avah* refers to the person who expresses the desire even for something which is not present and which is not outwardly beautiful. The person himself experiences a longing for it.... It collocates with *nefesh*: *ta'avat ha-nefesh* (longing of the soul) but never: *ḥemdat nefesh*."

Then she quotes Wertheimer: "*Ta'avah* refers to the human desire without benefit of visual contact. *Ḥimud* is the stimulation of desire by visual contact..."

As to Jacob, I will now elaborate on his views,[71] stating more than

68. Translation taken from Nehama Leibowitz, *Studies in Shemot*, Part I (1976, translated by A. Newman), p. 345.

69. Ibid.

70. Benno Jacob was not an Orthodox Jew, but she often quotes him. See Rabbi Hayyim Angel, *Peshat Isn't so Simple* (2014), p. 38.

71. His views are expressed in his article "The Decalogue," *JQR* 14, 1923/24,

what is included by Nehama. Jacob first writes that it is not true that the God of Israel is indifferent towards sentiment or inclination, and judges only based on actions. He brings many verses that show that God judges individuals based on what is in their heart. He concludes: "Because the law is aware that action springs from the mind and receives from it direction, aim, character and value, therefore it addresses itself with its exhortations to the heart, so that it be one with God."

Jacob then writes: "There is not a single passage in the Bible where חמד signifies 'snatch to one's self,' and the passages which are adduced for it prove just the opposite."

Then he notes that חמד is quite often mentioned in connection with words like ראה, מראה and עין. He cites Gen. 2:9, Josh. 7:21, Isa. 53:2, 1 Kings 20:6, Ezek. 24:16 and 24:25, and Lam. 2:4. You are finding something beautiful and desiring it but the opinion arises first through inspection.[72]

But the desire reflected in אוה is considerably different. "The difference is this, that the occasion for חמד is inspection, for אוה imagination, the reference being therefore to imagined estates and pleasures...." The body part doing the אוה is usually the נפש, not the eyes.

Then he makes the critical observation that אוה is often expressed in the *hitpael*, as in the tenth commandment. Why should that be the case? We have all looked at that tenth commandment for decades and wondered about חמד versus אוה, but we have forgotten to notice that אוה was in the *hitpael*. The command was not לא תאוה, but לא תתאוה. A large percentage of the time in *Tanakh*, perhaps a majority, the *hitpael* is a reflexive stem, meaning that it indicates that the person is doing something to himself.[73]

So what is the import of the *hitpael* of אוה? Jacob explains that it means "to nourish in one's heart the desire for something, through a

pp. 141–87. His discussion of the tenth commandment starts on p. 166.

72. He also points out that in Arabic it means "to praise, thank" and that it is from this meaning that Muhammad derived his name.

73. The *hitpael* has other functions as well, which I will not go into here. I have discussed the *hitpael* extensively in my article on התפלל in *Roots and Rituals* (2018).

vivid presentation in one's phantasy. . . ." So now we understand! אוה means you have a desire for something that is not based on a visual inspection. The reason the *hitpael* is being used is that you are actively building up your desire for the object that you had not seen (or at least is not in front of you at the time). A perfect of example of אוה being used is Numbers 11:5, where the people cry out: "We remember the fish that we used to eat in Egypt . . ." The previous verse had described this situation as: התאוו תאוה.

Jacob also suggests that we should not be so technical and apply חמד only to the wife, and אוה only to the other objects. While חמד is mentioned only in connection with the wife, and אוה is mentioned only in connection with the other objects, an expansive view of parallelism can imply that we should treat both verbs as applying to all objects.

* * *

Several decades ago, I heard the following homiletical *devar Torah*. The land of Israel is called *eretz ḥemdah* in the *Birkat Ha-Mazon*, based on the use of the phrase at Jer. 3.19; Zech. 7:14, and Ps. 106:24. Let us assume that we would follow the *Mekhilta* and Rambam and conclude that one has not violated *lo taḥmod* unless one has come into possession of the object. This would mean that the desire alone to live in Israel does not make it *eretz ḥemdah*. One would have to live there in order to fulfill this description!

* * *

Mitchell First is a personal injury attorney and Jewish scholar. He used to use his imagination to postulate distinctions between לא תחמד and לא תתאוה. Now he no longer needs to!

10. חמשים: The Meaning of חמשים (*Ḥamushim*) at Exodus 13:18

At the beginning of *Parshat Beshallaḥ*, we are told that the Israelites were *ḥamushim* when they went out of Egypt.

This word is often translated as "armed." What other choices are there for the translation? *Ḥamushim* appears three other times in *Tanakh*: at Josh. 1:14 and 4:12 and at Judges 7:11. We need a meaning that works for all these passages.

Aside from meanings related to "five," the root חמש also has a meaning like "belly." See the passages in 2 Sam. at 2:23, 3:27, 4:6, and 20:10. There individuals are stabbed in the *ḥomesh* and killed. The Brown-Driver-Briggs lexicon interprets the word as "belly," as does the Koehler-Baumgartner lexicon. "Belly" is also the meaning of the cognate in Akkadian.[74]

At *Sanhedrin* 49a, חמש is interpreted as "fifth rib." This is stated to be a very dangerous place because it is the location of the liver and the gall bladder. But it is unlikely that those four people stabbed in *Tanakh* were stabbed precisely in the fifth rib. The general term "belly" fits better.

So how are we going to translate our word at Exodus 13:18? Does it have a meaning related to "five" or to "belly," or perhaps it has an entirely different meaning?

A tannaitic source, the *Mekhilta*, gives the following interpretations: (1) מזויינים (=armed), citing Josh. 1:14, and it explains further: armed with five different types of arms; (2) מזורזים (whose meaning is discussed below), citing Josh. 4:12–13; (3) one in five; (4) one in fifty; and (5) one in five hundred.

Interpretations #3, 4, and 5 do not fit the context of *ḥamushim* in the other verses. They can easily be ruled out.

As to interpretation #1, it is not translating *ḥamushim* as "armed." Rather, it is deriving the "armed" meaning from the "five" root and the context.[75]

As to interpretation #2, מזורזים could mean a few things: e.g., strong, quick, or enthusiastic. Verses 4:12 and 4:13 are both cited. It seems that the statement is interpreting the *ḥamushim* of Josh. 4:12 in light of the *ḥalutzei tzava* of 4:13. But how did this source understand *ḥalutzei*? We do not know, as this itself is a word with varying interpretations.

Targum Onkelos has ומזרזין. This word could have a few meanings, similar to מזורזים."[76]

74. See H. Tawil, p. 113.

75. Interpretation #1 is also found at JT *Shabbat* 6:4 with an erroneous text.

76. Onkelos lived around the early 2nd century. His statement does not have to be interpreted in light of the *Mekhilta*. On the other hand, material was added

Rashi translates our word as מזויינים (=armed). He does not explain how *ḥamushim* came to have this meaning.

Ibn Ezra also takes the "armed" approach, writing: *ḥagurei ḥomesh la-milḥamah*. Probably he means they wore their swords on this *ḥomesh* area.[77] See similarly Radak, *Sefer Ha-Shorashim*, and S.D. Luzzatto. (Similarly, in English we have the word "armed," based on the assumption that weapons were carried with one's arms.)

But if *ḥamushim* meant "armed," where did the Israelites get their weapons? The Egyptian army (a possible arms source) had not drowned yet. Also, no mention is made of weapons at the parting of the sea and the impression given there is that only miraculous intervention could rescue the Israelites.

Other suggestions I have seen include: traveling in groups of fifty or five, or with five different leaders assigned to them. Also, some interpret *ḥamushim* as "equipped" (perhaps the "armed" meaning expanded to "all necessary equipment"), or "ready for battle" or "dressed for battle." Others interpret *ḥamushim* in light of the *ḥimmesh* of Gen. 41:34, e.g., provided with food. (But the meaning of this word at Gen. 41:34 is itself unclear.) Many other suggestions have been offered.

Rabbi Dr. J.H. Hertz quotes a suggestion that *ḥamushim* comes from an Egyptian word: *chams*, which means "lance." But this suggestion does not seem to be accepted by scholars today.[78]

* * *

The reason I wrote this article is to offer a different suggestion, one that does not seem to be mentioned in Jewish sources until modern times. In Arabic, there is a word that means "army" and this word is similar to the Hebrew חמש. Usually, references to Arabic are from the time of the Quran (early seventy cent.) and later. But this word is

---

to the text of Onkelos over the next few centuries. If so, we should perhaps read this *u-mezarzin* in light of the *mezurazim* of the *Mekhilta*.

77. I am not sure precisely how Ibn Ezra understood *ḥomesh* when he wrote *ḥagurei ḥomesh la-milḥamah*.

78. For more suggestions, see William H.C. Propp, *Exodus 1–18* (Anchor Bible), pp. 487–488.

already found in South Arabic. We have inscriptions in South Arabic from the (late) biblical period.

The suggestion I am offering is that *ḥamushim* in our verse means something like "in military formation." I am not sure who first suggested this, but here are some who have:

- Brown-Driver-Briggs lexicon (1906): "in battle array." The lexicon mentions that there was a similar Arabic word that meant "army" and that an army may have been composed of five parts.
- Umberto Cassuto: "on the basis of the Arabic, in proper military formation. They went not like a mob of slaves escaping from their masters, in confusion and disorder, but well organized..."[79] In further support of this interpretation, he cites Exodus 12:51 where it is stated that God took the Israelites out *al tzivotam*.[80]
- Ernest Klein: "armed, equipped... possibly... refers to the division of the army into five parts: van,[81] body, rear and two wings. Hence related to Arab. *ḥamis* (=army; properly 'army divided into five parts')..."[82]
- *Daat Mikra*: This source first translates *ḥamushim* as מזויינים. But it also briefly mentions our interpretation: *arukhim be-seder ke-maḥanot tzava*. Their commentary to Josh 1:14 explains further: *arukhim be-seder tzeva'i le-fi ḥamishah ḥalakim*, and then enumerates the sections: front, two wings, center, and rearguard. See similarly Soncino to Judges 7:11, and the Koehler-Baumgartner lexicon. (This lexicon uses the phrases: "army in five parts," "van, rear, body, two wings," and "lined up for war." It also mentions with approval the suggestion "groups of fifty.")
- Many contemporary English translations by Gentile authors translate *ḥamushim* as "in battle formation," "in battle array," "in marching formation," and "in orderly ranks."

79. Translation by Israel Abrahams, pp. 156–57.
80. But the precise meaning of this phrase is not clear.
81. "Van" is short for "vanguard" and means the front part of the army (and is related to the word "advance").
82. E. Klein, p. 221.

Even assuming that the word *ḥamushim* was originally derived from the (assumed) five sections of a standard ancient army, it is reasonable to suppose that, by the time of Exodus 13:18, the meaning had already expanded and included "marching in an organized way like an army," without any implication of five sections.[83]

Regarding the other occasions *ḥamushim* is used in *Tanakh*, we can interpret it with related meanings: "as an army" and "army." See Josh. 1:14, 4:12 and Judges 7:11.

* * *

Mitchell First is a personal injury attorney and Jewish history scholar. When language issues arise, he is arrayed with his linguistic resources in proper formation, ready to solve them.

11. חרש: The Multiple Meanings of חרש (Deaf, Mute, Cut, Plow)

I was always bothered by how a word can mean both "deaf" and "mute." From some statements in rabbinic literature (e.g., Mishnah *Terumot* 1:2) one gets the impression that this was the case for the word חרש. Moreover, statements like Mordechai's statement to Esther at 4:14: "*ki im haḥaresh taḥarishi*..." are often translated as: "But if you will be silent..."

It is possible to postulate that the word חרש had some abstract meaning like "person with a limitation." But generally language does not work like that. Words start with a specific meaning and then expand. In writing this column, I finally figured out how to understand this word. The word has a fundamental meaning of "to be deaf." But I can easily explain how the "silent" meaning arose.

If one looks at the Even-Shoshan concordance, one sees that the letters חרש are used as a noun nine times. **The references always seem to be only to deaf individuals**. Here are a few examples:

83. As I write this in early 2021, a common word is "quarantine." It originally referred to a period of 40 days that a ship suspected of carrying contagious diseases was isolated in port in 14th-century Italy. Another word which has lost its numeral connotation is "decimate." It originally meant "to kill one tenth." I thank Rabbi Alec Goldstein for the latter example.

- Lev. 19:14: "Do not curse the deaf [*ḥeresh*]." Surely in the verse's plain sense, it is referring to cursing a "deaf" individual. He is one who would not know if you cursed him.
- Psalms 38:14: "I am as a deaf man [*ḥeresh*], I hear not; I am as a dumb man [*illem*]; his mouth does not open."
- Isa. 35:5 "The ears of the deaf [*ḥershim*] shall be opened."
- Isa. 42:18: "Listen, deaf ones [*ha-ḥershim*]."

I also noticed that when the word has a meaning like "silence," it is always in the *hiphil* (=causative) construct.

I then realized what was going on. **When you are silent, you are causing yourself to be deaf to someone else's statement**! I then found such an explanation in the Radak. In his *Sefer Ha-Shorashim*, entry חרש, he writes: *kullam mei-inyan 'ḥeresh,' ki ha-shotek hu ke-ilu eino shomea mah yedabru ha-aḥerim ve-oseh atzmo ke-ḥeresh* (=they all come from the "deaf" meaning, since one who is silent it is as if he does not hear what the others are saying, he makes himself into a deaf person).[84]

Since you are causing yourself to be deaf, I would have expected all these "deaf" meanings to have been expressed in the *hitpael*. But for whatever reason it arose in, or evolved into, the *hiphil*. Perhaps because you are making yourself deaf to someone else, it is slightly different than an ordinarily *hitpael*.[85]

A few times, חרש occurs in the *kal*. See, e.g., Psalms 28:1: *Tzuri, al teḥerash mi-meni* (=my rock, do not be deaf to me). The other *kal* occurrences are at Psalms 35:22, 39:13, 50:3, 83:2 and 109:1, and Micah 7:16. In such cases, the best approach is to interpret all these with the "deaf" meaning. See, e.g., Radak to Psalms 28:1. See also the *Daat Mikra* to this verse, and their comment in note 1 which states clearly that the meaning in the *kal* is "be deaf," and the meaning in the *hiphil* is "be silent." [86] The Koehler-Baumgartner lexicon also takes this approach.

---

84. Earlier than Radak, I found this view in Ibn Janaḥ. But after mentioning it, he decides not to adopt it.

85. There is a *hitpael* at Judges 16:2; the best interpretation is the second one offered by *Metzudat David*.

86. See also the comments of Rav S.R. Hirsch on Ps.28:1: "חרש literally means

Nevertheless, in some of these verses in the *kal*, חרש is often (erroneously) translated with the "silent" meaning.[87]

I am not claiming that every single time we see חרש in the *hiphil*, we have to look for an underlying meaning of "making oneself deaf to something." For example, it is hard to see such a meaning at Gen. 24:21 and Ex. 14:14. In such cases, we can say that the word simply evolved to have the meaning of "be silent." But in the case of Esther 4:14, such an underlying meaning is particularly poignant: "But if you **make yourself deaf** [to what is going on] at this time, then relief and deliverance will arise to the Jews from another place...."

In conclusion, there are many roots that meant "to be silent" in Biblical Hebrew, including שקט, שתק, חשה, הסה, דמם, and דום.[88] But חרש was not one of them![89]

* * *

There is another interesting issue that arises in conjunction with the root חרש. Aside from the "to be deaf" meaning, it also has a meaning: "to cut, engrave, plow." It also refers to one who is an "engraver, cutter, craftsman." It seems very hard to find a common ground between the "deaf" meaning and these other meanings.[90]

It turns out that we don't have to! Scholars now realize that the Hebrew letter ש reflects a merger of two different earlier (="Proto-

---

'to remain deaf' to a call to speak or to act, to 'give no ear' to such a call." See also *Daat Mikra* to Gen. 34:5.

87. The *Daat Mikra* itself commits this error at 50:3, forgetting its own instruction at 28:1, n. 1! (Perhaps the sections had different authors?)

88. Regarding שקט, E. Klein writes, p. 678, that it originally meant "drop down." Regarding הסה, it derives from הס, and is of imitative origin. See E. Klein, p. 157. (In English, we might say: "hush.")

89. Before its meaning expanded.

90. Here are some clever attempts at connections that have been made: (1) the silence reflected in חרש reflects a digging into one's mind; (2) the silence reflected in חרש is a silence that is preparatory to action, as one considers what to do next; (3) the craftsman is one who is thinking silently about what he intends to do; (4) the deaf have to plow their own fields of thought, for no seeds are planted in the soil of their brains; and (5) plowing prepares a land for agricultural use; then the meaning expanded to anyone who deliberately ponders his actions, and from there it expanded to anyone who is quiet.

Semitic") letters. One of them had the "sh" sound. The other had a "th" sound.[91]

While the one with the "th" sound typically became a שׁ in Hebrew, it typically became a ת in Aramaic. This is the explanation for why the word for "three" has the root Sh-L-Sh in Hebrew and T-L-T in Aramaic.[92]

Scholars suspect that, in the case of the "deaf" meaning of חרשׁ, the last letter came from the Proto-Semitic "sh," while the last letter of the "cut, engrave, plow" meaning came from the Proto-Semitic "th." (We even have evidence in *Tanakh* for the "cut, engrave, plow" meaning with the letters חרת. See Ex: 32:16.)

Other examples of pairs of words with שׁ that look similar, but which should not be connected are: *shemen* and *shemonah*, and *shalaḥ* and *shulḥan*. Based on the evidence from Ugaritic and Aramaic, scholars suspect that the latter of both of these pairs was a "th" in Proto-Semitic.

* * *

Mitchell First is a personal injury attorney and Jewish history scholar. As an attorney, he keeps his ears open. As a scholar, he keeps his mouth closed and prefers to write articles.

12. טוטפת: The Meaning of טוטפת: Pendant or Headband?

This word appears three times in *Tanakh* (Ex. 13:16, Deut. 6:8 and 11:18.)[93] We all know that it means "phylacteries." But what does that

---

91. I would like to acknowledge the post at balashon.com of Jan. 29, 2007, on the letter שׁ, from which I am getting this material.

92. There are many more words like this, e.g., Hebrew *shor* (=ox) versus Aramaic *tor*.

93. The widespread way the *Ḥumash* is published today is that Deut. 6:8 lacks the initial *vav* and the other two verses have the initial *vav*. This is not the way the words are spelled in the standard printed editions at *Men.* 34b, *Zev.* 37b, and *Sanh.* 4b. I do not intend to address this issue. See further *Minḥat Shai* to Deut. 11:18.

Jeffrey H. Tigay, who wrote a leading article on the meaning of the word *totafot* (cited below), believes the word was intended as a singular, despite the

mean? That deserves a separate column! Let me start again. We all know that *totafot* means *tefillin*.[94]

But how do we understand that word *totafot*? Forgive me but I am not going to discuss the interpretation found in *Menaḥot* 34b relating it to "two" in the Coptic and African languages, which is the first interpretation brought down by Rashi. It seems too homiletical as it only produces the number "four" and does not describe the object itself. I am going to discuss two views that try to fit the word within Hebrew or other Semitic languages.

Scholars today look at that pattern of letters in **טטפת** and believe that they reflect an original root of **טפטפ**, where the first **פ** dropped. As a parallel, let us look at that biblical word **כוכב**=star. We now know from other Semitic languages that it derives from an original **כבכב**.[95] (By the way, the mishnaic word **לולב** probably derives from an original **לבלב**, "to blossom"![96])

But what does our hypothetical original **טפטפ** mean? There are two widespread approaches, although each is not without its problems.

One approach believes that **טפטפ** derives from an original **נטפ**.[97] This is a well-known root in *Tanakh*. It means "to drip." (It is also probably the root of the word **טיפה**, "drop.") From this root, we have the word **נטיפות**, a kind of decoration that men or women wear. See Jud. 8:26 and Isa. 3:19. Since the root is **נטף**, scholars believe that it must be a kind of pendant that drips downward, and was worn on the head, neck or ear.[98] **טטפת** may just be a word related to **נטיפות**, from the same root.

Another widespread approach to **טפטפ** sees its root as **טופ**. In Arabic, this root has a meaning like "encircle." For this approach, see,

---

Masoretic vocalization of the word as a plural. Interestingly, at Ex. 13:16 the word is preceded by והיה. In contrast, in the two verses in Deuteronomy, it is preceded by והיו.

94. I have addressed both the words "*tefillin*" and "phylacteries" in a separate article.

95. See the article by Tigay cited below.

96. See E. Klein, p. 297.

97. See, e.g., E. Klein, p. 241 and other scholars cited in the article by Tigay.

98. See the further discussion in the *Daat Mikra* on Ex. 13:16, and the Soncino on Judges 8:26.

e.g., S.D. Luzzatto on Ex. 13:16, Brown-Driver-Briggs, and the detailed article by Jeffrey Tigay cited below that advocates this approach.[99] In this approach, טטפת means something like "headband."

There are two weaknesses with the first approach. We would prefer to find a root for *totafot* that did not have a *nun* as its initial root letter (even though initial *nuns* do often drop). More importantly, *tefillin* do not drip downwards from the head. In response to this, we can suggest that, although the word may have originated as a description of pendants that drip downwards, the word subsequently expanded its meaning to include items worn that do not drip downwards.

As to the second approach, ordinarily we would prefer not to base suggestions on parallels in Arabic. Although Arabic is a Semitic language, our sources for Arabic are usually from the time of the Quran (early 7th cent.) and later, long after the period of the *Tanakh*. Moreover, a word that has an "encircle" meaning and implies "headband" does not, at first glance, fit with *tefillin*, an item focused on the front of the head. A response would be that items on the front of the head typically do not stay in place unless they are attached by an encirclement on the head. Therefore, a term that means "encircle" can be viewed as appropriate.

* * *

A few other thoughts:

- I mentioned above that *totafot* appears three times in *Tanakh*. But what about the concept of *arba parshiyot* (=four sections) that discuss *tefillin*? The explanation is that in the first *parshah*, Ex. 13:1–10, where we would expect *totafot*, we have *zikkaron* instead (*u-le-zikkaron bein einekha*). Ibn Ezra focuses on this and deduces that *totafot* must have a meaning related to *zikkaron*. But we can

99. Rav S.R. Hirsch, comm. to Deut. 6:8, agrees that it seems that the root is טופ. But then he looks to Chaldean for its meaning. (It is very rare for Rav Hirsch to look at a Semitic language other than Aramaic. Rabbi Matityahu Clark, in his *Etymological Dictionary of Biblical Hebrew: Based on the Commentaries of Samson Raphael Hirsch* (1999), intro. pp. xi-xii, implies that Rav Hirsch would almost never do so. He writes that "Hirsch's basic thesis is that the לשון הקודש, the language in which the Torah was given, is a self-contained entity that did not borrow from other languages.")

respond that a word could still have a specific meaning and only in a general sense serve as a *zikkaron*.

- With regard to the root נטפ=drip, this root later evolved into a "speak/preach" meaning (with the *nun* dropping). See, e.g., Ezek. 21:2 and Micah 2:6. (When one speaks, one's words flow/drip out. See similarly Deut. 32:2.) Rashi, in his second explanation, quotes the 10th-century grammarian Menachem Ibn Saruk for the view that *totafot* derives from the "speak" meaning of the letters טפ in the verses cited above.[100]
- Karaites did not wear *tefillin*. They understood *totafot* similar to the way Ibn Saruk did, as "preaching between your eyes."[101]
- With regard to a possible Egyptian origin of the word *totafot*, some have suggested a relation to the Egyptian D-D-F-T, which means "snake," including the uraeus snake often worn on the headdress.[102]
- Mishnah, *Shabbat* 6:1 and 6:5 refer to a טוטפת (*totefet*) worn by women. This word seems to mean something like an "ornament," one without any religious significance.[103] Based on this word, one can suggest that the biblical *totafot* may have meant "ornament." But more likely, this word for an ornament worn by women was just an expansion from the biblical word *totafot*.

* * *

A final "drop of wisdom" (and humor!): A well-known controversial view of Rashbam is that the idea of binding God's words on one's

100. This "speak" interpretation is also based on the parallel verse which has the word *zikkaron*. The root זכר sometimes means "to mention." See, e.g., Gen. 40:14 and Jer. 20:9. But Rashi adds that seeing the *totafot* being worn would remind people about the miracle of the Exodus and cause them to speak about it. This is not found in Ibn Saruk. See Aharon Maman, "*Peshat* and *Derash* in Medieval Hebrew Lexicons," *Israel Oriental Studies* 19 (1999), pp. 343–357. Tosafot, *Menaḥot* 34b, s.v. לטוטפת, suggests that *totafot* has a meaning relating to "seeing."

101. See Maman.

102. For further Egyptian origin suggestions, see the concordance of S. Mandelkern (suggesting a relation to the gods Thoth and Ptah), and some of the eleven suggestions in the *Torah Shelemah* (cited below).

103. As one scholar has written: "There is…no reason to imagine that the Mishnah's *totefet* was an inscribed object."

arm and head is only a metaphor. He cites Song of Songs 8:6: "set me **as a** seal on your heart."[104] According to Rashbam, the plain sense of Exodus 13:9 is merely instructing the Israelites to preserve the memory of the Exodus **as if** it were imprinted on their hand and as an adornment between their eyes. Supposedly, a non-observant scholar was once asked whether he wore the *tefillin* of Rashi or of Rabbenu Tam. He responded: I wear the *tefillin* of the Rashbam![105]

* * *

For further material, see Menaḥem Kasher, *Torah Shelemah* 12: 277–280 (appendix to *Bo*), and Jeffrey H. Tigay, *Journal of Biblical Literature* 101/3 (1982) pp. 321–331.

* * *

Mitchell First is an attorney and Jewish history scholar. His next project is to try on a pendant and a headband and see which feels more like *tefillin*.

13. יד: The Meaning of יד in יד ושם (Isa. 56:5)

The name of this Holocaust Remembrance Center in Jerusalem comes from Isaiah 56:5. Here is the first part of this verse: *Ve-natatti lahem*

---

104. See his comm. to Ex. 13:9.

105. I am not in any way claiming that Rashbam did not wear *tefillin*. I am only presenting his understanding of the plain sense of the verse. Amnon Bazak, *To This Very Day* (2020), p. 393, writes "it is clear that Rashbam's intention was not to challenge the commandment of wearing *tefillin*." See his references there for further discussion. Moreover, Rashbam states clearly elsewhere that when he offers a plain sense interpretation that is different than the halakhic one, it is the halakhic interpretation that is the essential one. See his comments at the beginning of Exodus chapter 21 and Bazak, pp. 389–90. Bazak points out that the correct text of the end of the Rashbam here is probably *halakhah okeret mikra* (based on *Sotah* 16a). See also the note in the *Torat Ḥayyim* edition. See also Rashbam's comm. to Gen. 1:1: "All the words of the Sages and their *derashot* are correct and true." (But this did not stop him from writing a commentary whose goal was plain sense interpretation! For a recent discussion, see the article by Mordechai Z. Cohen in *Regional Identities and Cultures of Medieval Jews* [2018], pp. 93–121.).

be-veiti u-ve-ḥomotai ***yad*** *va-shem*... (= I will give them in my house and within my walls a monument and a memorial[106]). Why is *yad* typically translated as a "monument" here?

The answer is that *yad* seems to have the meaning "monument" in two other places in *Tanakh*: at 1 Sam. 15:12 and 2 Sam. 18:18.

The context at 1 Sam. 15:12 is that Saul had just defeated Amalek. Verse 12 reads: "Samuel rose early to meet Saul in the morning; and it was told to Samuel, saying: Saul came to Carmel, and, behold, he is setting up for himself a monument..." The monument was surely to commemorate his recent victory over Amalek. The Hebrew for the last phrase is **הנה מציב לו יד**.[107]

The context at 2 Sam. 18:18 is the killing of Absalom and that a heap of stones was built over his dead body. (Soncino comments: "as a monument of shame over the rebel's grave.") We are then told, in a contrast, that Absalom had in his lifetime set up a **מצבת** because he had no sons. The verse continues: *va-yikarei lah* ***yad*** *Avshalom ad ha-yom ha-zeh*." Translation: "it is called Avshalom's *yad* (=monument) until this day."

As to how the word *yad* means "monument," this is a difficult question, as the cognates to *yad* in the other Semitic languages do not have the "monument" meaning.

It has been suggested that monuments in ancient Israel originally had the shape of a raised hand (e.g., the upper part of the monument

106. I gave the phrase *yad va-shem* a literal translation above, thereby implying that these are two different nouns. (I followed the 1917 translation of the Jewish Publication Society of America.) But more likely the phrase should be translated as "a *yad* that serves as a *shem*" (=a monument that serves as a memorial). This is the interpretation adopted in the *Daat Mikra*. The phrase is likely a "hendiadys" (=one through two). In a hendiadys, the two words are separated by a conjunction but in fact one word modifies the other. There are hundreds of examples of these in *Tanakh*. See, e.g., Isa. 19:20, Lev. 25:47, and 2 Sam. 20:19. I would like to thank Rabbi Menahem Meier for explaining this to me. (The purpose of the hendiadys form is one of emphasis.)

107. What follows shortly thereafter in verse 14 is Samuel's famous rebuke of Saul: "*u-meh kol ha-tzon ha-zeh*...." Many have observed that the *meh* of *u-meh* was likely meant to sound like the sound of sheep!

was rounded).[108] Alternatively, the term might have originated with monuments depicting a hand, perhaps the hand of God giving a blessing or the hand of the individual in prayer.[109] Or perhaps it was a shortened form of *matzevet yad*, the original meaning "a *matzevet* as a sign." *Yad* does mean "sign" in *Tanakh*. See Ezek. 21:24 (and the Soncino commentary there). I also have one more suggestion which I will make below.

Going back to Isaiah 56:5, the context here is also of interest. The *yad va-shem* that God is giving is addressed to the *sarisim* (=eunuchs) who kept the commandments and presumably did a lot of good deeds, but had no children. God promises to establish them a *yad va-shem* which is "better than sons and daughters." As the *Daat Mikra* commentary points out, probably it was a big *zekhut* for them that the memorial will be in God's Temple and walls.

There is another interesting use of the word *yad* at Deut. 23:13. The context here is the holiness of the military camp. At verse 14, we are told to have a יתד (=paddle, trowel) to use to dig and cover up our excrement.

But the verse that concerns us is the prior verse, verse 13. This verse tells us what to do when we have to urinate in the military camp[110]: *ve-yad tihiyeh lekha mi-ḥutz la-maḥaneh*, and then the verse continues: ויצאת שמה חוץ. Those last three words are so innocuous that I never realized they were alluding to relieving oneself![111]

But what is the meaning of *yad* in the first part of verse 13: "you shall have a יד for yourself outside the camp"? Some interpret *yad*

108. For attempts at supporting this archaeologically, see M. Delcor, "Two Special Meanings of the Word יד in Biblical Hebrew," *Journal of Semitic Studies* 12 (1967), pp. 230–34.
109. Ibid. Especially interesting is one at Hazor which depicts two raised hands.
110. This is the view of *Daat Mikra*. But this verse may be referring to both bodily functions.
111. R. Hirsch translated: "thither shalt thou go out." The ArtScroll Stone has "to there you shall go out, outside." The Jewish Publication Society has: "whither thou shalt go forth abroad." In contrast, *The Living Torah* of R. Aryeh Kaplan uses the word "lavatory" in its translation: "You must designate a place outside the camp to use as a lavatory."

here as meaning "a place."[112] Others interpret it as meaning a "sign,"[113] or perhaps it is an elliptical way of saying "a sign pointing to a place." But the interpretation that I like best is that *yad* here is an elliptical way of saying מקום על יד (=a place on the side.)[114]

In many places in *Tanakh*, *yad*, *al yad*, and *el yad* are used to mean "side." See, e.g., Ex. 2:5, Psa. 140:6, Prov. 8:3, and 1 Sam. 4:13 and 4:18.

Now that we are reminded that *yad* sometimes means "side," I will offer the suggestion that in the case of monuments, perhaps they were originally placed on the "side" of the objects they were commemorating. Hence, *yad* came to be a term for a monument.[115]

* * *

Mitchell First is a personal injury attorney and Jewish history scholar. He hopes there will be an interesting *matzevah* at his grave. Perhaps it can be called *Yad Rishonah*.

14. ירח: The Meaning of *Yareaḥ* (=Moon)

Most nouns in Hebrew derive from a verb. Let us try to figure out what verb was the root of ירח. Unfortunately, ירח never functions as a verb in *Tanakh*. But wait. With a slight alteration, we can see the verb ארח. This verb means: "travel, wander." It turns out that the widespread scholarly view of the Hebrew word ירח is that it is related to this root ארח. Most likely, in the ancient world, the moon was viewed as the "wandering/traveling object in the sky."[116]

What about that place name יריחו? I have seen it suggested that it derives from ירח as well. There was much moon worship in ancient times in the near East. I have seen the suggestion that that was what

112. See, e.g., Onkelos, *Sifri* 257, Rashi, and *Daat Mikra*.
113. The sign might even be in the shape of a hand.
114. See, e.g., Brown-Driver-Briggs, p. 390. See similarly *TDOT*, vol. 5, p. 402.
115. For additional material on this topic, see *Encyclopedia Mikra'it*, vol. 3, entry יד, p. 464.
116. See, e.g., *TDOT*, vol. 6, p. 356.This view is also mentioned in the concordance of S. Mandelkern and in the dictionary of M. Jastrow.

was going on at that site originally. Yeriḥo is a very old city. It existed for thousands of years prior to Yehoshua.

Now let us look anew at the following Biblical words with the root ארח:

- אורח (*oreaḥ*): The original meaning of this word is not "guest." It is "wanderer, traveler."
- אורח (*oraḥ*): This word means "path" because it is something that one wanders/travels along or because the path itself wanders along.
- ארחה (*orḥah*): This word means "caravan," derived from the "wander/travel meaning." It only appears two times in *Tanakh*. One time is at Gen. 37:25 (story of Joseph): *orḥat Yishmieilim*. The other time it appears is at Isa. 21:13: *orḥot*.
- ארוחה: Here the etymology is in dispute. The word appears six times in *Tanakh* with a "food" meaning. One time (Jer. 40:5), it seems that the word means "food for the journey." But one cannot read this "food for the journey" meaning into four of the other times it is used. It is possible that the meaning expanded to mean "food, portion" in general. Or perhaps the word has a completely different etymology based on an Akkadian word that means "to consume, destroy."[117]

Most likely, the verb to "wander, travel," in (the hypothesized original language of) Proto-Semitic, was ורח.[118] But in Hebrew, roots generally do not begin with *vav*,[119] so Proto-Semitic *vav* almost always turns to *yod* in Hebrew. In this particular root, the initial *vav* also turned into an *aleph*.

* * *

A later development of the word ירח in *Tanakh* is the "month" meaning. A month is the period of time (29 days and a fraction) that it takes

---

117. Both possibilities for its etymology are mentioned in Koehler-Baumgartner and in E. Klein. M.Z. Kaddari puts it in a separate entry. Brown-Driver-Briggs categorizes it with the other ארח entries but does not explain how this one consistently fits.

118. *TDOT*, vol. 6, p. 356.

119. For example, if one looks at the concordance of S. Mandelkern, one finds only three root entries: וו, וזר (with a question mark), and ולד.

the moon to grow from a crescent, attain fullness, and then wane to its original state.

What is the root of the word תאריך=date?[120] Does it have anything to do with ארך=length? So far it seems that the word was first used in Hebrew by R. Abraham bar Ḥiyya (c. 1100). He spelled it with a כ as the last letter. But scholars have pointed out, based on the spelling of its Arabic cognate, that the Hebrew word should have been spelled with a ח. Once we realize this, then we understand that this word derives from ירח with its "month" meaning.[121]

* * *

Since we discussed the moon, we should also discuss the sun. (We don't want the sun to be jealous!) We all know the verb שמש=to serve. Interestingly, this verb appears nowhere in the Hebrew portion of *Tanakh*. (It is found one time in the Aramaic portion of *Tanakh*, at Dan. 7:10.)

One approach to שמש=sun is that the word is a primary noun.[122] I.e., it is not derived from any verb; rather, the noun preceded the verb. Many scholars then take the next step and theorize that since the sun was worshipped by some, the verb *shamash* arose in Aramaic with the meaning "to serve the sun." Then in a later stage, it expanded to mean "to serve" in general.[123] (Admittedly this is all speculation, but it is interesting speculation!)

* * *

Mitchell First is a personal injury attorney and Jewish history scholar. Did you know that the book *Goodnight Moon* has already sold over 50 million copies?!

---

120. The material in this paragraph is based on the post at balashon.com of Jan. 22, 2008. This is also where I first learned about the connection between ירח and the root ארח.

121. Abraham bar Ḥiyya lived in Barcelona, which was part of Arabic Spain. (He was a philosopher, mathematician, and astronomer.) If he introduced the word, would not he have known to spell it with a ח? The post at balashon.com asks this question but offers no answer.

122. See, e.g., Koehler-Baumgartner, p. 1589. But others disagree and make some attempts to relate it to a verb.

123. Klein, p. 668. But Klein mentions other theories as well.

15. כהן: Insights into the Words כהן and כמר

1. Ancient Israel was not alone in using the word כהן for a priest or leader. This word had this meaning in other societies as well. This is evident from many places in *Tanakh*: e.g., Malkitzedek (Gen. 14:18, *khohein le-eil elyon*), Poti Fera (Gen. 41:45; *kohein on*), Yitro (Ex. 3:1, *kohein Midian*), Matan (2 Kings 11:18, *kohein ha-Baal*), and *khohanei Dagon* (serving the Philistine god, 1 Sam. 5:5). There are many more such verses.

Outside of *Tanakh*, we find the term used for priests in some of the other ancient Semitic languages, such as Ugaritic and Phoenician.

2. Typically in Biblical Hebrew, a verb has three letters and the noun is formed by adding a *mem* (or *tav*) as the first letter. For example, the noun מקדש (=temple) is derived from the verb קדש.

In the case of the noun כהן, if the verb preceded the noun, then we would expect the noun to have taken the form מכהן. Since it did not, this suggests that the noun preceded the verb.[124] The *Tanakh* does use the verb לכהן, but since it came after the noun, it means merely: "to function as a priest."

When the noun precedes the verb, the task of determining the root is harder as it is not just a matter of chopping off the initial letter. I will mention a few speculative suggestions before I mention the most likely one:

- כהן comes from the root כהה (*dim*). The latter was a word used in the leprosy context (see, e.g., Lev. 13:6), and initially priests were involved in medical matters.
- Another attempt to connect to כהה: Even though the Torah commands our priests to often wear clothing made of white linen (בד), perhaps the priests of other ancient religions wore dimmer/darker clothes.
- There is an Akkadian word *kanu* which can mean "bow down, worship."
- There is a Syriac word *kahhen* which, in addition to meaning "priest," means "bring abundance, make happy." (Syriac is a type of Aramaic.)

124. See, e.g., *TDOT*, vol. 7, p. 66, E. Klein, p. 271, and S. Mandelkern.

But the most likely explanation is that the root of כהן was כון.[125] This root has meanings like: "set up, prepare, establish, stand." This fits because the כהן was the one who was responsible for setting up and preparing the religious procedures, and standing before God.

Rav S.R. Hirsch looks to an even a broader meaning of the root, preparing the people. Here are his inspiring words at Genesis 14:18:

> כהן from root כון... הכין, to get a thing ready for a special purpose. נכון, that which is suitable... כהן, that one who (by teaching, example and symbolic procedure) **influences people**[126] that they become כן, that they correspond to the Will of God, are ready and fixed for godliness. The Jewish priest has not to make God and godliness satisfy human requirements... but to shape men and human matters to satisfy God's requirements....

3. A few times in *Tanakh*, people who are merely important advisors (without priestly lineage) are referred to with the term כהן. See, e.g., 2 Sam. 8:18, which describes the sons of David as כהנים.[127] The parallel passage at 1 Chron. 18:17 removes the word כהנים and writes instead: *ha-rishonim le-yad ha-melekh.*

Of course, at Exodus 19:6, the entire Israelite people are referred to as ממלכת כהנים. There are surely many interpretations here. I will just offer the one in *Daat Mikra*: In the Jewish religion, the priests have a closer relationship with God than the Israelites do, have additional obligations, atone for the sins of the nation and teach the nation. So too, compared to the other nations, the Israelites have the *shekhinah* on them alone, have additional obligations, atone for the sins of the other nations, and are obligated to teach them about God.

---

125. This view is not yet completely accepted in the scholarly world. It is the view of E. Klein, p. 271, and M.Z. Kaddari, p. 49, and they were preceded by S. Mandelkern. Koehler-Baumgartner has "etym. uncertain,? כון." Although this work places a question mark here, it does not suggest any alternatives.

On the other hand, *TDOT*, vol. 7, p. 66, mentions the suggestions related to Akkadian and Syriac, along with the כון suggestion.

126. Emphasis mine.

127. Rashi (Ex. 19:6) uses the above verse from 2 Samuel as support for his view that *kohanim* in general merely means *sarim.*

A well-known view of the Sages is that the seventy bulls offered on the holiday of Sukkot are to atone for the sins of the seventy nations.

* * *

It was mentioned above that sometimes כהן in *Tanakh* can refer to a non-Israelite priest or religious leader. But there is another word in *Tanakh* that is used only for such individuals. It appears only three times, always in the plural: כמרים. What is the etymology of this word?

The root כמר has a few meanings in *Tanakh*: (1) to heat/warm; (2) to cast a net, snare; and (3) black, darkness (Job 3:5 and Lam. 5:10).[128]

The Brown-Driver-Briggs lexicon suggests that the "net/snare" meaning is related to a meaning "lay prostrate" and that this is the explanation for the word כמרים.

But there is another approach based on the "heat/warm" meaning. At Genesis 43:30, we are told about Joseph that נכמרו רחמיו (=his feelings were warmed) towards his brother. Rav S.R. Hirsch writes that the "warm" meaning of כמר here refers to "a deep emotion being excited." He continues:

> Probably from the same idea, pagan priests are called כמרים in contrast to כהנים. The Jewish כהן does not depend so much on devoutness, feelings. Jewish Divine Service is not designed to excite dark mysterious feelings. The Jewish Sanctuary makes its appeal primarily to the mind, the intelligence rather than to feelings.... One can weep copiously before God in prayer, and get up and be no hair breadth better than one was before. **The כמר, the pagan priest reckons on exciting feelings.**[129] But the כהן is to be כן to himself, and מכין to others, give them a firm clear basis on which to stand, a direction where to go.

What do modern scholars have to say? The term *kumru* for priests is a very old one. It is already found in documents from Mari. The Mari texts are from centuries before *Tanakh*, from the area of the

128. Since burnt items are black and dark, this meaning may be related to meaning #1.
129. Emphasis added.

modern Iraq-Syria border. These Mari texts are considered as having being composed in a Semitic language.

In the Mari texts, the suggestion is that the meaning of the title was "the excited one, the hot one.[130]" So modern scholars are partially agreeing with Rav Hirsch. They accept the "warm, excite" meaning of כמר as the explanation for the root, but focus on the quality of the priest himself.

Finally, the most recent discussion of the word argues that the above explanation is not satisfying and takes the position that כמר with its "priest" meaning is of non-Semitic origin. It comes from the Hurrian language. In Hurrian, *kumri-* denotes a type of priest.[131]

* * *

Mitchell First is an attorney, a Jewish history scholar and a כהן. He enjoys continually preparing and exciting his readers.

16. מדבר: The Origin of the Words מדבר (*Midbar*) and דביר (*Devir*)

It is very easy to intuit that the root of the word *midbar* (=desert) is דבר, since a typical way that Hebrew forms its nouns is by taking a three-letter verbal root and adding an initial *mem*. But our next question is much harder: what meaning of דבר generated this noun?

Of course, we all know the verb דבר=to speak. Could a *midbar* fundamentally be a place where people went to speak (to themselves!)? Creative but unlikely. We also know the letters דבר as one of the ten plagues. Could a *midbar* fundamentally be a place of plague?[132] Again, creative but unlikely.

130. Koehler-Baumgartner. *TDOT* adds the following (vol. 7, p. 65): "There is in fact evidence in the Mari texts that a *kumrum* was an ecstatic."

131. See Benjamin J. Noonan, *Non-Semitic Loanwords in the Hebrew Bible* (2019), p. 125.

132. I discussed the plague *dever* in a different article. There I pointed out that *dever* is not merely a plague on animals (as we are misled to think by the ninth chapter of Exodus). In the rest of *Tanakh*, *dever* is consistently a plague on humans that results in death or threatens death.

I am now going to present what I think is the most reasonable explanation. (But admittedly not everyone agrees with this.)

In Akkadian and Arabic, there is a root דבר which means something like "to push from behind and drive away."[133] With this in mind, when you look through *Tanakh*, you see that this was probably the meaning of the root at 2 Chron. 22:10: *va-tedabber et kol zera ha-mamlakhah* (=she drove away all the royal seed).[134]

Perhaps the root דבר has the "push from behind and drive away" meaning elsewhere in *Tanakh* as well.[135]

Based on the "push from behind" meaning, a later meaning also developed: "to subdue/rule over." See Psalms 18:48: *va-yadber amim taḥtai*, and 47:4: *yadber amim taḥteinu.*

When a shepherd was out with his animals, what he was doing was pushing them from behind and leading them in this manner. The explanation I am now offering is that a *midbar* was called this because it was fundamentally a place where one went to push from behind and lead one's animals in this manner.[136]

Radak, in his *Sefer Ha-Shorashim*, entry דבר, also understands *midbar* as a place where one leads animals. Although he does not mention anything about the Arabic root דבר (and Akkadian was not known to him), he does explain (citing Targum Onkelos) that in Aramaic, the root דבר is the equivalent of the Hebrew נהג (=lead). He concludes that a *midbar* is called this because this is where a shepherd is *noheg* his animals.

Even though we are used to thinking of a *midbar* as a dry area, it could have been any wide and open area that was used for pasturing animals. As S.D. Luzzatto writes (comm. to Ex. 3:1): "Perhaps because the term *midbar* was used for places of pasturage with no houses or trees but only wide, open space, the term was retained for dry

133. See, e.g., H. Tawil, p. 71, and E. Klein, p. 113.

134. There is a parallel to the above verse at II Kings 11:1. There the verb used is *va-te'abed* (she destroyed).

135. See in particular Ps. 127:5: *yedabru et oyvim*, and the *Daat Mikra* commentary, n. 7.

136. See, e.g., E. Klein, p. 317, and Koehler-Baumgartner, pp. 209–210 and 546–547.

desert places which are likewise wide and open without houses or trees."[137]

We now have a reasonable explanation of the origin of the word *midbar.* We also see that the letters דבר have at least three different meanings in *Tanakh*: speaking, pushing, and plague.

An interesting issue is whether the word for bee, *devorah,* has some relation to the "speak" meaning. I have seen it suggested that the root דבר originally meant "to buzz or to hum" before it meant "to speak," and that this is the relation to the word *devorah*![138]

* * *

The above is essentially what I wrote in my article on the meaning of *midbar* in my book *Roots & Rituals* (2018). I surveyed the main words with the root דבר, but I did not discuss the word דביר. I now see that I should have!

Devir is a word that we recite in every *Amidah*: *ve-hashev et ha-avodah li-devir beitekha.* It is in many other places in the liturgy as well (e.g., *Maoz Tzur*). What does it mean and where does it come from? It is nowhere in the Torah. It is only one time in Psalms (28:2). Other than that, it appears only at 1 Kings chapters 6, 7, and 8, and in its reiteration at 2 Chronicles.

It is evident from 1 Kings 8:6 that *devir* is just another way of describing the *kodesh ha-kodoshim.* The verse tells us that the priests brought the *aron* (with the *luḥot*): *el devir ha-bayit, el kodesh ha-kodoshim.* Moreover, when you look at any diagram of the Temple, you will see that the *devir*/*kodesh ha-kodoshim* is the room that is behind the *heikhal.*[139]

One possible explanation for דביר is that it is the room that holds the עשׂרת הדברות. But the verses refer to it as the room of the *aron ha-edut* and the *aron brit Hashem*. See, e.g., Ex. 26: 33–34, and 1 Kings 6:6 and 19. They do not refer to it as the place of the *dibrot* or the *devarim.* Therefore, this explanation is unlikely.

137. Translation from Klein edition.

138. See, e.g., E. Klein, p. 113, and Koehler-Baumgartner, p. 210.

139. It seems that *devir* was also used loosely with another meaning in 1 Kings. See, e.g., Rashi and *Daat Mikra* to 1 Kings 6:16 and 19–20, and *Metzudat Tziyyon* to 6:5.

But there are two better explanations. One is that it is the room from which God speaks. See, e.g., Ex. 25:22: *ve-**dibarti** itkha me-al ha-kapporet... asher al aron ha-edut* and Num.7:89: *ha-kol **mi-dabber** eilav me-al ha-kapporet asher al aron ha-edut.*[140]

The other explanation is that it is the room that is **behind** the *heikhal*, related to the "push from behind" meaning of the root דבר. Scholars prefer this latter explanation.[141] It reads well into 1 Kings 8:6. Moreover, it seems from that verse that *devir*, when it appears alone, may merely be short for *devir ha-bayit*=the back of the Temple building.

* * *

There is a passage on the meaning of *devir* in the Jerusalem Talmud, *Berakhot* chap. 4, section 5 (end). Two explanations are offered, although both are unclear. One perhaps connects the word to the *aseret ha-dibrot*. The other is very unclear: משם דבר יוצא לעולם. The ArtScroll edition gives two explanations of דבר here: (1) pestilence (as retribution to those who violate God's will,) and (2) lead, i.e., the pagan nations will submit to the Jewish people (based on Ps. 47:4).[142]

* * *

Mitchell First is a personal injury attorney and Jewish history scholar. When he wrote his article on *midbar* in his 2018 book, he was looking all through *Tanakh* for verses that might have a "behind" meaning for דבר. But he overlooked דביר! The answer was literally under his nose (=in his *siddur*) as he was reciting the *Amidah*!

---

140. See the detailed explanation of the *siddur* commentator *Iyyun Tefillah* (translated into English in B.S. Jacobson, *The Weekday Siddur*, 1978, p. 252).

141. See, e.g., Brown-Driver- Briggs ("hindmost chamber of temple"), Soncino and *Daat Mikra* to 1 Kings 6:5, E. Klein, p. 113, and Koehler-Baumgartner.

142. See also *Metzudat David* to 1 Kings 6:5 who seems to allude to the passage but spells the word דבור. See also *Tosafot Yom Tov* to Mishnah *Middot* 4:1 for a completely different version of the passage in the Jerusalem Talmud.

17. מכתם: What is the Meaning of מכתם?

Our subject is a word that appears only six times in *Tanakh*, only in the book of Psalms, and only in the first verse each time. Our word appears in chapter 16, and in chapters 56 through 60.[143]

It is such a difficult word that several etymological works are not willing to make any suggestion.[144] Long ago, the King James Bible (1611) did not translate it and merely wrote "*Michtam.*" This approach is still taken by some modern translations.[145]

The root would seem to be כתם. This root appears 9 times in *Tanakh* with the meaning "gold."[146] The root also appears at Jeremiah 2:22, which we will discuss.

Does the "gold" meaning get us anywhere? Some suggest that the meaning is: a psalm as honored or beloved as gold. See e.g., Ibn Ezra to 16:1, first suggestion. At 56:1, Ibn Ezra goes even further: the initial *mem* teaches that the psalm is **more honored** than gold. Rashi (in one of his approaches at 16:1) suggests that the gold meaning implies that the psalm was worn as an *atarah* (=crown or wreath). The implication is that the psalm was one that David regularly recited. Rav S.R. Hirsch (comm. to 16:1) suggests that gold is an allusion to the everlasting nature of the Psalm: "David has recorded for himself... an everlasting memorial, a tenet to which he would adhere forever."

Several of our Rishonim propose that *mikhtam* has a melodical or musical meaning. For example, Rashi (in one of his approaches at 16:1) suggests that it denotes a type of melody or rhythm.

---

143. Two times we have: *mikhtam Le-David.* Four times we have: *Le-David mikhtam.* Interestingly, one of the Rishonim, R. David b. Levi of Narbonne, called his own work *Mikhtam Le-David.*

144. See, e.g., Brown-Driver-Briggs and E. Klein.

145. See, e.g., Koren *Tanakh.*

146. This itself is an interesting word. One suggestion is that the word is derived from a Sumerian word that meant "goldsmith." *Daat Mikra* to Lam. 4:1 suggests that Ketem was the name of the country where the gold came from. H. Tawil (p. 173) mentions a different view that theorizes that *ketem* was the word for gold in the Ophir language, wherever Ophir was. (Three times the *Tanakh* refers to *ketem Ofir.*) See also the post at balashon.com of Aug. 27, 2006 on *katom* (=orange).

The introductory verses to the psalms often use liturgical and musical terms that are difficult for us moderns to understand. A survey of these terms is found in the *Encyclopaedia Judaica* at 13:1319–1321. Another such survey is found in the introduction to the *Daat Mikra* edition of Psalms. In this survey (pp. 5–6), the author distinguishes between two types of terms: (1) those that describe the different types of psalms, and (2) those that are melodical and musical instructions. (The survey in the *Encylopaedia Judaica* had lumped them all together.) The *Daat Mikra* commentary takes the position that *mikhtam* is of the first category. It puts it in the same category as: *mizmor* (this appears 57 times in the book of Psalms), *shir* (30 times), *maskil* (13 times), *tefillah* (5 times), *shiggayon* (1 time), *shirah* (1 time), and *tehillah* (1 time).

I am going to agree with *Daat Mikra* that *mikhtam* is not a melodical or musical instruction. For example, the melodical and musical instructions often have the word *al* preceding them (e.g., *al ha-gitit*, *al ha-sheminit*, *al maḥalat*, and many more). Moreover, one can see from 56:1 that *al yonat eilem reḥokim* is the musical instruction there. (It is undoubtedly the title of a song to whose melody the psalm was song.) *Le-David mikhtam* there (and presumably in all six of its occurrences) must be something else, of a more general nature.

There is an Akkadian root *katamu* that means "to cover." Based on this, some suggest that a *mikhtam* was a psalm of atonement.[147]

Based on this "cover" meaning, another view is that a *mikhtam* was a prayer that, when David originally composed it, was said silently (=secretly). I.e., David's lips were covered. Four out of the six times where *mikhtam* is used, it is used with a historical background and some of these backgrounds imply that a silent prayer was necessary. See, e.g., 57:1, "when he fled from Saul in the cave," and 59:1: "they watched the house to kill him." [148]

There is another direction that some take. The suggestion is that

---

147. This suggestion is mentioned at *EJ* 13:1320. But the Akkadian *katamu* does not have the connotation of atonement. See H. Tawil, p. 211.

148. See, e.g., B.D. Eerdmans, *The Hebrew Book of Psalms* (1947), pp. 75–76 and M.Z. Kaddari, p. 614. In this view, one can interpret the נכתם of Jer. 2:22, as "covered by a blot."

the root כתם meant "write" in Biblical Hebrew. Jeremiah 2:22 has the following: "Even if you wash yourself with nitre and take much soap, your sin is נכתם before Me." Now let us look at Jeremiah 17:1 "The sin of Judah is written (= כתובה) with a pen of iron. . . ." Although these verses are from different chapters,[149] one can suggest, based on the parallel, that the root כתם at Jeremiah 2:22 means "written." (Usually, the translations relate it to the root כתם in Rabbinic Hebrew, which means "stained.")

Accordingly, perhaps מכתם means a psalm that is "written." [150] There is another basis for a claim that מכתם means something that was written. At Tosefta *Shabbat* 18:4, we are told not to read certain מכתבין on *Shabbat*. There are at least two manuscripts that read מכתמים here.[151]

What could be the implication of a psalm being "written"? It seems unlikely that all the other psalms were oral. Could the implication be that it was to be recited silently? The fact that there is a musical instruction at 56:1 and 60:1 immediately preceding the *mikhtam* phrase refutes this.[152]

Perhaps the implication of "written" is that it was engraved on a stone as a way of publicizing it.[153] Support for this translation of *mikhtam* is found in the Septuagint. Here the translation into Greek of *mikhtam* is *stelographia*=an inscription upon a slab.[154] But we have to be cautious in the weight we give to the Septuagint. Those Jewish translators living in Egypt only had a limited understanding of Biblical

149. Also, the Hebrew word used for "sin" differs in each.

150. See, e.g., S. Mandelkern, M.Z. Kaddari, p. 614 and H. Tawil, p. 211. See also the post at balashon.com of Aug. 27, 2006.

151. See Louis Ginzberg, in the *Louis Ginzberg Jubilee Volume* (1945), vol. 1, pp. 169–171.

152. The obscure phrase at 57:1, 58:1 and 59:1 also probably reflects a musical instruction.

153. See Ginzberg, and EJ 13:1320. It is also the preferred translation in *Daat Mikra*. See their comm. to Ps. 16:1, n. 1. At the end of their note, *Daat Mikra* also mentions suggestions related to "gold": as beloved as gold or written in gold letters.

154. See also Targum to Ps. 16:1 and *Daat Mikra*. Elsewhere, the Targum translates מכתם differently.

Hebrew. The fact that their interpretation bears some resemblance to our suggestion may only be fortuitous.

Note also that at Isa. 38:9, a prayer of Hezekiah is referred to as a מכתב.

It would be very reasonable to interpret כתם as being related to כתב (=write). The letters *mem* and *bet* are both bilabial consonants, sharing a place of articulation.

In modern times, the Koehler-Baumgartner lexicon adopts "inscription" as its main definition, but also mentions the "secret prayer" definition.[155]

* * *

Mitchell First is a personal injury attorney and Jewish history scholar. He likes to ponder those difficult technical terms in the book of Psalms.

18. מנחה: The Meaning of the Word מנחה

In Biblical Hebrew, most nouns are derived from verbs. So when you see a noun and want to know what it originally meant, the first step is to determine what verb (=root) underlies it.

Hebrew often adds an initial מ to create the noun. Accordingly, in our word מנחה, our initial thought should be that the root is נחה. This root means "to lead" and a *minḥah* would be an object that leads or is lead. Yet this does not sound correct.

Years ago I read S.D. Luzzatto who wrote (comm. to Gen. 4:3) that a *minḥah* is something that "an inferior gives to a superior to appease him and set his mind at rest (להניח דעתו) if there is a possibility that the inferior has offended him."[156] Luzzatto states that the root of the word is נח.

Luzzatto's understanding of the philosophy behind the word sounded very reasonable to me. I am merely going to pretend that he

155. For another approach to מכתם, interpreting it in light of *maskil*, *mizmor*, and *shigayon*, see H. Tawil, pp. 211–12.

A few homiletical interpretations of מכתם are found at *Sotah* 10b.

156. Translation from the Klein edition.

wrote that the root was נוח. This is the conventional root that people use today when they refer to the Hebrew root for the verb "to rest."

But there is a problem with Luzzatto's approach. The traditional mishnaic vocalization of the plural is *menaḥot* (as opposed to *minḥot*).[157] Grammarians explain that this points to the root being מנח.

But there is no root מנח in Hebrew. There is such a root in Arabic and this root does mean "to give, to loan."[158] But generally our sources for Arabic are much later, i.e., starting from the time of the Quran (early 7th century CE). We cannot assume from an Arabic root in post-talmudic times that there was once a biblical root in Hebrew of the same meaning.

Scholars today analyze ancient Semitic languages from early biblical times to see if they can find such a root. It turns out that there was a noun *mnḥ* with the meaning "gift" in Ugaritic, and it is possible that there was even a verb with such a meaning.[159]

But if there was a verb מנח in the Hebrew of the time of the *Tanakh*, it would be surprising that it never appears in *Tanakh*. Moreover, if there was a Hebrew verb/root מנח at the time of the *Tanakh* and that it meant something like "to give," typically a noun that is derived from such a root would have an initial מ or ת added.

Let us look at how some of our traditional interpreters have dealt with the word מנחה.[160]

---

157. Although the word *minḥah* is used in a plural form in *Tanakh* at Ps. 20:4, Amos 5:22, and Num. 29:39, these references include possessive suffixes. The word does not appear in the simple plural form in *Tanakh*. We learn the vocalization of the plural from the manuscripts of the Mishnah with vocalization.

But I admit that I do not understand why the vocalization in the Mishnah manuscripts is given so much weight. The earliest Mishnah manuscript is the Kaufmann manuscript. It dates to only the 10th or 11th century, and its vocalization was inserted centuries later!

158. See *TDOT*, vol. 8, p. 407.

159. See *TDOT*, vol. 8, pp. 408–09 and Koehler-Baumgartner, p. 601. For one possible relevant text in Akkadian, See *TDOT*, vol. 8, p. 409.

160. Most of the over 200 occurrences of the word in *Tanakh* are in a sacrificial setting. I am not interested in that word מנחה. I am making the reasonable assumption that this reflects a later development of the word.

Why our afternoon prayer is called מנחה in the Mishnah and thereafter is a separate issue. On this issue, see *TDOT*, vol. 8, pp. 419–20, 1 Kings 18:36, Psalms

Rashbam (comm. to Lev. 2:1) writes that the meaning of מנחה is דורון (= gift).[161] He implies that the root is נחה by citing to the נחה of Ex. 32:34. But when one looks up this verse, one sees that נחה here means "lead."[162]

Radak discusses the word in his *Sefer Ha-Shorashim* in his entry for מנח. His intuition tells him that the root is נחה. (He probably means נחה with the meaning "rest.") But the plural form *menaḥot* forces him to conclude that the root is מנח.

R. Hirsch discusses the root in several places. For example, in his comm. to Lev. 2:1, he first suggests that if the root is נחה, the meaning is an object that reflects "a recognition of the 'Leadership' of the receiver." But he admits that the plural form points to the root being מנח. Since there is no such Hebrew root, he is forced to conjecture what such a root might mean. He theorizes that it would be a root that reflects "homage" and "allegiance" to the receiver.

At Gen. 4:3, he opines that a *minḥah* is "a gift given as a sign of the recognition, the allegiance of a subordinate to a superior." But he admits that how to derive this from the actual letters is difficult.[163]

Rabbi Matityahu Clark, in his work based on the commentaries of R. Hirsch, includes the word in his entry for מנח. So too do the lexicons of Brown-Driver-Briggs and Koehler-Baumgartner, and the concordance of S. Mandelkern.[164]

Now let us try to draw some conclusions. Luzzatto's approach that relates מנחה to the verb נוח=rest is intuitively very satisfying. Perhaps the word did originate as something that helped put the receiver's

---

141:2, and Ezra 9:5. See further Lawrence H. Schiffman, "*Minchah*: A Halakhic and Historical Analysis," in Daniel Z. Feldman and Stuart W. Halpern, eds., *Mitokh Ha-Ohel:Tefillat Ḥol* (2014), pp. 323–328, at p. 325, and the references there. He adds: "An equivalent of the *Minchah* prayer was part of the daily liturgy of the Dead Sea Scrolls sectarians."

161. This word derives from the Greek word for "gift," as in the name Theodore (= gift of God).

162. Perhaps he meant that in this verse God tells Moses to lead the people to the land of Israel, and the land of Israel is a gift.

163. He makes additional comments on the meaning of מנחה at Gen. 43:11 and perhaps elsewhere.

164. See similarly, E. Klein, p. 357 and M.Z. Kaddari, p. 629.

mind at rest. Luzzatto has a response to the grammatical problem raised. Even though the original root did not include an initial מ, over time the מ in the noun form became treated as if it was part of the root. This already occurred by the time of the Mishnah. That is why the plural in the Mishnah and thereafter became *menaḥot*, as if there was a root מ there initially. Luzzatto cites the example of the verb תרם, to give *terumah*. The original verb was רום=to raise. This generated the noun תרומה. Then the ת became treated as if it was part of the root and a new verb developed, לתרום.

There are over thirty times in *Tanakh* that the term *minḥah* is used as a gift in settings not connected to sacrifices. It seems that a *minḥah* is given for many different reasons, e.g., respect, thanks, homage, and friendship. Although one can perhaps argue any meaning from these many occurrences, Yaakov's *minḥah* to Esav at Gen. 32:21 (*akhaprah fanav ba-minḥah*) and Yaakov's instruction to his sons to offer a *minḥah* to Yosef when they return for a second visit (Gen. 43:11) seem to particularly support Luzzatto's approach. A *minḥah* is something that is meant to set the receiver's mind at rest, especially if there is a possibility that the giver has offended him.[165] The meaning could have expanded to other gift contexts thereafter.

I do not find convincing the approach that מנחה derived from a Hebrew verb/root מנח, with the meaning "give." It is unlikely that there was a Hebrew verb/root מנח with the meaning "give" at the time of *Tanakh*. It never appears in *Tanakh*.[166]

* * *

165. See similarly 1 Sam. 26:19. Many more examples can be brought.

166. But I do admit that there is another possibility, namely, that Hebrew borrowed the noun *mnḥ* from Ugaritic, but never borrowed the verb. This seems to have occurred in connection with the noun מלאך=messenger, which appears many times in *Tanakh*. When Ugaritic was discovered in the early 20th century, we learned that they had a verb לאך= "to send." See *EJ* 2:957. This verb never appears in *Tanakh* and perhaps never made it into the Hebrew of the time of the *Tanakh*. But the noun מלאך did make it into *Tanakh*. Perhaps the same thing happened with their noun *mnḥ*. It would not be surprising that the verb did not make it into *Tanakh*. When words are borrowed from one language to another, it is typically nouns that are borrowed, not verbs.

Mitchell First is a personal injury attorney and Jewish history scholar. His mind is at rest now that he has completed this article.

19. מס: Taxes or Forced Labor?

The Grammar of God (2015) is a very interesting book by Aviya Kushner. She is someone who grew up in Rockland County with a very good knowledge of Hebrew. Later in life, she ended up studying the King James Bible in a graduate school course in Iowa among non-Jews. She was shocked at the inadequacies of the King James Bible translation and wrote the above book about it and about the inadequacies of other English translations of the Bible.

As one example, when she got to Exodus 1:11, *sarei missim*, she noted that the translation in the King James Bible was "taskmasters." She wrote (p. 85): "But 'taskmasters' is not what the literal Hebrew says. The Hebrew word means 'tax masters.'...This tax, in Exodus 1:11, is a most unpleasant one. It is a tax so high it cannot be paid in money; it must be paid in bodily labor."

I thought her comments were clever and mentally filed them away for a future essay. Now that I have researched the biblical word מס, I realize that she erred. The word occurs 23 times in *Tanakh* (in either singular or plural form).[167] If we focus on the earliest twenty-one of these verses, there is usually some contextual evidence that the reference is to physical labor.[168] For example, at Genesis 49:15, we have ויהי למס עבד. At Deut. 20:11, we have יהיו לך למס ועבדוך. At Josh. 16:10, we have the same phrase as at Gen. 49:15. At Josh. 17:13, we have ויתנו את הכנעני למס. At Isaiah 31:8, we have ובחוריו למס יהיו. In none of

See Ben Noonan, *Non-Semitic Loanwords in the Hebrew Bible: A Lexicon of Language Contact* (2019).

167. These are: Gen. 49:15, Ex. 1:11, Deut. 20:11, Josh. 16:10 and 17:13, Judges 1:28, 1:30, 1:33, and 1:35, 2 Sam. 20:24, 1 Kings 4:6, 5:27 (twice), 5:28, 9:15, 9:21 and 12:18, 2 Chron. 8:8 and 10:18, Isa. 31:8, Prov. 12:24, Lam. 1:1, and Est. 10:1. Another instance may be Deut. 16:10. (See the discussion in Tawil cited below.)

168. The Brown-Driver-Briggs lexicon does a good job of showing this.

these twenty-one verses is there any indication that the reference is to a financial payment.

The second to last reference chronologically is Lamentations 1:1.[169] Here "forced labor" is probably the meaning as well. See, e.g., the Brown-Driver-Briggs lexicon, the Anchor Bible volume on Lamentations, and the Koehler-Baumgartner lexicon.[170] The import of this verse is that the former "princess of the provinces" (*sarati bamedinot*) is now being humiliated by forced labor of its people."[171]

So the "tax" meaning, if it exists at all in *Tanakh*, is a **later meaning** of the word. (Whether the word means "tax" in its latest use in *Tanakh*, at Esther 10:1, is a separate issue.[172]) Fundamentally, the word means something like "forced labor on a governmental project at a location outside of one's home town." Most likely, the word originated with forced labor of a nation's own people and then expanded to forced labor of a conquered people.[173]

The sophisticated word usually used to convey these ideas is

169. Chronicles was completed in the Second Temple period, but the references there are merely parallels to passages in Kings.

170. This is also the view of the *Daat Mikra* but it is stated much too briefly. Many other modern scholars follow the "forced labor" interpretation, as does the *Encyclopedia Mikra'it*, vol. 5, p. 56. It is also the view of Yaakov Klein and Nadav Na'aman (see footnote below). See also Yair Zakovitz and Avigdor Shinan, *Megillat Eikhah-Peirush Yisraeli Ḥadash* (2017), p. 29. I thank Rabbi Jay Goldmintz for this reference and for his insights into the word מס in the various verses.

171. But there is no evidence of forced labor of the Jews exiled to Babylonia. One possibility is that the author of this verse at Lam. 1:1 just assumed that forced labor was their fate. Another possibility is that the reference is to non-deported Jews utilized in forced labor for the Babylonian officials governing Judea from their center at Mitzpah.

172. I discuss this in a separate essay.

173. See Yaakov Klein, *Eikhah: Im Mavo U-Peirush* (2017, *Mikra Le-Yisrael* Series), pp. 128–29. (These pages are in an appendix where he discusses the meaning of מס throughout *Tanakh*.) I thank Prof. Reuven Kimelman for this reference. See similarly Nadav Na'aman, "From Conscription of Forced Labor to a Symbol of Bondage: *MAS* in the Biblical Literature," in Y. Sefati et al, eds., "*An Experienced Scribe who Neglects Nothing*"; *Ancient Near Eastern Studies in Honor of Jacob Klein* (2005), pp. 746–758.

When the *Tanakh* refers to the person in charge of the מס, it is referring to *corvée.* See, e.g., the comments on Ex. 1:11 of Rabbi Dr. J.H. Hertz in his Pentateuch. Similarly, *Daat Mikra* on Ex. 1:11 defines *mas* as: *gius la-avodat kefiah.* See also *Daat Mikra* to 1 Kings 4:6.[174]

Kushner is not the only source to make this understandable error in translating *mas.* If you look at the Even-Shoshan concordance, the only definition it gives for *mas* is *tashlum ḥovah le-otzar ha-medinah* (=obligatory payment to the government treasury). It seems that anyone overly influenced by modern Hebrew and Rabbinic Hebrew will make this error in translating the word in *Tanakh.*

If one assumes that the word מס comes from Hebrew and tries to figure out its root, the theories abound. Some suggestions are: (1) מסס, (2) נסס, (3) מכס, (4) נשא, and (5) נסה.[175]

But the widespread scholarly view today is that it is a foreign word. The Brown-Driver-Briggs lexicon had stated that it was probably a foreign word but did not make a suggestion. Now scholars usually connect it with the word *massu* found in texts from approximately the 17th or 16th centuries BCE at the site Alalakh in southern Turkey and a few centuries later in one of the many texts from El-Amarna, Egypt.[176] All these texts are in the Akkadian language.[177] These texts describe workers who were conscripted to work at locations outside of their home towns.[178]

* * *

Mitchell First is personal injury attorney who pays his taxes. His income from being a Jewish history scholar is negligible.

---

the person in charge of the conscription, not the person who supervises the actual work. Na'aman, p. 750.

174. See also Tosafot, *Ḥag.* 8a, s.v. וישׂם.

175. See, e.g., Rashbam and S.D. Luzzatto to Ex. 1:11, Rav S.R. Hirsch to Deut. 16:10, and the מס entries in M. Jastrow, S. Mandelkern, and Koehler-Baumgartner.

176. See, e.g., Y. Klein and N. Na'aman.

177. The language of all these texts is considered to be "peripheral Akkadian." For further explanation, see *EJ* 15:933.

178. See N. Na'aman, pp. 747–49. The etymology of the word *massu* is unknown. Tawil (pp. 217–218) suggests that it originated as a word for "basket" and "basket carriers."

20. מסכנות: The Meaning of ערי מסכנות (Ex. 1:11)

Exodus 1:11 is the only time the word *miskenot* appears in the *Ḥumash*. But it appears 6 other times in *Nakh*, in various forms. Usually it appears with the word *arei*=cities.

From the various contexts (see especially 2 Chr. 32:28), it seems like the meaning is "store cities." But what is the root of מסכנות? S.D. Luzzatto (comm. on Ex. 1:11) is willing to postulate a switch of letters. He wants to understand the word as if the root was כנס (=gather). But this far-reaching switch is farfetched!

Let's see what happens if we stick with the Hebrew root that we have. There are three different סכן roots in *Tanakh*. One is סכן with the "danger" meaning. This meaning only appears one time, at Ecclesiastes 10:9.[179] It does not explain our word *miskenot*.

There is another root סכן with a meaning like "pauper." This root appears a few times in Ecclesiastes and once at Deut. 8:9. On the simplest level, this also does not seem to have anything to do with our word *miskenot*. (Admittedly, Rav Hirsch on Ex. 1:11 comes up with a very clever connection: *miskenot* means "years of need." The cities were built for years of need: "hunger-years"!)

The third סכן root is the main meaning of the root in *Tanakh*. It means something like: "useful, benefit, be accustomed to." (E.g., the סכנת to David at 1 Kings 1:2). Moreover, there is one place, Isaiah 22:15, that this root perhaps implies economic management. Therefore Rashi and many others cite it to explain our *miskenot*. This verse reads: "Go, get thee to הסכן הזה (=this *sokhen*) to Shevna who is over the house." [180] Of course, I would feel better about this explanation if there were more occurrences of this root in *Tanakh* that implied economic management.

But there is an entirely different approach that one can take to

179. Based on its language, the scholarly consensus is that it is a late book. See *EJ* 6:349.

180. The Targum uses a word from the root אוצר. Rashi writes *ke-targumo* and then cites Isa. 22:15 and interprets סכן there to be *gizbar ha-memuneh al ha-otzarot*.

miskenot. It relies on Akkadian, but only as a first step towards seeing the original Semitic and Hebrew root.

Specifically, there is an Akkadian verb *shakanum* that means "to deposit, to lay an object down." This verb led to certain nouns like *mashkantum*, a storage place. This is likely the same word as our *miskenot*, just that it utilizes "sh" instead of "s." But we can recognize the Semitic and Hebrew root שכן in *shakanum*.

Accordingly, perhaps the root of our *miskenot* was originally שכן. We all know this root. It means "dwell, lay down."[181] Now we understand our word! A storehouse is where things are laid down! Of course, this relation to שכן is only a suggestion, but it is a very reasonable one and is adopted in the Koehler-Baumgartner lexicon and by Ernest Klein.[182]

* * *

Mitchell First is personal injury attorney and Jewish history scholar. This book was not stored in a storehouse prior to its delivery to you. Rather, each book that is ordered is individually printed.

21. משפחה: Is There a Connection Between משפחה and שפחה?

This is a question that has been troubling me for decades (along with whether there is a connection between מלחמה and לחם![183]) Both *mishpaḥah* and *shifḥah* derive from the root שפח, so our initial presumption should be that there is a connection. Yet, the Brown-Driver-Briggs lexicon, which discusses both in adjacent entries (under

181. E. Klein, p. 658, records the interesting suggestion that שכן is really a Shaph'el form of כון and literally means "cause to be set up, cause to be established."

182. See Koehler-Baumgartner, p. 606 and E. Klein, p. 361. (Unfortunately, in the former, there is a major "typographical" error. Instead of writing that *shakanum* meant "deposit," the word erroneously printed is "defeat.") See also U. Cassuto, p. 11, M.Z. Kaddari, p. 634, and H. Tawil, pp. 218–219.

Daat Mikra at Ex. 1:11 translates our word as מחסנים. The root חסן means "store." But it does not attempt any (farfetched) etymological connection to כנס.

183. This one I discussed in *Roots and Rituals* (2018).

the root שפח), makes no attempt at a connection. Also, *Theological Dictionary of the Old Testament* has an entire article on the word *mishpaḥah* and no mention is made in this article of the word *shifḥah*. Moreover, their article on *shifḥah*, by a different author, explicitly denies a connection, declaring that "the two Hebrew nouns are unrelated etymologically."

Similar (but not as rejecting) is the Koehler-Baumgartner lexicon. Their *mishpaḥah* entry makes no mention of *shifḥah*. Their *shifḥah* entry refers to the possible connection between the two words but calls it "questionable."[184]

Radak, in his *Sefer Ha-Shorashim*, includes both in his entry for the root שפח, but he too implicitly denies that they are connected. We see this because after he discusses the "handmaid" meaning, he discusses the "family" meaning, but he prefaces the latter with the phrase ועניין אחר (=a different matter). Those familiar with this work understand that this is his way of denying a connection, even though he has placed the words in the same entry.

(Among the Rishonim, Rashi usually presumes that words with the same three-letter root are connected and tries to determine the underlying connection. But many of the other Rishonim, especially in the Sephardic world, did not think like this. Sephardic Rishonim were often influenced by Arabic. In Arabic, words with the same root letters are often not connected.[185])

Going back to *shifḥah* and *mishpaḥah*, some scholars today do see a connection. They generally take the following approach. There is a biblical root ספח and this root sometimes has the meaning of "join, attach." See, e.g., Isa. 14:1 and 1 Sam. 2:36.[186] If ספח had the "join, attach" meaning, perhaps שפח had it too. A שִׁפחה is attached to a family, and a מִשפחה is a group of people who are attached to one another. Some who

184. Also worth mentioning is Kaddari. He has separate entries for each word, far apart (i.e., *mishpaḥah* is an entry that begins with מ). Neither entry mentions the other word.

185. See Richard Steiner, "Saadia vs. Rashi: On the Shift from Meaning-Maximalism to Meaning-Minimalism in Medieval Biblical Lexicology," *JQR* 88 (1998), pp. 213–258. Steiner taught at Yeshiva University for decades.

186. In modern Hebrew, נספח is an appendix/attachment.

take this approach are S. Mandelkern, p. 1221, M. Jastrow, pp. 857 and 1614, and Rav S.R. Hirsch, comm. to Lev. 25:5 and Num. 1:2.[187] This approach is also taken by the Academy of the Hebrew Language.[188]

Rav Hirsch, in his commentary on Gen. 8:19, makes the following comment: "[N]ote how the שפחה, that person who, in the non-Jewish point of view, stands at the very lowest social grade, in the Jewish point of view, as is expressed in the name they give her, is raised to a member of the family."[189]

A ramification of whether שפחה and משפחה are connected is how one should translate the former. Those who believe that the words are not connected are free to translate it as something like "slave." Those who believe that the words are connected might translate it with a more elevated word.[190]

The Academy of the Hebrew language suggests that a שפחה was attached to the family for her entire life and also points to Genesis 16 where Hagar was given the role of building a family for Abraham. This implies an attachment and elevated status for the שפחה.

They also point out that in Latin, there is a similar phenomenon. *Familia* is the word for family, and *famulus* and *famula* are the words

---

187. Klein relates them in his entry for each (pp. 394 and 674), but does not explain how.

188. See their website hebrew-academy.org.il and their post on the word משפחה of 2/2/14.

189. In response to Rav Hirsch's observation, my *ḥavruta* Josh Teplow pointed out that in English, we have a word "bond," which, in a slavery context, can have the negative connotation of "bondage." But in a different context, e.g., "bonded with the family," has a more positive connotation. The connotation of a word can change from context to context.

190. There was a view that theorized that a שפחה was the lowest rank of maidservant; this type of maidservant was required to pour water over the hand of her master. This view is based on the conjecture that the שפח of שפחה was related to שפך, the verb for "pour." Fortunately, Koehler-Baumgartner writes that this view "is no longer recognised."

There is no male form of שפחה. But eleven times the word is used in connection with the word עבד. Thus the *TDOT* entry for שפחה is willing to conclude (vol. 15, p. 406) that the word means "an unfree female dependent of comparable status." Of course, the *Tanakh* contexts only imply what the word meant in the *Tanakh*, and not what the word's original meaning may have been.

for male and female slaves. (The English word "familiar" is also related to these words.)

My gut feeling tells me that our proposed connection between שפחה and משפחה, namely that both come from an "attached" meaning, is correct. I believe this, despite the fact that a connection is largely denied by perhaps most scholars today. Sometimes, in these etymological issues, one has to go with one's gut feeling!

In fact, we are lucky that most modern scholars deny a connection. If they believed that there was a connection, they might have theorized that ancient biblical society was so patriarchal that the head of the family viewed all his household members (משפחה) as slaves! (I am sure that there is someone out there who theorizes this!)

* * *

On an "adjacent" topic, let us briefly mention an unusual aspect of the word משפט. In Hebrew, the word means "sentence" in both the judicial and grammatical contexts. In English, the word "sentence" also has these dual meanings. Why should this be the case? As yet, I have no answer.[191]

* * *

Mitchell First supports his *mishpaḥah* as a personal injury attorney, and his *shefaḥot* as a Jewish history scholar.

22. נס: Insights into the Word נס (=Sign, Miracle)

1. The noun נס appears 21 times in *Tanakh* in various forms. In the view of the *Daat Mikra* (commentary on Exodus 17:15), in none of these times does it mean "very wondrous sign" or "miracle." Its main meaning is "flag, pole, sign." (But admittedly, Rashi and some other commentaries do give it the "very wondrous sign" or "miracle" meaning at Ex. 17:15 and sometimes elsewhere, as I will discuss below.)

2. נס developed the "very wondrous sign" and "miracle" meanings

191. A first step is to determine when the Hebrew word *mishpat* took on the meaning of "sentence" in a grammatical sense. This is not a biblical or talmudic meaning of the word.

at some point after *Tanakh*,[192] as an expansion from its initial meaning. It has these new meanings in the Mishnah. See, e.g., *Berakhot* 9:1 (*makom she-ne'esu bo nissim le-Yisrael*). The expanded meaning developed in Aramaic as well. It also often has these new meanings in passages in the liturgy that date from tannaitic times and thereafter.[193]

3. Two times in *Tanakh* we find a verb related to נס. One is at Psalms 60:6: "You gave to those that fear you *nes le-hitnoses*... (=a banner to display)." The other is at Zech. 9:16 (*mitnosesot*). The issue for etymologists is: which came first the noun or the verb?

In Hebrew, normally the verb precedes the noun. A verb comes into existence and then an initial *mem* or *tav* is added to turn the verb into a noun. For example, there is a verb זבח, to slaughter. An initial *mem* was added to this to create the noun: מזבח, the place of slaughtering. There are hundreds of cases like this. In the case of נס, however, since the noun does not fit the above form, many scholars believe that the noun came first and the verb followed.[194]

4. It is sometimes suggested that the noun נס, with its basic meaning of "flag, pole, sign," has some etymological connection with the root נשׂא, "to lift." [195]

5. A root נסה with the meaning "test, trial" appears many times in *Tanakh*. But נס, either in its original meaning (flag, pole, sign) or in its expanded meaning (very wonderous sign, miracle) is probably not connected with this root.[196]

6. I am willing to accept the view of the *Daat Mikra* expressed in statement #1 above. Now let us use this newfound knowledge. At Exodus 17, there is a story about the Israelites being able to defeat

---

192. See, e.g., E. Klein, p. 418 and *TDOT*, vol. 9, p. 438. The Dead Sea scrolls only have a few references to the word נס and the expanded meaning does not seem to be found there.

193. See, e.g., the passage in the מודים paragraph in the *Amidah*.

194. See, e.g., S. Mandelkern, p. 750 and *TDOT*, vol. 9, p. 438. Also, the verb probably only exists in the *hitpael* form, which is unusual.

195. See, e.g., S. Mandelkern, p. 750 and E. Klein, p. 418.

196. *TDOT*, vol. 9, p. 438. I have seen the suggestion that the way ancient people tested things involved raising and lifting them. But this is still far away from the "flag, pole, sign" meaning.

Amalek as long as Moses was able to hold up his hands. He stood at the top of a hill holding up a *matteh Elokim* with both hands.[197] The story concludes with Moses building an altar there and calling it *Hashem nissi*. Rashi (following the Targum) writes that the meaning is that God did a miracle for us there. But Rabbi Aryeh Kaplan, in *The Living Torah*, gives the simplest translation: "God-is-my-Banner." Many others have taken such an approach, not accepting a "miracle" meaning here.[198]

7. Another interesting verse to test the theory of the *Daat Mikra* is Deuteronomy 4:34. Here we have two words that could be given a "miracle" meaning: נסה (*nisah*) and מסת (*masot*).[199] *The Living Torah* translates both as "miracles," [200] and Rashi translates the first with "miracles" and the second with "tests."[201] But many others do not give a "miracle" meaning to either.

* * *

A synonym to נס is אות. This word appears seventy-nine times in *Tanakh* (in various forms). It originally meant "sign" but already in *Tanakh* it expanded into "very wondrous sign, miracle." It occurs with this meaning numerous times in *Tanakh*. See, e.g., Deut. 13:2, Ex. 4:8, and Ex. 4:17.[202]

* * *

---

197. On the simplest level, perhaps the sight of the *matteh Elokim* served as a source of inspiration and courage to the fighting Israelites. But compare Mishnah *Rosh Hashanah* 3:8.

198. See, e.g., Rashbam, Radak, S.D. Luzzatto, Rav S.R. Hirsch, and Rabbi Dr. J.H. Hertz.

199. Everyone will agree that *massot* should be understood as *mansot*.

200. "Has God ever done **miracles**...with such tremendous **miracles**, signs, wonders...?"

201. "Has any god performed **miracles**...with **tests**....?

202. The Even-Shoshan concordance counts 37 entries of אות with this meaning. (It is important to realize that Even-Shoshan's "meanings" are only suggestions, and are often wrong. But I admit that I find his attempts to categorize the words' meanings very helpful and thank him for his Herculean efforts.)

What about that innocuous word את? Often defined as "the mark of the accusative." Here is what we find in E. Klein, p. 60: "The orig. form [of את] prob.

I would like to acknowledge the Nov. 10, 2006, post "Nes and Nisayon" at balashon.com which provided some of the ideas for this column.

* * *

Mitchell First is miraculously able to be both a personal injury attorney and a Jewish history scholar, although the former is a trying experience and tests his patience.

23. נפש: What is the Meaning of וינפש (Ex. 31:17)?

In our Kiddush every Shabbat morning we recite the following from Exodus 31:17: "For in six days God created the heaven and the earth and on the seventh day *shavat va-yinnafash*." We know the meaning of *shavat*.[203] But what is the meaning of that last word?

At the outset, I have to point out that the letters נפש are used as a noun over seven hundred times in *Tanakh*. But only three times do they function as a verb. Aside from our verse, one of the other occasions is 2 Samuel 16:14: "The king and all the people that were with him came weary,[204] *va-yinnafesh sham*." (The reference is to King David at the time of the rebellion of Absalom.)

The other occasion is Exodus 23:12: "Six days you shall do your work and on the seventh day you shall rest so that your ox and donkey shall rest, *ve-yinnafesh* the son of your handmaid, and the stranger."

As a noun, common meanings of נפש in *Tanakh* are: "life," "living being," and "person." But the noun also has the meaning "throat" in *Tanakh*. The evolution was probably: throat > life > living being > person.[205] The throat is the organ for breathing and eating.

Examples of the "throat" meaning of *nefesh* in *Tanakh* include:

---

was '*iwyath*... which ultimately derives from base אוה (=to sign, mark), whence also אות (=sign)." Whoever imagined that את had such an interesting pedigree!

203. To cease from work.

204. *Ayefim*.

205. H. Tawil, p. 244. Probably the word started out as a noun, and not as a verb. See *TDOT*, vol. 9, p. 498.

- Isa. 5:14: "*She'ol* has opened wide its throat and parted its mouth to a measureless gap."
- Ps. 69:2 and 124:4: "Water reached to the throat."
- Ps. 105:18: "His feet were subject to fetters, an iron collar was put on his throat."

In Akkadian, one of the meanings of their verb that is cognate to נפש is "breathe" and one of the meanings of their cognate noun is "throat."[206] Also, in Ugaritic, their cognate noun includes a "throat" meaning.[207]

In *Tanakh* itself, an example of a noun with a breathing-related meaning is: *nafsho geḥalim telahet*=his breath kindles coals. See Job 41:13 (referring to Leviathan).

The *Tanakh* also has expressions with the combination of קצר + נפש several times. At least one of these may have had the literal meaning of "shortness of breath."[208]

I have also seen the suggestion that perhaps every time the *Tanakh* uses *nefesh* to mean "person," it literally means "breather"!

* * *

After that lengthy introduction, how has our two-word phrase at Ex. 31:17 been understood over the centuries?

- Onkelos: *shevat ve-naḥ*
- Rabbi S.R. Hirsch: "ceased to create and withdrew unto Himself."[209]
- R. Aryeh Kaplan: "ceased working and withdrew to the spiritual."
- Brown-Driver-Briggs: This work makes two suggestions for our verb. The second suggestion is "refresh oneself." This suggestion is followed by many, including *The Complete ArtScroll Siddur*, which has: "was refreshed." This was also the translation in the King James Bible (1611).

---

206. *TDOT*, vol. 9, pp. 500–01.
207. Ibid., p. 502.
208. See Num. 21:4, and Ḥizzekuni and S.D. Luzzatto. See also H. Tawil, p. 245.
209. This is in contrast to working on something external to Himself. R. Hirsch gives a similar explanation at Ex. 23:12 regarding the son of the handmaid and the stranger: they "come to themselves." See his elaboration there.

- Rambam: *Va-yinnafash*: "that which He desired was accomplished, and what He wished had come into existence." See *Moreh Nevukhim*, 1:67.[210]

But as you may suspect from my lengthy introduction, the best answers give our word a "breathing" meaning.

One suggestion is "catch one's breath." For example, Rashi on 31:17 uses the phrase *she-meshiv nafsho u-nshimato*. Similarly, Ibn Ezra writes *ke-mi she-yigga ve-yashiv nafsho* (shorter commentary[211]). Even though God's creations were with words and not through physical effort, the Torah speaks *bi-lshon bnei adam*. It is **as if** God stopped His work and took time to catch his breath.[212]

But perhaps a bit more simply, we should translate *shavat va-yinnafash* as "ceased his work and **breathed easily**."[213] As we might say colloquially today, "He took a breather!"

* * *

Mitchell First is a living and breathing personal injury attorney and Jewish history scholar.

24. נצח: The Multiple Meanings of the Word נצח: Eternal, Strength, Supervise

The precise meaning of נצח is relevant to us in our daily prayers. In the prayer *Va-yevarekh David* (just before *Yishtabaḥ*), we assign to God

210. Friedlander translation. Rambam can offer this interpretation because *nefesh* sometimes means "will" and "desire." See his discussion earlier at 1:41.
211. The shorter commentary is not found in the standard Mikraot Gedolot. It is found in the *Torat Ḥayyim*.
212. See also the comments made by Rabbi Dr. J. Hertz on Ex. 23:12. Hertz did not comment on our verse, surely relying on what he had written earlier.
213. See, e.g., *TDOT*, vol. 9, p. 504 and M.Z. Kaddari, p. 723 (נשם לרווחה). See also Brown-Driver-Briggs, first suggestion: "take [a] breath." H. Tawil, p. 244, translated *va-yinnafash* as "relax." In English, we have the expression: "rest and relaxation." This sounds a bit like *shavat va-yinafash*. But "relax" is not a word related to "breathing."

"*ha-gedulah, ve-ha-gevurah, ve-ha-tiferet,* ***ve-ha-neitzaḥ****, ve-ha-hod.*" This is a quotation from 1 Chronicles 29:11.

Our first task is to determine what נצח means in this verse. In *Tanakh*, the root usually means "eternal."[214] In contrast, in Rabbinic Hebrew, the root is typically used with a "strength, victory" meaning. Could the root have a "strength, victory" meaning in this late biblical verse?

Let us closely examine the meanings of the noun נצח in *Tanakh*. The noun appears 45 times.[215] The Even-Shoshan concordance gives 40 of these 45 occurrences the meaning of לעולם (=eternal). Aside from these, in two occurrences (both in Isaiah chapter 63) the word seems to have a meaning related to "blood." [216]

Let us look at the three remaining occurrences. One is the famous phrase at 1 Samuel 15:29: *neitzaḥ Yisrael lo ye-shaker ve-lo yinaḥem.* ולא ינחם means "he will not change his mind." This strongly suggests that the entire phrase should be translated as: "The Eternal One of Israel will not lie and will not change his mind." This is how Malbim and *Daat Mikra* interpret the verse.[217]

Another is Lamentations 3:18: אבד נצחי. While a "strength" meaning is possible, נצחי here is parallel to תוחלתי which means "my hope." Therefore, the more probable meaning of נצחי here is "my eternity." This is how Rashi understands it.

Finally, we have our verse in Chronicles. Admittedly the traditional commentaries give it strength-related meanings here. But how likely is

---

214. But unlike the word *olam*, which can refer to both the extended future and the extended past, נצח always refers to the future.

215. Usually, the vocalization is *netzaḥ*. Four times the vocalization is *neitzaḥ*. There is no difference in meaning. The same vocalization issue occurs with many other words in *Tanakh*, such as the word את. It is a function of the trop.

216. This meaning may derive from a meaning like "eternal life force." Alternatively, there is an Arabic cognate with the meaning "sprinkle." See *TDOT*, vol. 9, p. 530. The two instances where נצח has a meaning related to "blood" may be related to this meaning.

217. Admittedly, many of the traditional commentaries interpret the phrase with a meaning related to "strength" or "victory." They were probably influenced by the Targum, and by the "strength, victory" meaning that is widespread in Rabbinic Hebrew.

it that the word has such meanings here if it does not mean "strength" anywhere else in *Tanakh*? (The only possible exception is Daniel 6:4, in the Aramaic section of *Tanakh*, as I will discuss below.)

The Complete ArtScroll Siddur translates our word in *Va-yevarekh David* with the strength-related word: "triumph." Every other English siddur and English siddur commentary that I have seen does something similar.[218]

But if you agree with my analysis above, the numerous other times that נצח appears in *Tanakh*, it has a meaning related to "eternal." This strongly implies that this should be its meaning in this occurrence. I.e., we are assigning "Eternity" to God. Malbim is one who agrees with this interpretation. [219] It is also significant that the word נצח is not placed next to the word *gevurah*, but between the words *tiferet* (=splendor, glory) and *hod* (splendor, glory, majesty).[220]

(But shortly I am going to suggest an entirely different approach to the נצח of 1 Chronicles 29:10, which is more consistent with this placement.)

What is the origin of the Rabbinic meaning "strength, victory"? It is the meaning of the word in the Aramaic language. This meaning is already found, prior to Rabbinic Hebrew, in at least one of the Dead Sea scrolls.[221] Of course, it is possible that this meaning already existed in Hebrew at the time of Chronicles, a late book of *Tanakh*.[222] But,

218. After I wrote that sentence in a column a few years ago, Shulamis Hes showed me the beautifully illustrated siddur *Nehalel beShabbat* (2013). This siddur translates the נצח of *Va-yevarekh David* as "permanence."

219. See his commentary here which also refers to his earlier comments on Isa. 57:16. Malbim does not agree with my claim that נצח never has a strength-related meaning in the Hebrew section of *Tanakh*. See, for example, his *biur ha-milot* at Job 34:36. I thank Rabbi Chaim Sunitsky for this reference.

220. In contrast, in the rabbinic prayer *Yishtabaḥ*, נצח is placed next to *gedulah* and *gevurah* and obviously means something like "strength, victory."

221. See 1QM 4:13 (referring to God's victory). The "strength, victory" meaning may be found in other Dead Sea scroll passages as well. See *TDOT*, vol. 9, p. 532. As indicated there, often the meanings of these passages are disputed. The *TDOT* article (vol. 9, p. 530) also notes that a meaning like "victory" is found in Phoenician. But the article does not explain from what century or give any more detail.

222. It is possible that נצח has a strength-related meaning at Ben Sira 43:5. This

as I suggested above, a strength-related meaning at 1 Chronicles 29 does not fit the context.

Are the "eternal" and the "strength, victory" meanings connected? (After all, Hebrew and Aramaic are related languages.) Certainly, things that are "eternal" are also often "strong," so a connection is very possible.

נצח is found one time in the Aramaic section of *Tanakh*, at Daniel 6:4. Here, the meaning may be a meaning related to "strength,"[223] but others believe that the meaning here is "distinguished himself." Aramaic has a meaning of נצח as "shine, bright."[224] If the meaning here is "distinguished himself," this may have derived from the Aramaic "shine, bright" meaning. [225]

A meaning in Hebrew of נצח as "shine, bright" is found in Ben Sira, at 32:10 and 43:13.[226] Accordingly, *Theological Dictionary of the Old Testament* suggests that the meaning of the word at 1 Chronicles 29:11 is "radiance." [227] Similarly, the Koehler-Baumgartner lexicon suggests "splendor, glory." These fit the context better than "eternity." Perhaps these are the best interpretations, even though נצח does not have such meanings elsewhere in the Hebrew section of *Tanakh*.

Now let us deal with that ubiquitous word למנצח (=for the *menatzeaḥ*). This word appears 55 times in the book of Psalms (and one time in Habakkuk). What does *menatzeaḥ* mean? נצח is used as a verb several times in *Tanakh*. See, e.g., Ezra 3:9: לנצח על עשה מלאכה. From the context here and in the several other verses, it clearly means "to supervise." So למנצח almost certainly means: "to the [musical]

is a difficult verse. The Hebrew of Ben Sira dates to approximately 200 BCE.

223. See, e.g., *Daat Mikra*.

224. See, e.g., M. Jastrow, pp. 927–28.

225. The Jewish Publication Society translation of 1917 is "distinguished himself." The Soncino commentary explains: "The root *netsach* in Aramaic originally means 'to shine,' and so 'to be illustrious.'"

226. Perhaps this meaning arose in Hebrew under the influence of Aramaic.

227. *TDOT*, vol. 9, p. 532. (On p. 530, the article had suggested "Glory.") In his forthcoming work on the daily liturgy, *The Rhetoric of Jewish Prayer*, Reuven Kimelman suggests "brilliance, splendor."

supervisor." What follows it is an instruction about how the psalm is to be performed.[228]

It seems difficult to connect this "supervise" meaning of נצח with the "eternal" meaning.

But some connect the "supervise" meaning with the "shine, bright" meaning. A suggestion is that from the "shine, bright" meaning came a "distinguish oneself" meaning. One who distinguishes himself then becomes the supervisor.[229]

So far, I have mentioned four different main meanings of נצח: (1) eternal, (2) supervise, (3) shine/distinguish oneself, and (4) strength/victory. Surprisingly, the Brown-Driver-Briggs lexicon, the Koehler-Baumgartner lexicon, and Ernest Klein are all willing to assume a relationship between all of them. Yet, they do not provide any explanation! I prefer the view of the article in *Theological Dictionary of the Old Testament* (vol. 9, p. 530): "philologists are uncertain as to their relationship."

* * *

One reason I have always been interested in the root נצח is because it is found in one of the most famous stories in the Talmud, the story of R. Eliezer and the oven (*Bava Metzia* 59b). Here the Sages decide that the *halakhah* must always follow the majority of the Sages. They reject the opinion of R. Eliezer, even though R. Eliezer has a *bat kol* descend from heaven and state that the *halakhah* is always in his favor. We are told that, upon hearing all of this, God concludes: נצחוני בני. From the context of the story, these two words obviously mean "my children have defeated me." But a famous homiletical interpretation makes the alternative suggestion that the proper translation here is: "my children have eternalized me." I.e., by making the determination of the *halakhah* subject to the majority of the Sages (and not Divinely

228. See, e.g., *Daat Mikra* to Hab. 3:19, and Soncino to Ps. 4:1 ("In the Psalm headings it refers to the director of music. He receives his instruction regarding the accompaniment of the Psalm in the words that follow.")

229. See the commentary of Keil and Delitzsh, quoted in the post at Balashon.com of Feb. 8, 2015. To my ears, this explanation sounds farfetched.

fixed at the outset), the *halakhah* is thereby made flexible and can last eternally.[230]

* * *

The verse *Neitzaḥ Yisrael Lo Yeshaker* was the source for the name of the ניל״י group, which was active from 1915–17. It was founded by four Aaronsohn's: Aaron, Alex, Sarah, and Rivka, together with Rivka's fiancé Avshalom Feinberg. This group spied for Britain against the Turks. As I was writing this article, I began to wonder: Did they choose the name for the group because they believed נצח had the "strength/ victory" meaning? Or did they understand the word with the "eternal" meaning? Or perhaps they chose the word because they liked the multiple meanings? Since this was an espionage group and they did not file public records, I suspect we will never know.

* * *

Mitchell First is a personal injury attorney and Jewish history scholar. He hopes to write illuminating and strongly convincing articles eternally.

25. נשק: The Two Meanings of נשק: "Kiss" and "Be Equipped"

נשק is an interesting root because it has two different meanings: "kiss" and "be equipped." From the latter, it also means "equipment/ weapons."

Let us call the "kiss" meaning נשק-1. This "kiss" meaning occurs many times. But there are a few times when the root seems to mean "touch" or "join together." For example, perhaps it means "touch" at Ezekiel 3:13 (to be discussed below), and perhaps it means "join together" at Psalms 85:11: *tzedek ve-shalom nashaku*.[231] There is also

---

230. See *Shenei Luḥot Ha-Berit* (17th cent.), *Toledot Adam*. See also Vilna Gaon (18th cent.), *Divrei Eliyahu*, commenting on the above passage in *Bava Metzia*. I would like to thank Rabbi Avi Horowitz for these references.

231. Also, the *nashaku* is parallel to *nifgashu* earlier in the verse.

The "kiss" meaning is also difficult at Prov. 24:26 and Job 31:27. For example, the latter has the hand "kissing" the mouth! This is the wrong order. A scholar

evidence for this "join together" meaning in Arabic. An issue that arises in the case of נשק-I is whether the original meaning of the root was "kiss" or whether it was "touch/join together" (the much rarer meaning in *Tanakh*). There is a disagreement between scholars on this issue. [232]

Let us call the "equipped, equipment, weapons" meanings נשק-II. These occur only 13 times in *Tanakh* (and never in the Torah).

Could נשק-I and נשק-II be related? After all, the purpose of military equipment is to create a physical contact with the enemy, even though it is a hostile contact!

I always thought that the two roots were related. Even in English, we have an expression "kiss of death." This led me to think that the "military equipment" meaning was a euphemism of some sort. But now that I have researched this topic, I see that the widespread view is that these two roots are **not** related.[233]

On the other hand, the essay in *Theological Dictionary of the Old Testament* (vol. 10, p. 73) is a bit more neutral, stating that "the etymological connection between [them] needs more precise investigation."[234]

S. Mandelkern is one source that takes seriously the possibility that

---

has suggested that the meaning of *yishak* and *tishak* in these verses is "seal up" (=similar to "join together"). In Job, it is the mouth that is being "sealed up." In Proverbs, it is the lips. The implication is one of silence. Accordingly, Prov. 24:26 should be translated: "He who responds with correct words will silence [hostile] lips." Similarly, the latter half of Job 31:27 should be translated: "[if] my hand ever silenced my mouth." See the article by Jeffrey Cohen in *Vetus Testamentum* 32 (1982), pp. 416–424.

Another difficult use of the term is at Psalms 2:12 בר נשקו.

232. For example, M.Z. Kaddari, p. 737, takes the position that the original meaning was "kiss," while E. Klein, p. 429, takes the position that the original meaning was "to touch, to fit, join."

There is another view, based on Arabic, that the original meaning of the root was "to smell." See, e.g., Brown-Driver-Briggs, and E. Klein, p. 429.

233. For example, all of the following sources separate them: Brown-Driver-Briggs, E. Klein, and M.Z. Kaddari.

234. There were also several entries for the root in Koehler-Baumgartner. I found their entries particularly confusing. They also included several question marks. This allows for the possibility of relations between their entries.

the two different נשק roots are related. He suggests that the connection is חבור וקשור. He does not explain further. But perhaps he means that נשק did not originally mean "kiss" but "join together" and perhaps military equipment was considered something attached to you.[235]

Rabbi Matityahu Clark, in his *Etymological Dictionary of Biblical Hebrew Based on the Commentaries of Rabbi Samson Raphael Hirsch*, puts four meanings of the root in the same entry: "equipping," "arming," "touching," and "kissing," citing examples of verses that reflect each meaning. He defines the root as having the fundamental meaning of "prepare." But he does not provide any further explanation.[236]

Of course, Rabbi Clark **always** puts words with common roots in the same entry, since, based on Rav Hirsch's approach to words, he assumes that words with common roots **must** be related. As I have mentioned in many articles, this is a very problematic approach, in particular for a dictionary. Words with common roots are often related, but not always. Moreover, when Rav Hirsch writes and attempts to unite two roots, he is a commentator writing prose. Everyone knows that his commentary is just his opinion. But Rav Clark's book is in dictionary form, giving the impression that what he writes is widely accepted.[237]

There was an interesting remark by Rav Hirsch in his commentary to the *yishak* of Gen. 41:40.[238] He rejects the meaning "kiss" here. Then

235. A friend suggested to me that an unwanted kiss may be viewed as hostile and aggressive, in particular, in today's "Me Too" world. This would be another possible way of connecting our two נשק roots!

236. As I write this, I am beginning to see what he may have had in mind, but I don't want to speculate. Often, but not always, one can see how Rabbi Clark unifies the words by his particular choice of word definitions.

237. Nevertheless, I have always found Rabbi Clark's book easy to use and very helpful. It just must be used with tremendous caution since many of his definitions are based on his uniting roots that should not be united.

238. *Yishak* here is a difficult word. Pharaoh tells Joseph*: ve-al pikha yishak kol ammi.* Many scholars today relate this ישק to the משק at Genesis 15:2. There Eliezer is described as the *ben meshek* of the house of Abraham. Of course, we do not know what this word משק means. But from the context, it is evident that it means something like "feed, support, manage." (See, e.g., Onkelos, Rashi, and S.D. Luzzatto.) It is possible that that word משק derives from נשק-II.

My friend Josh Waxman suggested humorously that the import of the

he writes "it is definitely preferable to take the other meaning of נשק viz. to make preparations, equip oneself." This would have been a perfect opportunity for him to explain how he views the relationship between the two roots. But unfortunately he did not do so.[239]

* * *

Finally, an interesting use of our root is at Ezekiel 3:13. (This is the verse that follows the famous *barukh kevod Hashem mimkomo*" at 3:12.) Here we are told that Ezekiel heard the noise (קול) of the *kanfei ha-ḥayot* (=wings of the *ḥayot*) as they were משיקות one to another. (The root letter *nun* often drops in the first position, so this word should be understood as the equivalent of *manshikot*.) Were the wings of the *ḥayot* "kissing" one another? Perhaps the meaning here is merely "touching." Another interpretation is that they were so close it was **as if** they were kissing.

But how would the meaning in any of the above translations result in a noise? For this reason, the Targum translates the word as if the root letters were in a different order. It uses a word from the root נקש. This root means "knocking." In this translation, the wings of the *ḥayot* were knocking against one another, thereby producing the noise. Of course, ordinarily we do not want to transpose letters to get a workable translation!

* * *

Mitchell First is personal injury attorney and Jewish history scholar, occupations that have little connection.

26. סלה: What is the Meaning of סלה?

We have all recited this simple word thousands of times in our prayers. But what does it mean?

To give you some background, it appears seventy-one times in

---

phrase *ve-al pikha yishak kol ammi* is that Joseph was instructed to be in charge of the ancient Egyptian dating service!

239. Perhaps he discusses his view of the relation somewhere else in his commentaries.

Psalms, and three times in Habakkuk (all in chapter 3). It appears nowhere else in *Tanakh*.

It never appears at the beginning of a verse, but occasionally comes in the middle of a verse (Ps. 55:20 and 57:4, and Hab. 3:3 and 3:9). Otherwise, its position is at the end of the verse.[240]

There is a statement by a Tanna at *Eruvin* 54a that *selah* has a meaning like ועד and נצח, i.e., something that will continue forever. The statement cites the last part of Psalms 48:9 as a support: "God will establish it עד עולם סלה." While this verse fits the "forever" meaning, the "forever" meaning does not fit all seventy-four occurrences of the word.

How have the *Nakh* commentaries interpreted the word *selah*? Let us look at several commentaries on Psalms 3:3, where the word first appears. *Metzudat Tziyyon* interprets it as לעולם (=forever). Malbim interprets it as indicating a הפסק and סיום הענין. Ibn Ezra thinks the word means something like "it is so," an affirmation of what preceded it. He also mentions an ancient view by a non-Jewish translator that the word has no meaning but is used as a filler so that the length of the line will match the melody.[241]

An interesting suggestion was made by some scholars that the word was derived from סל=basket and that *selah* was the instruction for a basket-shaped drum to be beaten![242]

After surveying the various views, *Daat Mikra* to *Tehillim* concludes that most likely, the word was an instruction to the singers or musicians about raising the singers' voices or music level.[243] I agree. The word probably derives from the biblical root סלל=raise.[244]

This view was expressed long by the Radak (d. 1235). See his comm.

240. Four times it appears at the end of the entire psalm. It may appear more than once in the same psalm.

241. See further Uriel Simon, *Four Approaches to the Book of Psalms* (1991), p. 295.

242. See *EJ* 13:1322, and the concordance of S. Mandelkern. The former has a long discussion of the word and concludes: "No solution to the enigma of *selah* is possible in the present state of our knowledge."

243. See their comm. to Psalms 3:3, note 3, and see further their comm. to Hab. 3:3.

244. See, e.g., Isa. 57:14, Ps. 68:5, and Prov. 4:8. Often in this root, a *lamed* will

to Psalms 3:3 and his *Sefer Ha-Shorashim.* As pointed out by Radak, evidence for a musical instruction approach is that *selah* only appears in the book of Psalms and in the third chapter of Habakkuk. This chapter of Habakkuk ends with the words *la-menatzeaḥ be-neginotai.* This ending indicates that this chapter of Habakkuk is of a similar genre to what is found in Psalms. In all of *Tanakh,* if we find a word only in Psalms and in Habakkuk chapter 3, this is strong evidence that it is a word relating to a musical instruction, and not a regular word.

I mentioned earlier that there was a statement by a Tanna that *selah* had a meaning like "forever." The Targum also adopts the "forever" explanation.[245] For these reasons, when the word *selah* is used in our rabbinic prayers, it is invariably used with the meaning "forever." A prominent example of this is that *selah* occurs three times in the daily *Amidah* with the implicit meaning of "forever."[246] Another prominent example of this "forever" meaning is the סלה באמת just before the morning *Shema.*

I mentioned above that the word *selah* appears seventy-one times in Psalms, and otherwise only appears in the third chapter of Habakkuk. What other word has a similar distribution? The word is למנצח. Aside from its one appearance in the book of Habakkuk, it appears fifty-five times in the book of Psalms. (I discuss this word in a separate article.)

* * *

Mitchell First writes scholarly articles for the Jewish Link and is an injury attorney who takes the other side to the brink. *Selah*!

---

drop, as in the first two verses cited. (In contrast, in the last verse cited, there is an extra *samekh*!)

245. See, e.g., Targum to the *selah* at Ps. 3:3: לעלמין.

246. See the *kedushat ha-shem* blessing, and the end of the *hoda'ah* blessing (two times).

27. ספר: The Multiple Meanings of ספר

The root ספר has a few meanings in *Tanakh*: the verbs "count," and "tell a story," and the nouns *sefer* (= letter or scroll), and *sofer* (scribe). A major issue is whether all these meanings are related.

Let us first address the easy question. Is there a relationship between "count" and "tell a story"? There is such a phenomenon in English as well: "to count," and "to recount" a story. Also, an "accountant" works with numbers, and a newspaper "account" is a retelling of a story. The word "tell" also had an original meaning of "count." Think of a bank "teller."

A relationship between the words for counting and telling a story is found in other languages as well, such as German, Dutch, Danish, French, Italian, and Spanish.[247] These languages are Indo-European languages, not related to Hebrew and the other Semitic languages.

The simplest explanation for all of this is that a story is the sum of details and in telling a story, there has been an enumeration and ordering of all the details. As one scholar has nicely put it: "To count is to put numbers in their proper order, and to tell a story or relate an incident is to put events in their proper order, first things first and last things last."[248]

(In Hebrew, it means "to count" in the *kal*: *lispor*, and to "recount, enumerate, tell a story" in the *piel*: *le-sapper*.)

* * *

Now let us move to the hard question. Are the nouns *sefer* and *sofer* related to the "count" meaning?

First, it is critical to define the nouns properly. The meanings of *sefer* in *Tanakh* are: an inscription, a document, a letter, and a scroll. A reasonable assumption made by scholars is that the fundamental meaning of all of these is "a writing." (The word *sefer* appears 185 times in *Tanakh*. It never means "book," like a bound modern book, but it sometimes means "scroll."[249])

---

247. See, e.g., the column of Philologos of Jan. 12, 2014 in the *Forward* and E. Klein, p. 626

248. Philologos, ibid.

249. For example, this may be its meaning at Num. 21:14 which refers to *sefer*

As to *sofer*, it probably originally meant one who writes such a *sefer*.[250] (The people with this title in *Nakh* are often ones working for the king.[251])

There was no verb ספר in Biblical Hebrew that meant "to write."[252] So how do scholars explain the origin of the noun *sefer*, with its meaning: "a writing"?

Early on they took the approach that the noun *sefer* with this meaning was a loanword from Akkadian. See, e.g., the Brown-Driver-Briggs lexicon of 1906. The explanation was that there was a word in Akkadian *shipru*, with the meaning "message, letter," derived from the verb *shaparu*=to send, write. This was viewed as the source for the Hebrew word *sefer*. If the Hebrew noun *sefer* was derived from Akkadian, then the Hebrew noun had no connection to the "count" meaning of the Hebrew verb.

In later decades, it was discovered that ספר was also used in Ugaritic with a meaning like "writing."[253] Ugaritic is a more likely source for Hebrew words than Akkadian. So a revised suggestion was that the Hebrew noun *sefer* was derived from a Ugaritic noun that meant "writing."[254]

But an alternative suggestion has been made. Perhaps the noun

---

milḥamot Hashem.

As Hebrew evolved and came under foreign influences, the nouns *ketav* and *iggeret* came into use and the meaning of *sefer* gradually became restricted to "scroll."

250. See Koehler Baumgartner, p. 767 and *TDOT*, vol. 10, p. 309. At *TDOT*, p. 322 a few other unlikely suggestions are made.

With regard to the *ha-sofer* title given to Ezra (at 7:6), this may have had a different connotation. See *Daat Mikra* and Koehler-Baumgartner. Scholars have observed that the word *sofer* perhaps had a broader connotation in the post-exilic period.

251. See, e.g., 2 Kings 12:11, Est. 3:12 and 8:9, and 2 Chron. 24:11. The word *sofer* does not appear in the Torah.

252. The Koehler-Baumgartner lexicon is willing to claim that Ps. 87:6 is a verse where the verb ספר means "make a written record." But even if the verb did have a meaning related to "write" in that verse, this would likely be a meaning of the verb that arose later, perhaps derived from the noun *sofer*.

253. See H. Tawil, p. 267.

254. Ibid.

sefer in Ugaritic did not originally mean "writing," but meant a "list of items." Only thereafter did it expand to have the general meaning "writing."[255] If this suggestion is correct, then we can connect the original meaning of *sefer* to the "count" meaning of the Ugaritic and Hebrew verbs ספר.[256] Whether this suggestion is the true explanation is an unresolved issue.[257]

* * *

A few other observations:

- There is a passage at *Kiddushin* 30a that *soferim* were called this because they counted all the letters in the Torah. The passage then gives a few examples, e.g., the *vav* in the word גחון (Lev. 11:42) is stated to be the midpoint of all the letters in the Torah.[258] But this is just a homiletical approach to the word. The biblical word *sofer* appears in contexts outside of Torah writing and that would not seem to involve the counting of letters. As I stated above, most likely it merely meant one who writes a *sefer.*
- At Psalms 56:9, we have both the "count" meaning (second word) and the "scroll" meaning (last word) in the same verse. But this is likely just wordplay.

* * *

What about the "cut" meaning of ספר? This meaning is not found in *Tanakh*. It is found in Aramaic and, like many Aramaic words, it slowly became incorporated into Hebrew.[259]

We also have ספיר (=sapphire, a gemstone) several times in *Tanakh*.

---

255. See *Theological Lexicon of the Old Testament*. vol. 2 (1997), p. 806.

256. See also Rav S.R. Hirsch to Gen. 5:1. R. Hirsch suggests that a *sefer* is a "summing together different things" (under one fundamental idea). Hence it is related to the count meaning of ספר.

257. See *TDOT*, vol. 10, pp. 309 and 328.

Archaeologically, it is the case that some of the earliest forms of writings are markings where items were counted. E.g., common people trading with one another.

258. This is not the case. Much has been written on this topic. For recent discussions, see James S. Diamond, *Scribal Secrets* (2019), pp. 112–16 and Amnon Bazak, *To This Very Day* (2020), pp. 180–82.

259. See, e.g., Mishnah *Avodah Zarah* 2:2 (haircuts by idol worshippers). Of

Most likely this is not a Semitic word and is a shortened form of *sanpir.*[260]

Finally, Arabic has a word *safar*=journey, related to the Akkadian "send" meaning mentioned above. This led to the Swahili word: "safari."[261]

* * *

Mitchell First is an expert in counting (chronology) and writing (etymology). He does not (yet) travel the spheric world and go on safaris.

P.S. For some light reading on the root ספר, see "The Hebrew Origins of Superman," *Biblical Archaeology Review*, May/June 1979, by James K. Brower.

28. עבר: Insights into the Root עבר

This is a very important root in *Tanakh*. It has basic meanings like "pass, pass over, cross over."[262] I cannot discuss every aspect of this root and will limit myself to a few.

1. The word עברה (*evrah*) appears many times in *Tanakh* with a meaning like "anger." For example, it is at Gen. 49:7: ועברתם (*ve-evratam*), regarding Jacob's rebuke to Simon and Levi. It also appears at Psalms 78:49 (a verse we recite at the *seder*): God sent upon them *ḥaron appo, evrah, va-za'am ve-tzarah*. What is the connection between the root עבר and "anger"?

There are several possible explanations. One is that an angry person has "crossed the line" of acceptable behavior. This seems to be the meaning of the expression in English. Alternatively, in English we have an expression "to be carried away by anger." Perhaps this is

---

course, I am not denying that a lot of storytelling goes on in a barbershop (=*misparah*), as my friend Yehuda Miller suggested to me!

260. The original form of the word in Old Indian was *sani-prijam*. It means "dear to Saturn." E. Klein, p. 454.

261. I learned this interesting insight from the post of April 18, 2006 at balashon.com.

262. See E. Klein, p. 462.

the explanation of our Hebrew idiom.[263] Finally, another possible explanation is that the anger overflows out of the person.[264]

2. The word עבור (*avur*) appears two times in the book of Joshua (5:11 and 5:12) in the expression עבור הארץ. From the context it means "produce of the land." This phrase appears nowhere else in *Tanakh*. Can we find an underlying "passing" or "crossing" here?

Perhaps there is a cross over in the sense that the produce "grows out of the land."[265] A different approach is suggested by Radak. The produce from שנה שעברה is called עבור, while the produce from the שנה הבאה is called תבואה.[266] Finally, another view explains the word with an Akkadian cognate. The Akkadian cognate, *eburu*, has the meaning "harvest, crop." [267] The last is the most widespread approach to the word.[268] In fact, עיבור (*ivur*) and עבורא (*ivura*) are Aramaic words for "grain."[269] Targum Onkelos consistently translates the Torah's דגן with such a word.

I have seen the suggestion that the reason that the unusual word for produce of the land was used in these verses was that Joshua 5:10 had used the words ערב (evening) and ערבות (plains). The goal was to find a word for "produce" that sounded somewhat similar. [270]

3. A big challenge is the word בעבור which appears 49 times in *Tanakh*. It has meanings like "on account of," "for the sake of," "because of," and "in order that."

The Brown-Driver-Briggs lexicon suggests: "perhaps originally

---

263. See, e.g., E. Klein, p. 462.

264. See, e.g., Brown-Driver-Briggs. See also the comments of Rav S.R. Hirsch to Deut. 9:8: "*Evrah*, the highest degree of rage, formed from the point of view of coming out of oneself; passing beyond oneself…"

Surprisingly, the Koehler-Baumgartner lexicon puts all the "anger" entries in a different entry (עבר II), and makes a comment about an "uncertain" relationship between the two entries.

265. This view is implicit in M. Jastrow, p. 1065 (last line).

266. See his commentary to these verses and his *Sefer Ha-Shorashim*.

267. See H. Tawil, pp. 269–270.

268. See Tawil, ibid. See also Brown-Driver-Briggs, p. 721a, M.Z. Kaddari, p. 770, and *Daat Mikra* to Josh. 5:11.

269. M. Jastrow, pp. 1065–66 and *Daat Mikra* to Josh. 5:11.

270. See *Daat Mikra* to Josh. 5:11.

for the produce or gain of." It seems that the Brown-Driver-Briggs lexicon was basing its suggestion on the "produce" meaning of *avur*.

But it seems unlikely to base the etymology of the common word בעבור on that rare agricultural word עבור. A better view is that the word reflects the **movement** from purpose to accomplishment, or from cause to result.[271] See similarly Rav S.R. Hirsch, comm. to Ex. 20:17: "the **transition** to something, in the intention to achieve something."

4. What about the word עבירה (*aveirah*)? Where does this word come from? It is not found in *Tanakh*. Rabbi David Bashevkin writes:[272]

> The word *aveirah* is clearly derived from the biblical word *la-avor* [לעבר], to transgress. Although we do not find the noun *aveirah* in the Bible, we frequently find the term *la-avor* as a verb indicating that a sin has been committed. The absence of the word *aveirah* in biblical literature may be part of a larger biblical trend that avoids abstract nouns in biblical writing. For instance, in the Bible we find the term *sho'khain* [שכן], a verb denoting God's dwelling, but only in later rabbinic literature do we find the conceptualized noun *shekhinah* [שכינה], meaning the presence of God. Steven Fraade, Judaic Studies professor at Yale, develops the idea that many biblical verbs later emerged within Mishnaic literature as conceptualized nouns...
>
> According to Fraade, Mishnaic times marked a shift towards conceptualization of many biblical terms... From the verb לעבור – to transgress, emerged the conceptualized noun עבירה – a transgression. Sin, with this new word, was no longer an action; suddenly sinning had become a concept.

Bashevkin then asks why the word *aveirah*, not mentioned in *Tanakh*, became such a common term for sin? One possible explanation is that, as the legal boundaries between what was permitted and

271. See R. Laird Harris, et al, *Theological Wordbook of the Old Testament* (2003).

272. *Sin-a-gogue: Sin and Failure in Jewish Thought* (2009), pp. 8–9. When Bashevkin speaks, he tells his audiences that his book should be on their shelves, but it cannot be the only book on their shelves!

what was prohibited became clearer from biblical times to mishnaic times, it became fitting to use the term *aveirah*, since a sin is a transgression of a boundary.[273] (On a homiletical level, he adds that calling sin an *aveirah* ties it to the past, while repentance is seizing control of the future![274])

5. Eventually the root עבר ended up as a word related to pregnancy. I always wondered why. Only at age 61, as I was first writing this column for the *Jewish Link* newspaper did I learn the answer.

In *Tanakh*, there is only one hint to a "pregnancy" meaning. At Job 21:10, we have שורו עבר (*shoro ibbar*). The word *ibbar* here is used for a male animal making a female animal pregnant.

The verb is in the *piel*. A reasonable assumption takes this to mean "to cause to be pregnant." In Rabbinic literature, we typically have מעוברת (*me'ubberet*) a word that describes the condition of the female. According to E. Klein (p. 364), *me'ubberet* is a *pual* form; the *pual* is the passive of the *piel*. It seems that the "crossing over" that occurred in the *piel* form is the transfer of the seed from the male to the female.[275]

Now I know why no one discusses this topic! Of course, I am kidding. Surely very few people realize that this is the probable origin of *me'ubberet*=pregnant.

Before I researched this, I had a completely wrong idea of how עבר came to mean "pregnant." I thought the growth of the pregnant woman's belly made her considered "over the line"!

6. From the "pregnancy" meaning came the next expansion, to the

273. Ibid, p. 10.

274. Ibid, p. 11.

275. See, e.g., Brown-Driver-Briggs, p. 718b ("semen") and Koehler-Baumgartner, p. 780 ("to allow the semen to spread over"). See similarly M. Clark, *Etymological Dictionary of Biblical Hebrew*, p. 178, item 8. See also *Daat Mikra* to Job 21:10, and Rav S.R. Hirsch to Deut. 9:8. (In contrast, E. Klein, p. 462, had written that "to cause to be pregnant" was probably a "special sense development" of עבר "pass, pass over, cross over," but did not explain how.)

Koehler-Baumgartner also mentions a different interpretation of the verse in Job: "mount." I.e., the physical act itself involves a crossing over.

calendar meaning. In the Mishnah and thereafter, the word is used to describe a year that has an extra month.

* * *

Mitchell First crosses between being a personal injury attorney and a Jewish history scholar.

29. לחם עני: The Meaning of לחם עני: Did the Israelites Eat Matzah While They Were Slaves?

At the beginning of the Haggadah, we make the statement that our forefathers ate לחם עני while in the land of Egypt: "*ha laḥma anya di akhalu avhatana be-ara de-Mitzrayim.*" On the simplest level, this statement means that our ancestors ate matzah while they were slaves in Egypt.[276]

What is the source for this הא לחמא statement? Unlike some other parts of the Haggadah, this statement is not found anywhere in the Mishnah, Talmud, or Midrash, and seems to date to the Geonic period.[277]

Is there any evidence in *Tanakh* that our ancestors ate matzah as slaves in Egypt? The only possible evidence might be the term לחם עני at Deuteronomy 16:3. Let us investigate this term.

We need to look at the entire verse: "You should not eat *ḥametz* with it [=the *pesah* sacrifice]; seven days you should eat *matzot* due to it, *leḥem oni*, because in haste you exited from the land of Egypt; in order that you remember the day you left the land of Egypt all the days of your life."[278]

A common translation of *leḥem oni* is "bread of affliction." This is

---

276. It is also possible that the intent is to refer to the matzah eaten with the sacrifice or to the matzah eaten as they were traveling. On the latter, see Ex. 12:37–39, Num. 33:5–6 and M. Kasher, *Haggadah Shelemah* (1967), p. 5, n. 13
277. See Kasher, p. 48 and Shmuel and Ze'ev Safrai, *Haggadat Ḥazal* (1998), pp. 109–111.
278. The word עליו appears twice in this verse. I am giving it two different translations: "with it" and "due to it." I am following the approach of the *Daat Mikra*.

the translation of the Jewish Publication Society of America of 1917. They took it from the King James Version (1611).[279]

First, let us look at some of the traditional commentators. Sforno writes that *leḥem oni* refers to the bread that the Israelites ate while serving as slaves (=during the period of עינוי). Because the taskmasters were constantly rushing them, the Israelites did not have time to let their bread rise. *Bekhor Shor* and Ḥizzekuni write that *leḥem oni* refers to the bread being made at the time of the exodus in the manner of an עני (=poor person). It was made without all proper equipment and with insufficient time. Naḥmanides writes that our verse indicates there is a double implication in the commandment to eat matzah: it commemorates the matzah that they ate in haste while they were leaving, and the matzah that they ate while they were slaves.[280]

But on the simplest level, verse 16:3 is referring only to the time that the Israelites left Egypt and *leḥem oni* is a way of describing the bread that they ate at this time. The bread is of low quality because it did not have time to rise. This seems to be how *Daat Mikra* understands the phrase: *ve-ha-matzot leḥem oni hu, ki lo ḥametz*. In this view, *leḥem oni* does not mean "bread of affliction," but "**afflicted bread**"! Similar is the interpretation of Jeffrey Tigay, in *The JPS Torah Commentary: Deuteronomy*: "primitive, unluxurious fare that one would not normally eat." This is also the view of Ritva, in his commentary on the Haggadah.[281]

Also noteworthy are the comments of R. Hertz on לחם עני:

> So called because the bread was prepared while the people were in a state of stress and hardship, consequent upon their hasty departure from Egypt... There is, of course, an obvious association of ideas with servitude in Egypt.

---

279. The King James Version, followed by the 1917 Jewish Publication Society of America translation, surprisingly adds the word "even" in its translation: "even the bread of affliction." This is what is found in the Pentateuch of Rabbi Dr. J.H. Hertz as well, which uses this as its translation.

280. Nahmanides offers a different explanation for *leḥem oni* as well: to teach that it should not be *matzah ashirah*.

281. It is quoted in *Haggadah Shelemah*, p. 5: *ha-matzah mitkabetzet **u-mitḥaseret ve-einah matzlaḥat** ke-mo ha-ḥametz.*

R. Hertz does not explain further. But he has **not** stated that the Israelites ate matzah while they were slaves in Egypt. The **עני** in our verse can allude to the servitude **without** implying that they ate matzah while in servitude.

At Exodus 12:8, we are told to eat *merorim* with the *pesaḥ* sacrifice. The Torah never gives the reason. Could it be there merely to increase the appetite for the meat, as some have suggested?[282] Strikingly, at Exodus 1:14 we had been told "***va-ye-mareru*** *et ḥayeyhem be-avodah kashah.*" Almost certainly, the *merorim* we were commanded to eat with the *pesaḥ* sacrifice symbolize the bitterness of the servitude expressed in this verse. But this does not mean that we ate *merorim* as slaves!

The case of matzah is analogous. Words with the theme of **עני** are common in the servitude verses. See Exodus 1:11 (**ענתו**), 1:12 (**יענו**), 3:7 (**עני**), 3:17 (**עני**), and 4:31 (**ענים**).[283] Eating **עני לחם** can serve to remind us of the affliction of our ancestors, but this does not mean that they ate "afflicted bread" while they were slaves.

This also seems to be the view of Rashi. He writes on 16:3: "*leḥem she-mazkir et ha-oni she-nittanu be-Mitzrayim.*" He is following the view of the Tanna R. Shimon at *Sifrei*, sec. 130. This view does not claim that the Israelites ate matzah while they were slaves.[284]

Of course, it is possible that matzah was a food staple of the Israelite slaves. But we can only get to this result by speculation, and not by evidence from the verses.

Additional Notes

1. When we look through the balance of the Torah for the reason given for eating matzah, here is what we find:
   - At Exodus 12:8, the Israelites were commanded to eat the *pesaḥ* sacrifice with *matzot* and *merorim*. No specific reason is given

282. *Daat Mikra* seems to prefer this interpretation.

283. See also Gen. 15:13, Deut. 26:6–7, Isa. 48:10 and Neh. 9:9.

284. Here is R. Shimon's statement: *Lamah nikra "leḥem oni"? Al shem innui she-nittanu be-Mitzrayim.*

for the *matzot* or *merorim* here and this was before the Exodus story described later in this chapter.[285]

- At Exodus 12:17, we are told: "*u-shemartem et ha-matzot*"[286] because on this selfsame day I took your masses out of the land of Egypt.
- At Exodus 13:6–7, the commandment to eat matzah is mentioned near the verse with the phrase בעבור זה at 13:8. Verse 13:8 has a variety of possible meanings.[287]
- At Exodus 12:34 and 39 are verses describing the Israelites leaving in haste. But these verses do not connect this to the commandment to eat matzah. [288]

2. Matzah could have symbolized "haste" even before the story of the Exodus. At Genesis 19:3, Lot baked *matzot* for his two unexpected guests. Two other biblical narratives also imply that *matzot* were the kind of cakes that would customarily be baked hastily for unexpected guests. See Judges 6:19–22 and 1 Samuel 28:24.[289]
3. The etymology of "matzah" is much debated,[290] but one view sees the root of the word as אוץ, which means "urge" or "hasten." See, e.g., Genesis 19:15 and Exodus 5:13.
4. The famous statement of R. Gamliel in the Mishnah explains the reason for the commandment to eat matzah. But it turns out that the original text of the statement in the Mishnah is much shorter than what is in our Haggadot. (For the other two items as well, the text in the Mishnah is much shorter than the text in our Haggadot.)

---

285. Also, at 12:11, they were told that they were to eat the *pesaḥ* sacrifice "with your loins girded, your shoes on your feet, and your staff in your hand" and *be-ḥipazon*.

286. It is unclear whether the reference here is to the holiday or to the *matzot*.

287. See, for example, the essay in Nehama Liebowitz, *Studies in Shemot* (1976), Bo, section 5.

288. The commandment to eat matzah is mentioned again at Exodus chapters 23 and 34, Lev. chapter 23, and Num. chapters 9 and 28, all without any reason given.

289. See similarly Nahum Sarna, *Exploring Exodus* (1986), p. 86.

290. I discussed this issue in *Roots and Rituals* (2018), pp. 227–228.

When R. Gamliel states the reason for the commandment to eat matzah, all he states is *al shem she-nigalu.*[291]

* * *

As a scholar, Mitchell First knows the "poverty" meaning of עני. But fortunately, he is an attorney as well and afflicts others by filing suits against them.

30. ויפג לבו: פוג (Gen. 45:26): What Happened to Jacob's Heart?

In *Parshat Va-yiggash* Jacob's sons return home and tell Jacob that Joseph is still alive and that he rules over the entire land of Egypt. The text then reports Jacob's response: "*va-yafag libbo*, because he did not believe them." But in the next verse, after the sons explain more and he sees the chariots that were sent, we are told ותחי יעקב רוח. What exactly happened to Jacob's heart initially?

The root of ויפג is usually assumed to be פוג. This root only appears six times in *Tanakh*, and this is the only time the root appears in the Torah. Let us review the approaches taken by some of our commentators.

- R. Saadia Gaon translates it that his heart was **in doubt**.
- Rashi writes that Jacob's heart was נחלף. Almost certainly, Rashi means "**changed**."[292] In this approach, Jacob's heart changed from believing to not believing.
- Radak suggests חלש ונרפה. The meaning of both of these words is "**became weak**."
- Ibn Ezra writes: עמד לבו ודמם. I.e., his heart **ceased** working. He cites to Lamentations 2:18 where פוגת is parallel to תדם, implying a "rest, cease" meaning. He also cites to 1 Sam. 25:37: וימת לבו.

  Many commentaries agree with Ibn Ezra here. For example, here is an excerpt from Naḥmanides: "The movement of his heart

291. See Safrai, p. 34. The standard printed Mishnah has an extra two words at the end: אבותינו במצרים.

292. See the ArtScroll edition of Rashi. Compare the Metsudah and Silbermann editions.

> **stopped** and he was like a dead person. This is a known matter when joy comes suddenly. This is mentioned in medical literature that elderly and weak people cannot bear this. Many of them will faint when joy comes to them suddenly. . . ."[293]
>
> Rav S.R. Hirsch also adopts the "cease" approach. His interpretation is that Jacob's "heart stood still *in doubt*, for he did not believe them, he could not so quickly get used to the wonderful news they brought him."[294]

But others think that the root פוג is fundamentally one of "**coolness.**" I.e., Jacob's heart became cold because he did not believe them. One can see the meaning "cold" in Mishnah *Yoma* 1:7 (*ve-hafeg*). Perhaps one can read it into some of the biblical verses which use the root פוג, such as Psalms 38:9: *nefugoti*. See, e.g., the Soncino commentary there: "The root-meaning is 'to grow cool;' he feels the chill of death creeping over him." Solomon Mandelkern also believes that "coolness" is one of the primary meanings of the root. One of the Latin words he uses to define it is *frigere*. (Surely you don't need me to translate this one!)[295]

The *Daat Mikra* to Habakkuk 1:4 suggests that "coolness" is the meaning there. (But then, in a footnote, it suggests the alternative meaning of "cease.")

Closely related to the "coolness" meaning is a meaning of "**numbness.**" See, e.g., R. Aryeh Kaplan, *The Living Torah*, who gives that translation here ("became numb").[296]

Daat Mikra translates our ויפג with two words: נקפא והתעלף (= his heart froze and he became faint). I suspect that their first word is the translation of *va-yafag* and their second word is only there because we are later told that Jacob's spirit was revived.

---

293. There is a tradition recorded in one of the Rishonim that Naḥmanides himself was a physician.

294. See also Rabbi Dr. J.H. Hertz: "his heart stood still, unable to beat for astonishment."

295. For the "cease" meaning, Mandelkern cites the two verses in Lamentations: 2:18 and 3:49.

296. See also, M.Z. Kaddari, p. 849. This is one of the suggested translations at Ps. 38:9 as well.

As I stated earlier, our root פוג occurs five other times in *Tanakh.* At Lamentations 2:18, it very clearly means "cease," because of the parallel that follows, and one can read the "cease" meaning into several of the other verses. But at Psalms 38:9 it is very hard to read the "cease" meaning in. Here the verse begins: *nefugoti ve-nidkeiti.* The second word means "I became crushed." It is hard to read the first word as "I became ceased." That is why meanings like "I became weak," "I became cold," and "I became numb" have all been suggested here.

To sum up, with regard to Genesis 45:26 and Jacob's heart, I have offered interpretations of: doubt, change, weakness, ceasing, coolness, and numbness. But the root does not mean "doubt" elsewhere. As to "cease," the verse does not clearly describe a lengthy cessation of Jacob's heart. Moreover, if Jacob's heart really stopped, it is questionable that he would have been able to be revived so quickly. With regard to the balance of the interpretations, I think that the "coolness, cold" interpretation offers the smoothest reading of verse 26: "His heart turned cold because he did not believe them."

This is also the interpretation adopted by Targum Onkelos: "But the words left his heart cold..."[297] The Kohler-Baumgartner lexicon also adopts this interpretation.[298]

The *Tanakh*, at Psalms 39:4, refers to a "hot heart" (חם לבי). So a "cold/cool heart" can be an idiom as well!

* * *

I suspect that the original meaning of the root פוג was a "coldness, coolness/numbness" meaning, and that the "weak" and "cease" meanings are later developments. Something that is cold/cool and numb becomes weak and eventually ceases to function.

* * *

Modern Hebrew has the term *pag tokef.* If you are unfortunate, this is

297. Translation from the Drazin-Wager edition.

298. See Koehler-Baumgartner, p. 916, interpreting the meaning in our verse as "to turn cold." Also noteworthy is Sforno: *nitalef ve-ḥasrah ketzat defikat libo ve-ruḥo.*" *Nitalef* means "became faint." Sforno is combining two approaches: "weak/faint" and "cease." By his use of the word *ketzat,* Sforno is implicitly agreeing that a lengthy heart cessation is not implied in the verses.

what a clerk in Israel will tell you: "The authority [of your document] has expired." This meaning surely derives from the "cease" meaning of our root. [299]

* * *

Mitchell First is a personal injury attorney and Jewish history scholar. Writing this column reminds him that he should check his passport expiration date.

31. שתם: Bilam: The Prophet Who Was *Shetum Ha-Ayin*

What is the meaning of this root שתם? It only appears at Numbers 24:3 and 24:15. There is a term for a word that appears only one time in *Tanakh*: a *hapax legomenon*. (This is Greek for "once said.") Our word can loosely be described as a *hapax legomenon*, since the second instance sheds no additional light on the word.[300]

The way most rabbinic commentators and scholars make sense of the word is by pointing to the root שתם in the Mishnah and Tosefta. (Of course, the Mishnah and Tosefta date many centuries later.) At Mishnah *Avodah Zarah* 5:3, for example, the root clearly means "to bore/open a hole."

Accordingly, Rashbam writes: *patuaḥ ayin* [=open eye], *roeh marot Elokim*. He cites the above passage from the Mishnah. Long before, Targum Onkelos had translated: שפיר חזי (=sees well). Most rabbinic commentators and scholars agree with Onkelos and Rashbam and view the phrase as a description of Bilam's ability to have visions.[301]

---

299. I thank Yehiel Levy for pointing out this modern Hebrew expression to me.
I would also like to acknowledge the post of balashon.com of July 31, 2006 which gave me the idea for this column.

300. There is a special word for a word that appears two times: *dis legomenon*. I thank Leonard Berkowitz for this detail.

301. See, e.g., Ibn Ezra, Radak (*Sefer Ha-Shorashim*), Koehler-Baumgartner, and *Daat Mikra*. Perhaps one can argue that the use of the singular, העין, implies a defect in the other eye. But it is very easy to interpret העין here as "vision/sight," as opposed to a reference to the physical eye. Then the use of the singular here does not imply a defect in the other eye. Also, the use of the singular can

But there is another way of deriving a meaning from the שׂתם of Mishnaic Hebrew. Rashi cites the same Mishnah ("to bore/open a hole"). Yet he believes the meaning here is that Bilam's eye was removed, and that his eye socket looked open.[302]

The term *gillui einayim* (=uncovered eyes) is used in reference to Bilam at 24:4.This supports the "open" interpretation of שׂתם, and is some evidence against Rashi's interpretation of the openness.[303]

* * *

Aside from the "open" interpretation, it is interesting to see how others have dealt with our unusual word *shetum*:

- R. Yonah Ibn Janaḥ suggests that the openness is a way of describing someone who cannot sleep.
- Naḥmanides suggests interpreting *shetum* as if the root was שׂית, which means "set, place." (He cites to Exodus 10:1.) The import is that Bilam had the power to obtain anything he set his eyes on.
- Many others interpret the word as if the word was סתם. The meaning would then be "closed." But this is not a plain sense approach to the interpretation of the word.[304]

---

even imply both eyes. See, e.g., the use of the singular ידו at Ex. 17:11 in light of Ex. 17:12. I thank Michoel Chalk for these insights his thoughts on this issue.

302. There are two different readings in Rashi when he describes the damage. Most editions read נקורה (=put out). But there is another version נקובה (=punctured). The ArtScroll edition of Rashi prefers the latter.

The ArtScroll edition suggests an explanation for Rashi's thinking: Had the verse referred to Bilam's powers of prophecy, it would have read *patuah ha-ayin*, but *shetum ha-ayin* means that the eye was open in the sense that the eye socket looked open.

After he gives his first interpretation, the one that seems to be his preferred one, Rashi also cites the view of Targum Onkelos approvingly.

303. But there are ways that Rashi could respond.

304. In contrast, interpreting a *sin* as if it were a *samekh*, and vice versa, is common. Also, sometimes we can interpret a *sin* as if it were a *shin* and vice versa. E.g., perhaps the pronunciation evolved over time from *shin* to *sin* or vice versa.

If the meaning of our word at verse 3 and verse 15 was "closed," it has been suggested that prophecy only came to him when his eyes were closed, or that the procedure of prophecy required that the prophet close his eyes. *Or*

- Some scholars have suggested that the vocalization is not correct and that the two words should be vocalized as *she-tam ha-ayin*=whose vision is complete/perfect (from the root תמם).
- Finally, most interesting is the homiletical interpretation of Baal Shem Tov.[305] Bilam was blind in one eye so that there could at least be one place in his body where holiness and prophecy could reside!

* * *

I also must mention the passage at *Sanhedrin* 105a. Here the Talmud has: "Bilam was blind (*suma*) in one of his eyes, as it is written שתום העין." At first glance, it looks like the passage is interpreting שתום as סתום. But those words are not in the text. Accordingly, Rashi interprets the passage to be teaching that *ayin* is in the singular and it is from this that we learn that Bilam had only one working eye. The passage is not addressing שתום at all.[306]

Just as I was getting used to Rashi's interpretation, I found that there is a parallel to the passage in the Talmud in the *Midrash Tanḥuma* manuscript that was published by Solomon Buber.[307] In this passage, there is an additional phrase: אל תקרא שתום אלא סתום. It is at least possible that these five words were once in the passage in the Talmud. Or perhaps they are expressing what was once viewed as the interpretation implicit in the Talmud.[308]

* * *

On the subject of Bilam, I must point out that in 1967, at Deir Alla (=perhaps the biblical "Succot," about eight kilometers east of the

---

Ha-Ḥayyim suggested that Bilam had to make a habit of closing his eyes. If they were open, his looking at someone would damage them.

It is noteworthy that at Lamentations 3:8, the word *satam*, with the meaning "closed," is spelled with a *sin*, instead of a *samekh*.

305. Cited in Yehuda Nachshoni, *Studies in the Weekly Parashah* (1989), p. 109.

306. In his comments on *Sanhed.* 105a, Rashi does not mention the main interpretation he offered in his biblical commentary.

307. I found this through that wonderful site alhatorah.org.

308. A passage similar to the one at *Sanhed.* 105a is at *Niddah* 31a. The five words found in the Buber edition of *Midrash Tanḥuma* are not here either. If the *al tikra* phrase was once in the Talmud, either explicitly or implicitly, this style of interpretation is typically meant only homiletically.

Jordan River), archaeologists found an inscription describing visions of a "Bilam son of Beor," who is described as a חזה אלהן (= seer of the gods).[309] Its language is a dialect with a mix of Aramaic and Hebrew. The text can be dated to around 800 BCE. This date is several hundred years later than the biblical Bilam. But the text may just be a tradition of a vision of the biblical Bilam.[310] (Or was this a vision of a descendant several hundred years later? Perhaps being a חזה אלהן was in the family genes!)

119 pieces of text were recovered. (The text was originally painted in red and black ink on plaster affixed to a wall. The wall later collapsed, perhaps due to an earthquake.) Reconstructing the text is difficult, but a main part of the text is a story that one night the gods come to Bilam and tell him that the world will be destroyed. Bilam arose and wept. He tells his people the details of what the gods told him, using images of birds and other animals. Actions are taken by Bilam and his people and the disaster is averted.

Unfortunately, there was no depiction of Bilam's face with this inscription. If there was, perhaps our issue of the meaning of שתם could have been resolved!

* * *

Mitchell First is a personal injury attorney and Jewish history scholar. Both as an attorney and a scholar, he has the ability to "see through" weak arguments.

---

309. Words from the root חזה are used twice at Num. 24:4 in connection with Bilam.

Daat Mikra includes a photo of a portion of the inscription. A brief discussion of the inscription is found in a supplemental volume of the *Encyclopaedia Judaica* (17:188). There is much material on the inscription available online.

310. The biblical Bilam, hired to deal with the Israelites, made the trip from his hometown in far away Petor in Aram Naharayim. See Num. 22:5 and Deut. 23:5. Perhaps he was often hired to locations far away, due to his reputation.

32. תפלין: The Origin of the Word תפלין

We are all familiar with the word תפלין. But what did it originally mean?

If one looks at the Mishnah, usually the word appears in the plural, תפלין.[311] But several times the word appears in the singular. We have תפילה של יד at *Menaḥot* 4:1 and תפילה של ראש at *Mikvaot* 10:3. There is also תפלתו at *Megillah* 4:8.

Our first thought might be that *tefilin*[312] were called תפלה because they were worn during *tefilah*, or at least during the morning *tefilah*. Many take this view. See, e.g., Ernest Klein, *A Comprehensive Etymological Dictionary of the Hebrew Language*, p. 713: "so called because they are worn during the morning prayers on weekdays." But is this etymology correct? First of all, in tannaitic literature, תפלה often means merely the *Amidah*. But even if we interpret *tefilah* in its broader meaning, we all know that this etymology does not sound correct. It is evident from many passages in early rabbinic literature that *tefilin* (in some form) were typically worn by men during their routine daily activities. So how should we understand the term תפלה, the singular for the plural *tefilin*?

First let us deal with that term "phylacteries." The original Greek term, *phylakterion*, literally means: "means of protection." It was a way of referring to protective amulets. How did this word become the common English word for *tefilin*? In the New Testament (Matthew 23:5), we are told, as a criticism of the hypocrisy of the Pharisees: "They do all their deeds to be seen by others; for they make their *phylakterion* broad and their fringes long." Almost certainly, the *phylakterion* reference here is to *tefilin*.[313] The later church fathers also use this term to refer to *tefilin*.

---

311. The original plural form (at least in Palestine) was likely תפלים (*tefilim*). This is how the plural appears in various places in the Kaufmann manuscript of the Mishnah, the earliest one. This manuscript was probably composed in Palestine. It dates to the 10th or 11th century, but is viewed as doing a good job of preserving the spoken language of second-century Palestine.

312. When writing words like תפלה and תפלין in English, I am going to deviate from the conventional spelling and write them with one "L."

313. See Jeffrey H. Tigay, "On the Term Phylacteries," *Harvard Theological*

As to the word תפלה with its meaning "prayer," this is almost certainly a shortening from an original תפללה. The root of התפלל is the verb פלל with a meaning of "intervene, judge." פלל as a noun would be תפללה, but sometimes, as happened here, one of the double letters drops.[314]

Now let us return to our original question, why the singular form of *tefilin* is תפלה.

Marcus Jastrow believes that תפלה in the *tefilin* context means something like "attachment."[315]

The *Encyclopaedia Judaica* (15:902) mentions a suggestion that תפלה in the *tefilin* context is not from the root פלל, but from a different root, פלה. This is a root that means "separate, distinguish." The suggestion is that Jews distinguished themselves from non-Jews by wearing *tefilin.*

Another view claims that פלל also has the meaning of "proof." See Psalms 106:30 and its interpretation at *Sanhedrin* 44a. The suggestion is then made that *tefilin* serve as proof that the name of God is upon the wearer and leads to fear of the wearer by others.[316] This view is found at Tosafot, *Menaḥot* 34b, s.v. לטוטפת, and is cited in many later sources. But פלל does not mean "proof."

Another view suggests that פלל has the implication of atonement. Wearing *tefilin* helps the wearer achieve atonement (perhaps parallel to the *tzitz* worn by the high priest). [317]

However, the best explanation for תפלה in the context of *tefilin* is provided by Yehudah B. Cohn in his detailed study: *Tangled Up in Text: Tefillin and the Ancient World* (2008).

Cohn argues convincingly that there was a widespread view of *tefilin* as serving an amulet function in the tannaitic period, influenced

---

Review 72 (1979), pp. 45–52.

314. With regard to the use of the *hitpael* for this verb, I have written much about this elsewhere and disagree with the widespread view that it means "judge yourself." A different function of the *hitpael* is at work here. See my *Roots and Rituals*, pp. 240–47.

315. M. Jastrow, p. 1687.

316. See Deut. 28:10.

317. See the תפילין entry in *Encyclopedia Mikrait*, vol. 8 (1982), pp. 884–885 (also by Tigay).

by the widespread Hellenistic practice of utilizing amulets. The Semitic term for an amulet is קמיע. In the Mishnah, *tefilin* are often mentioned side by side with קמיע. See *Shabbat* 6:2, *Shekalim* 3:2, *Mikvaot* 10:2, and *Kelim* 23:1.

Cohn suggests that *tefilin* may have been viewed as amulets for long-life, since this is alluded to at Deuteronomy 11:21 (*lemaan yirbu yemeikhem...*), or they may have been viewed as general purpose amulets for protection.

Cohn points out that the first use of תפלה in either Hebrew or Aramaic to describe a material object is found in an Aramaic document from a Jewish community in Egypt. The document is estimated to date to 300 CE. It mentions ten תפלה of silver. Cohn writes: "The reference to *tefillah* as a material object is clear, and suggests an amulet, surely the most likely candidate for prayer in material form."[318]

Cohn continues: "This expansion of the original meaning of *tefillah* to describe objects that *functioned* as prayers can be analogized to the one experienced by the English word 'charm.'... [T]he function of the object came to be used to refer to the object itself."

So תפלה in the singular included the meaning of an object that functioned as an amulet[319] and *tefilin* is its plural. Of course, this interpretation of *tefilin*, and its singular, *tefilah*, is consistent with the meaning of the Greek word, *phylakterion*, a word commonly used for amulets.

The scholar Jeffrey Tigay writes: "It is true that the official understanding of *tefillin* was as educational and spiritual symbols.... But there is no lack of evidence that *tefillin* were ascribed apotropaic properties and used as such."[320] Tigay then cites the example of the Amora R. Yoḥanan who is mentioned as believing in the protective power of *tefilin* (*Berakhot* 23a–b).

---

318. See Cohn, p. 147. The document itself is included at Arthur Cowley, *Aramaic Papyri of the Fifth Century* BC (1923), #81, line 30. (Most of this work collects fifth century BC documents. But 300 BCE is the date that Cowley estimates for this particular document due to the many Greek names found in it.)

319. It is only when the object contained the biblical *parshiyyot* that the words *tefilah* or *tefilin* would be used to describe it. Other amulets would be described merely as קמיע.

320. *Harvard Theological Review*, p. 51.

Tigay continues: "This attitude does not indicate that *tefillin* first entered Judaism as amulets... it is but another case of the superstitious veneration which commonly adheres to sacred objects and practices." Tigay also cites the church father Jerome (c. 400, Palestine) who was very familiar with Jewish practices. Jerome writes: "Whoever has them, has them as a protection and reminder to himself." I.e., Jerome mentioned both aspects of *tefilin*: the biblical aspect and the protective aspect.

* * *

P.S. As to why the plural of תפלה is *tefilin* and not *tefilot*, I cannot say. But already in a Dead Sea text we have *tehillim* as a plural for *tehillah*![321] (By the way, Ibn Ezra calls the book of Psalms: *Sefer Tehillot.*[322])

* * *

Mitchell First is a personal injury attorney and Jewish history scholar. Maybe it is time already for him to discard his amulets.

33. Interesting Words in the Megillah

אגרת (9:26, 29)

This word only appears in Esther, Nehemiah and 2 Chronicles.[323] Everyone realizes from the context that the word means "letter." But why? There is a root in Hebrew, אגר that means "gather."[324] Therefore, many of the traditional commentaries believed that an אגרת was a collection of thoughts. But scholars now realize that the word is likely derived from the Akkadian word *egirtu* that means "a letter that is sent."[325]

---

321. This is found in the Dead Sea Psalms Scroll. In *Tanakh,* the plural of *tehillah* is always in a feminine form. See, e.g., Ex. 15:11.
322. See *Daat Mikra*, intro. to Psalms, p. 1, citing Ibn Ezra's introduction to this work.
323. But related words appear three times in the Aramaic section of the book of Ezra.
324. See, e.g., Deut. 28:39 (תאגר).
325. E. Klein, p. 7, H. Tawil, pp. 5–6, and *Daat Mikra*.

והאחשדרפנים (9:3)

This word has eleven Hebrew letters.[326] This makes it one of the three longest words in *Tanakh*.[327]

The original Persian word here is *khshatrapanan*. The meaning is "satrap" which comes from the Greek shortening of the Persian. The Megillah added an initial *aleph* to the Persian.

Something similar happened in the case of the name אחשורוש. His name in Persian was written as *Khshayarsha*, and the Megillah added an initial *aleph*.[328]

האחשתרנים בני הרמכים (8:10)

Here we have two one-time words. This is a well-known phrase because an Amora in the Talmud (at *Megillah* 18a) admits that even the amoraic Sages did not know the meaning of the phrase. But רמכים is found in Mishnah *Kilayim* 8:5, and is a kind of horse, so perhaps the amoraic statement was really focused on the first word. The solution to the first word was found in the mid-19th century, when Persian cuneiform was deciphered. The word means "royal/ governmental."[329]

אמן (2:7)

We are told that Mordechai was *omein* to Esther. How should we translate this word?

Of course, we all know this root אמן. Usually it means "trust/

---

326. The word appears two other times in the Megillah with fewer letters. It also appears one time in Ezra.

327. There are two other words with eleven letters. See Ezek. 16:47 and 20:44. (By the way, the word with the largest *gematria* in *Tanakh* is תשתרר at Num. 16:13. Its *gematria* is 1500.)

328. I have written much about this elsewhere. See my *Esther Unmasked* (2015), pp. 130–36. Interestingly, in Elamite cuneiform, the name was written with an initial "i" sound, and in Akkadian cuneiform, the name was usually written with an initial "a" sound. So the Megillah was not doing anything so unusual here by adding that initial *aleph* to the name of the king.

329. See E. Klein, p. 18, and Zvi Ron, *The Jewish Bible Quarterly* 36:1 (2008), pp. 33–38

believe." But one time in *Tanakh*, at Song of Songs 7:2, it means "craftsman." The "trust/believe" meaning and the "craftsman" meaning are not related, as the latter comes from Akkadian (borrowed from Sumerian, a non-Semitic language).[330]

OK, so what did Mordechai do for Esther? And what did Naomi do for Ruth's baby? (She is described as an *omenet* at Ruth 4:16.) Were they teaching their children crafts?

Many translate the word at Ruth 4:16 and elsewhere (e.g., Num. 11:12) as "nurse." But the application of this word to Mordechai (and other men, see, e.g., 2 Kings 10:1) is difficult!

Daat Mikra, in the case of Mordechai, offers מגדל and מחנך (raise and educate). But we would prefer not to invent new meanings for the root.

Here is the better approach. A fundamental meaning of the root אמן is "trust." The *omein* and *omenet* were individuals who were entrusted with the child and trusted with its care.[331] In this explanation, there is no reason to postulate a "nurse" meaning.[332]

אנס (1:8)

This verse reads: "The drinking was according to דת (law/custom/usage), no one was אנס (=compelled)." If you look at the main section of the Mandelkern concordance, you will see that this seems to be the only time this word appears in all of *Tanakh*. However, a word with the same three letters, but with a different vocalization, appears at Daniel 4:6, in the Aramaic section of *Tanakh*. Mandelkern does indeed list this word in his separate Aramaic section. This is a reminder that when using the Mandelkern concordance, one must always check both

330. See H. Tawil, p. 24 and E. Klein, p. 35. But I did see one source that did not realize this (or did not accept it) and translated the אמן of Song of Songs 7:2 as a "dependable worker"!

331. See *TDOT*, vol. 1, p. 294.

332. Because *omein* has been commonly thought to mean "nurse," the 1917 Jewish Publication Society of America translation (included in the Pentateuch of Rabbi Dr. J.H. Hertz) was forced into the following translation at Num. 11:12: "as a **nursing-father** carries the suckling child"! The word *omein* is, of course, male, unlike *omenet*.

the Hebrew section and the very thin Aramaic section that covers sections of the books of Daniel and Ezra.[333]

The word at Daniel 4:6 may or may not be related to the word at Esther 1:8. Its meaning is subject to varying interpretations.[334]

With regard to the meaning of אין אונס at Esther 1:8, there are two interpretations. One is that no one was forced to drink more than they wished. The other is the opposite: no one was forced to stop! Everyone was allowed to drink as much as they wished![335]

גורל (3:7 and 9:24)

This word appears many times in *Tanakh*. It means "lot." But what is its origin? The original meaning of the word seems to have been "small stone," suggesting that the casting of lots was originally done with small stones. Scholars deduce the word's meaning from Arabic, which has a similar sounding word for "small stone."[336] The English word "coral" probably ultimately derives from this Semitic root.[337] I also saw a suggestion that related our English word "gravel" to this Semitic root,[338] but others disagree.

דת (1:8 and elsewhere)

This word only appears in the books of Esther, Daniel and Ezra. Hebrew borrowed the word from Persian.[339] (Persian is not a Semitic language.) It means "decree, law, usage."

As to the word אשדת at Deut. 33:2, it is written as one word, not as two separate words. Moreover, since דת with the "decree, law, usage" meaning does not appear until the late books of *Tanakh*, it is very

333. Along with one verse in Jeremiah (10:11) and two words from Genesis (at 31:47).

334. See *Daat Mikra* to Dan. 4:6.

335. For further discussion, see *Daat Mikra*.

336. See E. Klein, p. 95 and *TDOT*, vol. 2, p. 450.

337. See E. Klein, p. 95.

338. See *TDOT*, vol. 2, p. 450.

339. E. Klein, p. 133, suggests an original Indo-European origin for the word.

unlikely that the אשדת of Deuteronomy, even if read as two separate words, has any connection with the "decree, law, usage" meaning.[340]

Of course, it is interesting that those who observe Jewish law today are called דתיים, even though this is a word with a foreign, non-Semitic origin. (דתיים is at least easier to say than *halakhiyim*, which might have been an alternative!)

הגלה: (2:6)

The root here is, of course, גלה. This root has two different meanings: "reveal" and "go away." Here the meaning is the latter. But the interesting issue is whether these two different גלה meanings have a common origin. Most scholars believe that there is a relation, but exactly what the relation is and which meaning came first is still subject to debate. I discussed this in *Roots and Rituals*, pp. 67–68.

הדו (*Hodu*)

This is the biblical term for India. The references to *Hodu* at Esther 1:1 and 8:9 are the only references to India in *Tanakh*. The name derives from the Persian name *Hindu*. But as often happens in Hebrew, the *nun* dropped. (The *dagesh* in the *dalet* reflects the fact that there was once a preceding *nun*.)

This area called *Hodu* in the *Tanakh* refers to the region near the Indus River. Modern scholars point out that this is in today's Pakistan.

The Hebrew word for turkey is *tarnegol hodu*. This means "Indian

---

340. Accordingly, "fiery law" is not the correct translation. So how should we translate these four letters? There are words in *Tanakh* with the letters אשדת that mean something like "slope of a mountain" or "waterfall." But these meanings do not fit the context in this verse.

Another approach was suggested by Richard Steiner. He believes these were two separate words. He postulated that דת was a shortened form of דאת. This word, a verb, would mean "flew." The meaning of the entire phrase would be "from his right, fire flew to them." (This way, we at least would have a verb in the phrase.) See Richard C. Steiner, "דת and עין: Two Verbs Masquerading as Nouns in Moses' Blessing (Deuteronomy 33:2, 28)," *Journal of Biblical Literature* 115 (1996), pp. 693–98.

chicken." Something like this is the name for the bird in many European languages, which is what led to the name in Hebrew.

But didn't turkey originate in North America? Why did Europe associate it with India? The explanation seems to be that the first Europeans who reached the Western Hemisphere thought that they were in India, so the people in Europe thought that this new bird was from India. This is also the explanation for the name "Indians" for the native people in America.

Finally, if there are people out there who think that Achashverosh reigned from "Turkey" to "Kush," I hope that this column serves to eliminate that thought! (As to Kush, this is probably Ethiopia.)

כרפס (1:6)

This is the only time this word appears in *Tanakh*. It is a loanword from Persian and means "fine fabric, linen." (Its earlier origin is Sanskrit, where it has the meaning "cotton."[341])

In the Mishnah, Tosefta, and Talmud, we have כרפס with the meaning of "plant," and "celery/parsley." This word may also ultimately derive from Persian but it derives from a completely different Persian word.[342] (Interestingly, the Mishnah, Tosefta, and Talmud never mention כרפס in connection with the *seder*.[343])

מדינה (1:1 and elsewhere): province, region

This word does not appear in the Torah but it appears in *Nakh*, starting with 1 Kings and in some of the books that date after that.

If you were inventing a word for "region," perhaps you might invent some word with a root like "neighbor" or "family." Alternatively, to mention a more negative approach, the French philosopher Ernest Renan once wrote that "a nation is a group of people united by a mistaken view about the past and a hatred of their neighbors." After

341. See Brown-Driver-Briggs. The word in Sanskrit is *karpasa*.

342. E. Klein, p. 287. Klein writes that it is probably borrowed from Persian *karats*.

343. The word is first mentioned in connection with the *seder* in the Geonic period (in the form כרפסא). See my *Roots and Rituals*, p. 227. It is mentioned as one of the permissible options for the *borei pri ha-adamah* at this stage.

that brief introduction, what exactly is the origin of this word מדינה? The answer is easily seen. That initial *mem* is not a part of the root. The root of the word is דין: to judge. What unifies the מדינה as a region is its common legal system with authority over its people.[344]

* * *

Mitchell First is a personal injury attorney and Jewish history scholar. He wants to start a new custom to travel to India on Purim, and eat turkey there. (Is this so different from traveling to Uman on Rosh Hashanah?)

34. The Difference Between R. Saadia Gaon and Rashi in their Approach to Words

When I write about a biblical word, I always assume that the word has one underlying meaning and that our task is to find it. There are many statements in Rashi that show that he takes this approach as well. Of course, sometimes it turns out that a word has a few different meanings. But that does not mean that my initial attempt was improper.

A few years ago, I came across an article by Richard Steiner, who was a professor at Yeshiva University for several decades. He pointed out that, prior to Rashi, a widespread assumption was that a word could easily have many meanings. He had an article published in 1988: *Saadia vs. Rashi: On the Shift from Meaning-Maximalism to Meaning-Minimalism in Medieval Biblical Lexicology.*[345] I would like to share some of his insights.

Aside from doing a translation of the entire Torah, Rav Saadia Gaon (d. 942) wrote a detailed commentary on the Torah. The commentary may have spanned the entire Torah, but there are also grounds for the view that it only spanned Genesis 1:1 to 28:9, and Exodus and Leviticus. (Only portions of the commentary have survived.)

Saadia includes semantic analyses in his commentary that go well beyond what is needed to clarify the meaning of the passage

344. E. Klein, p. 319.
345. *Jewish Quarterly Review* 88, pp. 213–58.

in question. The reason Saadia wrote so expansively was probably because there were not yet biblical dictionaries in his time.

Steiner writes further: "Saadia believed that words have many meanings, while Rashi held that they often have only one basic meaning. Saadia made the multiplication of meanings a cornerstone of his exegesis, while Rashi pursued a reductionist policy. In short, Saadia was a meaning-maximalist, while Rashi was a meaning-minimalist."[346]

What motivated Saadia to propose multiple meanings for words? Obviously, positing multiple meanings helps resolve contradictions in Tanakh.

But it also sometimes helps reconcile the Bible with our intellect. For example, if a certain interpretation of a word would describe God in a way that made no sense, one can give a different interpretation of the word. Steiner provides the following example. In the case of the root נחם, Saadia gives six different interpretations: regret, threaten, console, forgive, see, and consider. The usual meaning in the *nifal* is "repent/ regret" but Saadia avoids this interpretation when the verb applies to God. For those cases, he uses the meanings: threaten, forgive, see, or consider. Steiner explains Saadia's thinking: "An interpretation according to the usual meaning would imply that God is susceptible to change, but since our intellect tells us that this cannot be true, we are duty-bound to posit the existence of other, less common meanings." [347]

Finally, positing multiple meanings helped as a weapon against the Karaites. For example, the date of the Shavuot holiday depends on the interpretation of the phrase "*mi-maḥarat ha-shabbat*" at Leviticus 23:15 and 23:16. In the rabbinic interpretation, the phrase in the first verse does not mean the day after Shabbat (as the Karaites would have it), but "the day after the day of rest (=Passover)." In the second verse, "*mi-maḥarat ha-shabbat ha-shevi'it*" means "the day after the seventh week." In his commentary to Genesis 2:2, Saadia stresses that the biblical word *shabbat* may refer to holy days other than the Sabbath.

Steiner writes that Saadia's Torah commentary exhibits "a marked

346. Ibid., pp. 214–15.
347. Ibid., p. 218.

tendency to vary the translation of words to fit the context, resulting in smooth, coherent renderings." [348] One scholar has counted 47 different translations of *vav* in the commentary, each one attested to at least three times! (Also, in his discussion of the "Tree of Life," Saadia lists eight meanings for the word חיים!)

Steiner explains further: "Saadia's approach is adopted from Muslim exegetes, lexicographers, grammarians, and philosophers, who were heirs to a tradition going back to Aristotle[349]... Saadia was heir to several intellectual traditions in which semantic distinctions which today appear unnecessary were both commonplace and respectable. The principle, later to be enunciated by William of Ockham, that 'entities are not to be multiplied beyond necessity' did not play much of a role in discussions of meaning in those traditions."[350]

Steiner amply documents Rashi's different approach. He writes: "Rashi has a fondness for definitions of the form 'every occurrence of term X, whether pertaining to +Y or to –Y, has the meaning Z.' Some of these definitions may have been designed to challenge Menaḥem's claim, borrowed from the Muslim lexicographers, that a word can have two diametrically opposed meanings..."[351] Steiner cites the following comments of Rashi where Rashi attempts to find the underlying common meaning of a word or root: Num. 14:36–37, Deut. 22:9, Ezek. 16:43, and Hab. 1:10. (These comments are regarding the roots דבה, קדש, זמה and קלס.)

In Rashi's view, there is normally only one meaning to a word, which "the interpreter adjusts according to the context."[352]

What motivated Rashi's approach of meaning-minimalism? Steiner suggests that a major factor was early rabbinic literature. Steiner notes that tannaitic definitions are usually of the form אין... אלא. More significantly, Steiner points to a statement in *Sifre* Numbers:

348. Ibid., p. 222.

349. Ibid, p. 215.

350. Ibid, p. 235.

351. Ibid, pp. 238–39.

352. Steiner's favorite statement of Rashi on this subject is at Ex. 14:31, on the word יד: "Many meanings fit the word יד, but they are all the same as the meaning of an actual hand, which the interpreter adjusts according to the context." (P. 240, translation by Steiner.)

ein nezirah be-khol makom ela perishah. Rashi cites this seven times in his commentaries.[353]

I often use the *Sefer Ha-Shorashim* of the Radak. Radak lived in 12th century Provence. When one goes through the entry for each root, sometimes he gives an explanation to unite the different meanings. But many times he shifts gears mid-entry. He writes וענין אחר and provides a different meaning and makes no attempt to connect the different meanings. This always bothered me, as it seemed to me that he gave up too easily. After reading Steiner's article, I now understand. For centuries, there was an intellectual approach to words that was satisfied with different meanings. Starting with Rashi, there was a movement towards "meaning-minimalism." But, in being satisfied many times with different meanings of homonyms (=words that looked the same), Radak was following an ancient tradition as well.

Ibn Ezra lived a few decades after Rashi. He only cites Rashi by name thirteen times in his Torah commentary.[354] He traveled a lot and probably did not have constant access to Rashi's commentaries. Steiner quotes another scholar who concludes that Ibn Ezra too had a "marked tendency to minimize, to the extent possible, his recourse to the exegetical strategy of 'this word has to be interpreted in two senses.'"[355]

* * *

One of the reasons Biblical Hebrew has a lot of homonyms is that the Hebrew alphabet of 22 letters is a "reduced" one. Most likely, the original Semitic alphabet had 29 letters, just like Arabic. Accordingly, several of our Hebrew letters (*zayin*, *ḥet*, *ayin, tzadi*, and *shin*) are letters in which earlier different letters have coalesced. Words may look the same in our reduced alphabet but, in an earlier stage, one or more of the letters were different.

* * *

Mitchell First is a personal injury attorney, a Jewish history scholar, and a meaning-minimalist.

---

353. Steiner, p. 250.
354. Ibid, p. 251.
355. Ibid, p. 251, quoting Uriel Simon.

History

1. The Invention of the Alphabet

In an alphabetic writing system, each letter represents a sound. Where did the alphabet come from? Were there different alphabetic writing systems that arose independently in different parts of the world? Since the English word "alphabet" bears a striking resemblance to the Hebrew letters *aleph* and *bet* you should already be able to intuit the answer.

Two other ancient writing systems are hieroglyphic writing and cuneiform. Hieroglyphic writing started off with each picture representing a word. ("Hieroglyph" is a Greek word meaning "sacred carving.") The Egyptians used hieroglyphic writing. In cuneiform writing, wedge-shaped signs were impressed by a stylus on wet clay. The clay was then baked. The cuneiform signs could reflect both consonants and vowels. Both cuneiform and hieroglyphic writing pre-date alphabetic writing.[1]

* * *

The earliest alphabetical writings known to us come from around 1700

1. As to cuneiform writing, it was used by the Sumerians in Mesopotamia in the late fourth and the third millennium BCE. The Sumerian language was not a Semitic one. But the Akkadians settled in the area in the third millennium BCE and took over this writing method for their own language, which was a Semitic one. Even after the alphabetic writing system was later invented and used in the other Semitic languages, the Akkadians continued to use only the cuneiform writing system. With regard to hieroglyphic writing, it also long pre-dated the alphabet.

BCE from Egypt and the Sinai. Probably this was the time period and locale of the invention of the alphabet. There were probably either 27 or 29 pictorial symbols in the alphabet in its earliest stage.[2]

The idea behind the alphabet is that, in spite of the thousands of different words that people use when they speak, there are only a limited number of sounds that people use. All words are simply varying combinations of this limited number of sounds. The next step was to make a picture to represent each sound. Learning to write would then become a relatively simple procedure, as opposed to cuneiform where one had to know many signs (and writing was therefore the occupation of professional scribes).

The pictures were chosen so that they would immediately suggest to the reader the sound the picture was to represent. For example, for the sound "B," the picture would be of a house (*bayit*). For the sound "Y," a hand or forearm (*yad*). For the sound "C," a palm (*caf*). For the sound "M," water (*mayim*). For the sound "P," a mouth (*peh*). For the sound "R," a head (*rosh*). For the sound "Sh," a tooth (*shen*).

This is not evident in our time because the way our Hebrew letters look today is not the way they looked initially. There are many charts available that show what the Hebrew letters looked like in ancient times.[3] The original form of the letters is often referred to by scholars as "Old Hebrew," or "Paleo-Hebrew."[4] Many of the

---

2. See Joseph Naveh, *Early History of the Alphabet* (1987), pp. 30–31. The number 27 is suggested based on the evidence from Ugaritic. The number 29 is suggested based on the evidence from the ancient South Arabian dialects. (The Phoenician alphabet omitted several letters. Their reduced alphabet of 22 letters was adopted by the Hebrew and Aramaic scripts.)

3. But to truly understand the meaning of the original letter shapes one must look at a chart which has the sketches of the letters in the earliest periods. The chart in the *Encyclopaedia Judaica* at 2:683 does not go earlier than 1000 BCE. A better one is in Eli Barnavi, ed, *A Historical Atlas of the Jewish People* (1992), p. 19. This one includes sketches as early as 1500 BCE. Another good one is at p. 25 of Joseph Naveh, *Early History of the Alphabet* (1987). Here Naveh has printed a chart made by archaeologist William F. Albright which includes sketches from as early as the 17th century BCE.

4. In the Talmud, it is referred to as *ketav Ivri* and ליבונאה. On this unusual word, see R. Reuven Chaim Klein, *Lashon Hakodesh* (2014), pp. 188–92. The

letter-picture resemblances are obvious. Admittedly some are less clear or unknown.

Scholars believe that the Hebrews (=ancient Israelites) and the Arameans borrowed the alphabet from the Phoenicians (=Canaanites).

Regarding the change in the shape of the Hebrew letters, there is one tannaitic opinion that believes that there was a change in the script instituted by Ezra (5th century BCE) from the original Old Hebrew (=*ketav Ivri*) to *ketav Ashurit.*[5]

But the story of the change in script is more complicated than that. There certainly was not an overnight change of scripts. Rather, in the post-exilic period, in the Diaspora and in Judea as well, the cursive Aramaic script gradually replaced the ancient Hebrew script.[6] But the letters probably did not take on the square shape that we are familiar with until around 300 BCE or later.[7] It is only the Hebrew

---

later script is referred to in the Talmud as *ketav Ashurit.* The Talmud refers to only two categories of script.

5. This is the view of R. Yosi at *Sanhedrin* 21b–22a, found earlier at Tosefta *Sanhedrin* 4:5, and also at J. Talmud *Meg.* 1:9. These passages refer to two other tannaitic views. One is the view of R. Shimon ben Elazar who states that the script of the Torah has always been *ketav Ashurit.* The other is that of Rebbe (R. Judah Ha-Nasi) who believes that the Torah was given in *ketav Ashurit,* but then there was a sin (what sin and when are not stated). After they repented in the time of Ezra, *ketav Ashurit* was restored. On a literal level, the tannaitic passages are talking only about the script of the Torah, and do not have to be interpreted as general statements about the script in use everywhere in those times.

6. The Old Hebrew script was not completely abandoned. It still appeared thereafter on a variety of materials including coins. It still seems to have held a high nationalistic and religious status. At Qumran there is a text of a few chapters of Leviticus which is written entirely in the Old Hebrew script. The Old Hebrew script was also sometimes used for the writing of the four-letter divine name in texts otherwise written in the later script. A version of the Old Hebrew script is still used today by the Samaritans.

7. A leading paleography expert summarizes what happened: "The Jewish script is one of the offshoots of the late formal Aramaic cursive script. It emerged when the latter split into local scripts following the fall of the Persian empire in the second half of the fourth century BCE." See Ada Yardeni in *Scrolls from the Dead Sea*, eds. A. Sussman and R. Peled (1993), p. 130. Like

from this period and later that is readable to us non-specialists today. For example, the earliest Dead Sea Scrolls date to the late 3rd century BCE and they are readable to us non-specialists.[8]

Going back to the shapes of the letters, the *aleph* has the shape of the head of an ox. *Aleph* is the word for an ox several times in *Tanakh*. See, e.g., Deuteronomy 7:13 (*alaphekha*).[9]

Some of the first pictures for the letters were inspired by the pictures used in Egyptian hieroglyphs, such as the drawing of a human head to serve as a *resh*. This is consistent with the hypothesis that Egypt or the Sinai area was where the alphabet was first invented. The alphabet then spread eastwards to the rest of the Near East.

As to the westward spread of the alphabet, it spread via the Phoenicians to the Greeks. The Greeks traded with the Phoenicians and scholars have determined that the Greeks were using this alphabet already by the 9th century BCE. But the Greeks had a problem with the Phoenician alphabet. There were no vowels. Semitic languages did not need vowels because the three root consonants determined the essential meaning of the word. But the Greek language and the other non-Semitic languages were not structured this way.

The Greeks found a way of adapting this alphabet to their own language.[10] The Greek language did not have all the 22 sounds that the Phoenician/Hebrew/Aramaic alphabet provided letters for. This freed up some letters to be used as vowels. They used the sign for *aleph* for their vowel "A," the sign for *heh* for their vowel "E," the sign for *ḥet* for their sound "AY," and the sign for *yod* for their sound "EE." They also had no use for the guttural sound represented by the *ayin*. This

---

many scholars, Yardeni calls the earliest form of our modern square script: "the Jewish Script." This is done to distinguish it from the Old Hebrew script and from the next evolving stage, the Aramaic cursive script.

8. Of course, the texts in the Dead Sea corpus have no dates on them. Scholars must rely on historical, archaeological, and paleographical data to date them.

9. The singular form would be *elef*, although this form is never in *Tanakh*.

10. The tradition that the Greeks were taught the alphabet from the Phoenicians and made some changes to it is recorded in Herodotus v, 58 (5th century BCE). The fact that the Greeks did not understand the meanings of the names of the letters helped to facilitate them making these changes!

became their letter for the vowel "O." (The original form of this letter was an "O" shape, like an eyeball.)

From Greece, the alphabet spread to Italy and then to all European languages.

* * *

An easy-to-read book which explains a lot of this is Edward Horowitz, *How the Hebrew Language Grew* (rev. ed., 1993). More advanced is Joseph Naveh, *Early History of the Alphabet* (1987). Also interesting (but outdated) is William Chomsky, *Hebrew: The Eternal Language* (1957).

* * *

Mitchell First is a personal injury attorney and Jewish history scholar. Since the singular form for an ox in Hebrew was *elef*, he wonders whether the letter might have originally been called *elef* (at least in Hebrew).

2. The Order of the Letters in the Hebrew Alphabet

When I was younger I noticed that in the acrostics in the book of Lamentations the letter *pe* preceded the letter *ayin* in chapters 2, 3, and 4. This got me interested in the history of the alphabet. I then discovered that several abecedaries (=lists of the letters in order) in ancient Israel from the early biblical period came to light in recent decades and that *pe* preceded *ayin* in every one of them! Some examples are the Izbet Sarteh abecedary (c. 1200 BCE) and the Tel Zayit abecedary (c. 950 BCE). It now seems that *pe* preceding *ayin* was the dominant or even the exclusive order in ancient Israel in early biblical times.[11] Interestingly, both of these abecedaries include

11. In my writings on this issue, I have argued that it was the exclusive order in ancient Israel though the First Temple period, not just the dominant one. This has important ramifications for the acrostics in the fifth book of Psalms, since they uniformly follow the later *ayin-pe* order. See my articles referenced at the end of this article.

another unusual order: *ḥet* preceding *zayin*. (Unlike *pe-ayin*, we do not have evidence in the Bible for this one.)

This all leads to the question of whether there was an original order of the alphabet (either at the outset, or at a later stage), and if so, what was its rationale.[12]

Before we begin to answer, we must point out that the way the Hebrew letters look today is not the way they looked in early biblical times. There are many charts available that show how the letters looked in early biblical times. This earlier stage is called: "Old Hebrew" or "Paleo-Hebrew."[13] When you look at the shapes of the letters in Old Hebrew, you see, for example, that the original *aleph* looks like an ox's head (*aleph* means ox several times in Tanakh), *caf* looks like the palm of a hand, *yod* looks like a hand or arm, *ayin* looks like an eyeball, *pe* looks like a mouth, and *shin* looks like a tooth.

We cannot be confident that we even know the original names of all the letters. The names of the letters were probably established in the several centuries before 1000 BCE, while our earliest sources for the names of the letters comes from over 1000 years later.[14] Also,

12. Archaeology has already provided evidence of our alphabetical order from Ugaritic, a cognate language to Hebrew, discovered in the early 20th century in the area near the coast of Syria. Several abecedaries have been found in Ugaritic from approximately the 13th century BCE. This is centuries before the earliest acrostics in *Nakh*. (There are no acrostics in the Torah.)

On the other hand, archaeology has also provided evidence of an **entirely different** order for the ancient Semitic alphabet. This other order is known as the *halaḥam* order. It begins with cognates to the Hebrew *heh, lamed, ḥet,* and *mem*. This order was the standard order in ancient Arabia and Ethiopia, and scholars had assumed it was confined to that region. But in recent decades archaeology has found evidence of it in Beit Shemesh (from the 13th century BCE) and in Ugarit (coast of Syria, 14th–12th centuries BCE). These discoveries have forced scholars to rethink many of their assumptions about the early history of the alphabet. For a recent article suggesting evidence from 15th century BCE Egypt, see Ben Haring, "*Halaḥam* on an Ostracon of the Early New Kingdom?" *Journal of Near Eastern Studies* 74 (2017), pp. 189–196.

13. In the Talmud, it is called *ketav ivri* or ליבונאה.

14. The earliest source with the names of the letters is the *Nakh* portion of the Septuagint. The translation of the Torah into Greek took place in Egypt in the middle of the third century BCE. The translation of the *Nakh* is dated about one

scholars have observed that some of the names, such as *zayin* and *nun*, sound Aramaic, raising the possibility that these were not the original names of these letters.[15]

One scholar who has devoted much time to studying these issues is Aaron Demsky, who was a professor at Bar-Ilan University for many years. A recent book *Origins of the Alphabet* (2015) includes an article by him on this subject.[16] I will now summarize his theory of the order of the letters, which admittedly is only a conjecture.

In order to evaluate his theory one must look at a chart which has the sketches of the letters in the earliest periods. The chart in the *Encyclopaedia Judaica* at 2:683 does not go earlier than 1000 BCE. A better one is in Eli Barnavi, ed, *A Historical Atlas of the Jewish People* (1992), p. 19. This one includes sketches as early as 1500 BCE. Another good one is at p. 25 of Joseph Naveh, *Early History of the Alphabet* (1987).

Demsky believes that the letters *aleph* through *vav* reflect the homestead: ox, house, camel, door, human with raised hands, and hook on the door; *zayin* through *tet* reflect the field (he thinks that *zayin* was originally *zayit*; the name of the parallel Greek letter is *zeta*); *yod* through *lamed* reflect the hand (*lamed* is an ox goad, see Judges 3:31, which can be viewed as an extension of the arm); and *mem* through *samekh* reflect water (*mayim* is water; he has explanations for the subsequent two letters as well).

Finally, *ayin* through *tav* reflect the head (e.g., eye, mouth, head, tooth). Admittedly, he has to conjecture for the difficult letters: *tzadi* and *quf*. As to *tav*, it is a mark on the forehead. See Ezekiel 9:4.

One advantage to his theory is that the pairs *zayin* and *ḥet*, and *ayin* and *pe*, are each within the same group. That we find a different

---

century later. In certain sections of the *Nakh* where the Hebrew had acrostics, the Septuagint adds in the name of the Hebrew letter, transliterated into Greek. (The names of the letters were not added into the text itself.) Admittedly, our earliest manuscripts of the Septuagint are only from the fourth century CE.

15. Scholars also believe that the name *resh* is Aramaic. Since the name for the parallel Greek letter is "rho," this is some evidence that the original Semitic name for the letter may have been *rosh*.

16. "The Interface of Oral and Written Traditions in Ancient Israel: The Case of the Abecedaries," pp. 17–48. The book was edited by C. Rico and C. Attucci.

order of these letters in some of the ancient sources is therefore not so troublesome.

* * *

The following is a list of the alphabetical acrostics in *Nakh*: Proverbs 31:10–31 (*eshet ḥayil*), Lamentations chapters 1 through 4, and in Psalms: chapters 9–10 (the acrostic spans two chapters and is missing many letters), 25, 34, 37, 111, 112, 119 and 145. The acrostic in chapter 145 lacks a *nun* verse. The acrostics in chapters 25, 34, and 37 are missing letters as well. There are no such acrostics in the Torah.

If anyone is interested further in these acrostics, the *pe-ayin* order, and the ramifications of the *pe-ayin* order for the book of Psalms, see my three articles on this topic: (1) *Biblical Archaeology Review*, July-Aug. 2012, pp. 47–50 (short article but with pictures); (2) *Journal for the Study of the Old Testament* 38 (2014), pp. 471–85; and (3) in my book *Esther Unmasked* (2015), pp. 207–230. The last is the most thorough.

* * *

Mitchell First is an attorney and Jewish history scholar. Nowhere in his writings has he discussed the ramifications of the *pe-ayin* order for *gematria*. This is an open field for anyone who wishes to do the recalculations!

3. The Meaning of the Cryptic Verse at Exodus 2:23

At Exodus 2:23, there is a verse that we are all familiar with: "In the course of those many days, the king of Egypt died, and Bnei Yisrael sighed because of the *avodah*, and they cried out, and their cry for help rose up to God, from the *avodah*."

What is the connection between the king of Egypt dying and Bnei Yisrael sighing and crying out because of the work?

A widespread suggestion is that once the king of Egypt died and Bnei Yisrael saw that they were still not freed, they realized that their slavery was becoming permanent. This led them to sigh and cry out. Of course, the verse does not say this, but this is a good try.

Another suggestion is that when the king of Egypt died, they had to build a monument for him and a lot of work was involved. This too is clever, but it is not stated in the verse.

Many other weak suggestions have been offered. For example:

- When the king of Egypt died, the Egyptians mourned for him and perhaps the Israelites even had a day of rest. Bnei Yisrael were then able to exhibit their suffering externally, but they were not mourning for the death of the Pharaoh but for their own difficult condition.
- When the king of Egypt died, the Egyptians took their anger out on Bnei Yisrael and ordered them to work harder.
- When the king of Egypt died, the Egyptians blamed Bnei Yisrael for his death and ordered them to work harder.
- The verse, in an awkward way, is telling us that the next king was crueler than the first king.

But what is the true answer to our question? What is the connection between the death of the king of Egypt and Bnei Yisrael sighing and crying out? The best answer is offered by Rashbam and many modern commentators (e.g., Umberto Cassuto, and *Daat Mikra*, p. 36, note 1, first suggestion).[17] There is no connection! The remark about the death of the king is just a parenthetical background statement. Verse 2:15 had told us that Moses fled Egypt because Pharaoh wanted to kill him for his killing an Egyptian. But now the background has changed. There is a new Pharaoh and God can now call Moses back. The Israelites need to be led out and God can assure Moses that those seeking to kill him are dead (as He does at verse 4:19).

* * *

I have always been fascinated by a midrash on this verse at *Exodus Rabbah* 1:34 that stated that the king did not die but became a leper. Rashi quotes this midrash as well. (The "leper" interpretation is also found in Targum Yonatan.) Why should there be a midrash that interprets the word וימת to mean "he became a leper"?

There is a similar midrash in the case of King Uzziahu, where his

17. The view of Rashbam is also implicit in the brief statement of Ibn Ezra printed in the standard *Mikraot Gedolot*.

"death" at Isaiah 6:1 is interpreted as "becoming a leper." See *Exodus Rabbah* 1:34 and *Tanḥuma, Tzav*. But in the case of Uzziahu, there are verses at the end of chapter 26 of 2 Chronicles that refer to him becoming a leper, so the midrashic reinterpretation of his "death" at Isaiah 6:1 is not totally out of left field.

Here are a few explanations for the midrash on Exodus 2:23 that have been offered:

1. The Israelites should have been happy at the death of the Pharaoh. Since they were not happy, he must not have died.
2. The midrash also refers to Pharaoh having to slaughter Israelite babies and bathe in their blood as a cure for his leprosy.[18] By making Pharaoh into a leper who needs a cure, the midrash is able to portray his enslavement of the Israelites in an even crueler manner.
3. There was a tradition in ancient Egypt that the Israelites were kicked out of Egypt because they were lepers. See the second story of the Israelite enslavement and Exodus reported by the 3rd century BCE Egyptian historian Manetho (recorded in Josephus, *Against Apion* I, commencing para. 230). Our midrash was a polemical response to that tradition. (See Louis Ginzberg, *The Legends of the Jews*, vol. 5, p. 413.)
4. The story of those first fifteen chapters of the book of Exodus would have a much better message if the Pharaoh who enslaved the Israelites was also the one who was punished with the ten plagues and drowning at the sea. A literal reading of verse 2:23 ruins this symmetry. By reinterpreting the "death" at Exodus 2:23, the midrash is able to equate the Pharaoh of the Oppression with the Pharaoh of the Exodus and interpret the story as consistent with the general principle of *middah ke-neged middah*. See Avigdor Shinan, *Midrash Shemot Rabbah*, p. 99, note 37.

The last answer was very clever, but we can now do even better. The approach we will take is very similar to the last answer. A longer version of the midrash at *Exodus Rabbah* 1:34 was found in a work known as *Midrash Ha-Gadol*. *Midrash Ha-Gadol* emanates from

18. Pliny (1st CE) reports that the Egyptian kings would bathe in warm human blood to treat their own leprosy.

Yemen and often preserves older readings of midrashim. (See *EJ* 11:1515.) On our passage, it has additional statements at the beginning: "Could he have died? But a verse [Exodus 9:16] reads: "because of this I appointed you [to show you my power]. . . ." The import of this additional passage is that verse 9:16 implies that the entire story of the first 15 chapters of the book of Exodus involves only one Pharaoh. God appointed a certain individual as Pharaoh and then wanted to teach that same Pharaoh a lesson about His power. This explains why the passage that refers to his "death" had to be reinterpreted.

* * *

Mitchell First is a personal injury attorney and Jewish history scholar. He is not a believer in bathing in blood to cure leprosy.

4. Why Was Moses Commanded to Remove His Shoes at the Burning Bush?

In Exodus chapter 3, God sees that Moses went to look at the burning bush and then instructs him: "Do not come near. Remove your shoes from your feet because the place where you are standing is holy ground." We are not told how far the radius of holiness extended. Why did Moses receive this instruction to discalceate?[19] (Don't you love that word!)

One suggestion is that the problem was with Moses' sandals. Sandals, being fashioned from animal skins, were considered impure. (This solution assumes that there was a concept of impurity even before the Torah was given at Sinai.)

Another suggestion is that taking off one's shoes is a sign of respect. Sandals accumulated dust and dirt and may have been typically removed before entering a house. All the more so, it may not have been considered proper or respectful to come to a sacred place without first removing one's dusty and dirty footgear.

A third idea is presented by Rabbi S.R. Hirsch: "Taking off one's shoes expresses giving oneself up entirely to the meaning of a place,

19. A similar instruction was given to Joshua at Joshua 5:15.

to let your personality get its standing and take up its position entirely and directly on it without any intermediary." He adds that the priests in the Temple also had to function barefoot.

A fourth idea is that the removal of the sandals represents a renunciation of any claims to possession.[20] Walking with shoes was a way of taking possession. Yet man cannot take ownership of the place of a theophany, since those places exclusively belong to God. (This explanation also fits nicely with the idea that the priests in the Temple had to function barefoot.)

A fifth idea is presented by Rabbi Joseph Soloveitchik. "The shoe is the symbol of vulgarity and uncouthness, of superficiality, of raw power: 'upon Edom I cast my shoe' (Psalms 60:10). To understand holiness, to gain sensitivity, a person must remove his shoes." (Quoted in *Chumash Mesoras Ha-Rav*, p. 24.)

Finally, another suggestion is based on the idea that Moses was about to bring religious laws to the people. Therefore, he himself needed to be tested to see if he could accept the distinctions between "holy" and "profane" that religious law sometimes demands.

(The above discussion was based on Alec Goldstein, *A Theology of Holiness*, 2018, pp. 96–98.)

* * *

When Moses was commanded to take off his shoes above, the word used was שַׁל (*shal*). It means "slip off, drop off." Where does this word come from? It turns out that the root is נשל. This root appears only seven times in *Tanakh*, and three of these times, the *nun* is not even there. (Another example of this root is at Joshua 5:15 where Joshua receives a command similar to the one that Moses received.) This is a good place to remind everyone that a peculiarity of Hebrew is that in the command form, that first root letter sometimes drops. Another example is קַח (=take) where the initial ל drops. But only certain letters drop as first letters in the command form.

* * *

20. For more on this suggestion, see the 2021 article by Rachel Adelman, at thetorah.com: "The Burning Bush: Why Must Moses Remove His Shoes?" The author brings support from ancient Hittite legal documents for this approach.

This is a good place to discuss the perplexing statement mentioned above at Psalms 60:10. First the verse insults Moab. The verse calls it: *sir rachatzi*. The meaning seems to be "washbasin," a place where a conqueror might wash his feet. Then the second part of this verse reads: *Al Edom ashlikh na'ali*= Upon/Unto Edom, I will throw my shoe.

What is the symbolism of throwing the shoe here? I will mention a few suggestions:

- Throwing a shoe, which is an insult even in modern times, was also an insult in biblical times. (E.g., a master throws a dirty shoe at a slave so that the slave can clean it.) The meaning is that Edom will be treated with contempt.
- Throwing a shoe symbolized taking possession of their land.
- Throwing a shoe symbolized trampling and military defeating the other party.
- Throwing a shoe symbolized making the recipient your slave, since shoe removal was a task of a slave.

But others think that *na'ali* does not mean "shoe" here at all but means "my lock," or "my chain." The purpose was to trap them.[21]

* * *

Mitchell First is a personal injury attorney and Jewish history scholar. He usually keeps his shoes on and tries not to throw them.

5. Did the Israelites Borrow from the Egyptians at the Time of the Exodus?

At Genesis 15:14, God tells Abraham that his descendants will be strangers and slaves in a foreign land for 400 years and that the nation that they served will be judged by God. Afterwards they will come out with *rekhush gadol*.

Then, at Exodus 3:21–22 we have: "I will give this people favor (חן) in the eyes of Egypt. And it shall come to pass, when you go, you shall

21. See, e.g., Rashi and *Metzudat David*.

not go empty. Every woman shall ask (ושאלה) from her neighbor… articles of silver and of gold and raiment… and you shall spoil Egypt." Similar is verse 11:2.

Finally, at Exodus 12:35–36: "The children of Israel did according to the word of Moses, and they asked (וישאלו) of Egypt articles of silver and of gold and raiment. God gave the people favor in the eyes of Egypt. They let them have what they asked (וישאלום). They spoiled Egypt."[22]

This episode raises two fundamental questions: (1) In Rabbinic Hebrew, שאל usually means "borrow." Is this the story of an ancient trick by the Israelites, ordered by God?, and (2) What was the purpose of this entire episode?

To answer the first question, most commentaries believe that there was no deception here. The verb שאל has many meanings in *Tanakh*, including "demand" and "request." Therefore it need not mean "borrow" here. In fact, "borrow" is a rare meaning of this verb in Tanakh.

Regarding the second question, on the simplest level, the purpose of the episode was to fulfill God's promise to Avraham. God was merely constructing a situation that enabled Him to fulfill it. I would be satisfied with this answer. But the commentators write much more. For example:

- Several point to Deuteronomy 15:13–14 which records that after a Hebrew slave works for six years and is freed, he should not be freed empty-handed. Rather, he is to be supplied liberally from his owner's flock, threshing-floor and winepress. Perhaps this was not a new law instituted in Deuteronomy, but was a common practice at the time of the Exodus or even earlier in the time of Abraham. As one source (Umberto Cassuto) explains, this bounty to the freed slaves was required for absolute justice to be done. Although no earthly court could compel the king of Egypt to fulfill this obligation, the Heavenly court saw to it that this requirement of justice was carried out and directed the course of events to this

22. Another set of relevant verses is found at Psalms 105:37–38. But I would prefer to limit my analysis to the verses in the book of Exodus.

end. See, e.g., *Torat Ḥayyim* on Ex. 11:2, in the name of R. Ḥananel, Hizzekuni to Ex. 3:21 and most elaborately, Umberto Cassuto (comm. on Ex. 3:21–22).

- Rav S.R. Hirsch writes that during the three days of darkness, the Egyptians were completely helpless but no Israelite took the slightest advantage of their persons or possessions. When this plague ended and they found all their possessions untouched, God made their recognition of the moral nobility of the Israelites overcome their antipathy to them. They even gave the Israelites these gifts before the Israelites asked.[23] God also wanted the first foundation stone of the prosperity of His people to be acquired through recognition of their moral greatness by those who had hitherto despised them. [24]

  (Regarding the last three words of 12:36, וינצלו את מצרים, R. Hirsch suggests they mean that the Egyptians stripped themselves of their own treasures and gave them to the Israelites.)
- Rabbi Dr. J.H. Hertz writes that the Torah commands us not to abhor an Egyptian (Deut. 23:8). He takes the position that the purpose of this entire episode was to ensure that there would be a friendly parting so we could end up being able to observe this commandment. The Israelites would come to see that the oppressors were Pharaoh and his courtiers, and not the Egyptian people. (Rabbi Hertz is here following the approach of the scholar Benno Jacob. In this approach, the suggestion is made that the last three words of Exodus 3:22, ונצלתם את מצרים, should be translated as "and you shall save Egypt." The meaning is that the name of the Egyptians will be cleared and their humanity vindicated.
- Nehama Leibowitz and others before her pointed out that there is no unfairness here because the Israelites may have left property

23. See similarly *Mekhilta, Bo*, end of sec. 13.
24. The comments of Josephus (*Antiquities*, II, 314–315) are also noteworthy: "They even honored the Hebrews with gifts, some to speed their departure, others from neighborly feelings towards old acquaintances. So they departed, amid the lamentation and regrets of the Egyptians for having treated them so hardly." For the different approach of the earlier source, Philo, see his *Life of Moses*, I, sec. 140.

> behind in Egypt. Nehama writes (*Bo*, article 2): "This loss of possessions has been a blight that has dogged Jews throughout their expulsions, from Spain in 1492 to Iraq in the first years of the State of Israel. But in all these cases, their neighbors were not so kind as to let them have silver and gold articles in return for the wealth they had left behind, and not even on loan, at that."

Most interesting however is the view of S.D. Luzzatto (comm. to Ex. 3:22) who believes that the Israelites did trick the Egyptians here at God's command. The root שאל certainly means "borrow" sometimes in *Tanakh*, so it can have this meaning here. The Israelites had never told the Egyptians that they were not coming back. Moses had only requested a three-day trip to worship the Israelite God (5:3). As late as Exodus 10:26 (between the ninth and tenth plagues), it seems that Moses is still only requesting permission for a temporary departure to worship the Israelite God.

But what about the moral questions: How could God command such an act of trickery? Would not the Israelites be learning a lesson that trickery is something to be encouraged? On the contrary! Luzzatto writes that what was impressed upon them was that God despises evildoers and favors those who are crushed in spirit. What the Israelites would be learning is that if they themselves were to oppress others, God would avenge them and transfer their wealth to those others! The whole episode strengthened their hearts with reverence for God and love of justice.

The whole idea of Moses' request for only a temporary departure deserves a separate article.[25] But one can respond to Luzzatto that the Egyptian people were not privy to the exact words of the negotiations between Moses and Pharaoh. And at 12:33, just **prior** to the transfer of items to the Israelites at 12:35–36, the verse tells us: *va-teḥezak Mitzrayim al ha-am* ***le-maher le-shalḥam*** *min ha-aretz, ki amru kullanu meitim.* On the simplest level, this sounds like the Egyptian

25. There is an interesting post by R. Menachem Leibtag on this topic at tanach.org: "Let My People Go – A Hoax or a Mission?"

people were desirous of sending the Israelites off permanently, and they still gave them the various items.

* * *

Mitchell First is a personal injury attorney and Jewish history scholar. He does not recall if Charlton Heston asked Yul Brynner for only a three-day trip.

6. Achashverosh's Imposition of a מס at the End of the Megillah

Verse 10:1 reads: "*Va-yasem ha-melekh Achashverosh mas al ha-aretz ve-iyyei ha-yam*" (=King Achashverosh placed a מס on the land and on the islands.[26]) We have all wondered for years why the end of the Megillah includes this statement.

Note also the unusual term *ha-aretz* here. Which land is it referring to? Why does it not say that the tax was from *Hodu* to *Kush*? Does it mean that only the region of Medeo-Persia was taxed, aside from the *iyyei ha-yam*?

What follows are some suggestions that I have seen to explain the reference to taxation. (Some of this material comes from Erica Brown, *Esther: Power, Fate, and Fragility in Exile*, 2020.)

- These words were inserted to accord honor to the Persian government and to demonstrate that the Megillah does not deal solely with the triumph of the Jews.
- The taxation symbolizes Achashverosh's new power and success with the help of Mordechai.
- The taxation symbolizes that government was now back to normal.
- The taxation symbolizes that there is a more responsible government now, in contrast to the government in chapter one that was overly concerned with arranging a large party.

---

26. *Daat Mikra* comments that the word אי' in *Tanakh* is not limited to areas that are surrounded by water on all four sides. The word appears many times in *Tanakh* and is likely of Egyptian origin. See my *Roots and Rituals* (2018), p. 189.

- The taxation shows that, to the credit of Mordechai, the king's revenue now would be generated through peaceful taxation rather than from bribery and extortion.
- The taxation is there to teach that a government has more to gain by orderly taxation than by massacre and plunder of the Jews.
- The taxation reflects a reversal of a tax remission perhaps alluded to at verse 2:18.
- *Aretz* and *iyyei ha-yam* were close and far areas that were not under the rule of Achashverosh. But these areas feared him and were willing to pay taxes. This shows just how far the king's authority reached due to Mordechai's talents (Ibn Ezra).
- *Aretz* and *iyyei ha-yam* were close and far areas that were newly conquered by Achashverosh, due to Mordechai's efforts. The verse gives the credit to the king out of honor to him (Malbim).
- By ending with taxes, the Megillah demonstrates that Achashverosh was wicked from beginning to end.
- The taxation alludes to the attempt of Achashverosh=Xerxes to raise revenue to compensate for his losses in his war against the Greeks which ended in his defeat.[27]

* * *

I discuss the word מס in a separate essay. There I point out that the word occurs 23 times in *Tanakh* (in singular or plural form). All the other times, which all date earlier than our book, it seems that the word means something like "forced labor."[28] Even as late as Lamentations 1:1, "forced labor" is probably the meaning.[29]

Almost all sources (rabbinic commentaries and scholars) are

---

27. It always bothered me that there was no mention in the Megillah of Xerxes' war with the Greeks. This would at least be an allusion. This war took Aḥashverosh=Xerxes out of the country from the spring or summer of his fifth year through part of his seventh year. That is why it took him so long to choose a new queen.

28. It is likely a word of foreign origin.

29. See, e.g., Brown-Driver-Briggs, the Anchor Bible edition of Lamentation, and Koehler-Baumgartner. See also *Daat Mikra* (but it is stated much too briefly here). That "forced labor" is the meaning at Lam. 1:1 is also implicit in the Soncino comments on Esther 10:1 ("everywhere else").

willing to give מס its later meaning, "tax," at Esther 10:1. But if מס meant "forced labor" all 22 prior times, there should be a presumption that this is its meaning at Esther 10:1 until we have indications to the contrary.

Admittedly, וישׂם sounds like the placement of a tax. But this same verb is used at Judges 1:28 in connection with the "forced labor" meaning וישם את הכנעני למס.

The Soncino commentary is one source that gives מס the "forced labor" meaning at Esther 10:1 At the top, the translation of the Jewish Publication Society of America of 1917 had been "tribute." On the bottom is the comment of the Soncino edition: "Since the Hebrew word everywhere else means 'forced labour,' a better translation is 'imposed forced labour.'" [30]

They also include the following comment: "The thought is: Ahasuerus... could command the service of the continent of Asia and the coast of the Mediterranean."[31]

Perhaps the image of Achashverosh ordering widespread "forced labor" is an even greater image of strength than his ordering a tax.

But here we have וישם המלך... מס על הארץ, as opposed to וישם את הכנעני למס. Moreover, no clues are given in the verse as to what such a forced labor might have been for. In contrast, if מס merely meant a tax, no clues are required, as we understand that kings always need revenue. Therefore, the later meaning, "tax," is the preferable one here.[32]

Erica Brown, in her *Esther: Power, Fate, and Fragility in Exile*

---

30. P. 243.
31. P. 242. The comment here translates *ha-aretz* as "the continent of Asia." Another view, found in Adele Berlin, *The JPS Bible Commentary: Esther* (2001), is that the use of *aretz* and *iyyei ha-yam* together is an idiomatic expression for the entire world. See similarly Isaiah 42:4 and 42:10.
32. See similarly Yaakov Klein, *Eikhah: Im Mavo U-Peirush* (2017), pp. 128–29. (These pages are an appendix where he discusses the meaning of מס throughout *Tanakh*.) See similarly *Encyclopedia Mikra'it*, vol. 5, p. 56.

(2020), remarks poignantly that, by the time we are at the end of the Megillah: "Haman is no longer with us, but taxes are here to stay."[33]

* * *

The Hebrew spelling of Achashverosh in verse 10:1 differs from the spelling in the rest of the book. Here it is spelled without either *vav*: אחשרש. Prior to this verse, 24 times the name is spelled with two *vavs*, and four times with one *vav*. A reasonable explanation that has been suggested is that, by the time the author reached verse 10:1 and was not writing the main narrative anymore, he was copying from a different source (about Achashverosh's governmental activities) and this source had the different spelling.[34]

* * *

Mitchell First is an attorney who pays his taxes and is hoping to avoid forced labor.

7. The Absence of the Book of Esther Among the Dead Sea Scrolls

The book of Esther is the only book of the 24 books of *Tanakh* that is not found in the caves at Qumran. Not only have no fragments from the book been found, there are also no quotes from it in any of the non-biblical texts.[35]

Nevertheless, there are ways to show that the book was known at Qumran.[36] Scholars find vocabulary in books at Qumran that suggest awareness of the book.[37] I will give two examples. The words שאלתי and ובקשתי are found next to each other in a Dead Sea text (although one ends a phrase and the other begins the subsequent phrase).[38] The

33. P. 440.

34. This also might explain the reference to *ha-aretz ve-iyyei ha-yam*, instead of the reference to the large empire the way it was described earlier, as spanning from *Hodu* to *Kush*.

35. The non-biblical books at Qumran often quote from biblical books.

36. My discussion in the next two paragraphs is based on Koller (pp. 129–30).

37. This approach only works for texts that seem to have been authored in the Qumran community.

38. 11QPsalms-a 24:4–5.

phrase שאלתי ובקשתי appears in Tanakh only at Esther (5:7). Also, the phrase יבקשו לשלוח יד appears in a Dead Sea text.[39] The phrase לשלוח יד, an idiom for harming a person, appears in Tanakh only at Esther 2:21 and 6:2.[40]

The best example that suggests awareness of the book of Esther at Qumran is a Dead Sea text known as 4Q267. Here it seems (based on a reasonable conjecture regarding some missing words) that the scribe wrote *mi-yom le-yom u-mei-ḥodesh le-ḥodesh*, instead of merely *mi-yom le-yom*, as he was supposed to. The phrase he wrote is from Esther 3:7. The scribe's acquaintance with the book of Esther was so great that words from its text were in his mind while copying a different text![41]

Based on the above evidence and more, it seems that some in the Qumran community knew of the book. (Talmon, cited below, finds eight passages that are similar to passages in Esther.) But Aaron Koller, in his *Esther in Ancient Jewish Thought* (2014), writes: "[T]he book was certainly not considered authoritative within the Qumran community. The festival of Purim, explicitly ordained in Esther 9, was not on the Qumran calendar."

But we do not have a complete "Qumran holiday calendar" like we have a "Jewish holiday calendar" today! (Although we do have some fragmentary calendrical texts.) Scholars just make reasonable educated guesses as to what holidays the Qumran community observed, based on the limited evidence we have.

Scholars have observed that according to the Qumran 364-day calendar (divisible by seven) the 14th of Adar would have fallen on the Sabbath every year. This might suggest that the calendar was constructed in a way that deliberately chose to ignore the holiday, as the Qumran sect was very strict about the observance of Shabbat. But in order to make the holidays ordained by the Torah not fall on Shabbat

39. 4Q171 ii 18–19.

40. 2:21 begins the expression with: ויבקשו. 6:2 begins it with בקשו. This strengthens the argument for an allusion.

41. See Jonathan Ben-Dov, "A Presumed Citation of Esther 3:7 in 4QDb," *Dead Sea Discoveries* 6 (1999), pp. 282–84.

(except for week-long holidays where this could not be avoided), the sect was forced to have a calendar in which Purim fell on Shabbat.

The way Koller phrases the issue the question is not why the book of Esther is not found at Qumran, but why the Qumran community did not consider the book authoritative. Many suggestions have been offered. For example: (1) the lack of mention of God (although this is true of Song of Songs as well); (2) the lack of mention of the Temple; and (3) the book's condoning Esther's intermarriage with the king.

Also, the book implicitly refers to the Jews not observing Passover. The decree to destroy the Jews was issued on the 13th of Nissan (3:12). At verses 4:16–17, we are told that Esther requested that Mordechai instruct the Jews of Shushan to fast (night and day) for three consecutive days. It would seem that the Jews in Shushan fasted either on the 13th, 14th and 15th, or on the 14th, 15th, and 16th. Either way, this would mean that they did not keep Passover properly that year.

Koller summarizes a literal reading of the book as follows: it is an "apparently secular book, which attributes salvation to flawed religious figures operating with no God and no providence, violating Passover and the ban on intermarriage explicitly and probably all the other laws implicitly.... It is no wonder that the book was not found at Qumran. It is a wonder that it is found anywhere at all."[42] (He is obviously exaggerating. He later goes on to explain how the Sages improved the book and made it more consistent with the other biblical books. For example, they found allusions to God, and they linked Haman *Ha-Agagi* to Agag, king of Amalek at the time of Saul. In this way the book of Esther could be viewed as a continuation of the Israelite battle against Amalek.)

A different approach to the lack of the book of Esther at Qumran is taken by Shemarayahu Talmon.[43] He thinks the simplest approach is to assume that the book of Esther was not yet in the canon at the time the sect came to Qumran, perhaps in the middle of the second century BCE.

---

42. Koller, p. 135.

43. See his "Was the Book of Esther Known at Qumran," *Dead Sea Discoveries* 2 (1995), pp. 249–67.

There is other evidence that the book was a late addition to the canon. Ben Sira chapter 49 refers to a variety of biblical heroes, and it is usually believed that he was referring indirectly to the heroes of the biblical books in his canon. (Why else would Job and The Twelve Prophets be mentioned?)[44] Accordingly, we would have expected a mention here of Mordechai (or Esther), and Daniel.[45] Yet there is none. Ben Sira dates to around 200 BCE. (Although Ben Sira does not mention Daniel, the book of Daniel was found at Qumran, see below.)

* * *

It is certainly possible that the reason no copies of Esther survived at Qumran is just fortuitous and that perhaps the holiday was observed at Qumran. We do not have dozens of copies of each biblical book at Qumran. Here is the number of texts of each book of *Nakh* found: Joshua, 2; Judges, 3; Samuel, 5; Kings, 3; Jeremiah, 5; Ezekiel, 6; Proverbs, 2; Ruth, 4; Song of Songs 4; Ecclesiastes, 2; Lamentations, 4; Job, 3; Ezra, 1; and Chronicles, 1. (I did not include Isaiah, Psalms, and Daniel; for all of these, many texts were found. I also did not include the book of The Twelve Prophets.) The texts I referred to above are all fragmentary texts.

The book of Nehemiah is also not found at Qumran. But since Ezra and Nehemiah were viewed as one book in tannaitic times,[46] the lack of Nchemiah is usually not mentioned by scholars.[47]

* * *

For a while there was something on Wikipedia that stated that fragments from the book of Esther were found at Qumran. How did this get on Wikipedia? In 2018, around the time of Purim, the site "thetorah.com" published an article "Newly Deciphered Qumran

44. I discuss this Ben Sira passage in more detail below. See my article: "The Distinction Between *Neviim* and *Ketuvim* and Insights into the Canon."
45. With regard to the book of Ezra, he mentions Nehemiah so that suffices, since these could easily have been viewed as one book in his time.
46. This is evident from the tannaitic passage at *Bava Batra* 14b.
47. A few years ago, there was an announcement of a discovery of a text of Nehemiah from Qumran. But after investigation, it was decided that it was likely a forgery.

Scroll Revealed to be Megillat Esther." Anyone who read the article with any degree of attention would have realized that it was just a spoof. But someone who did not read it carefully put this "new find" on Wikipedia! Eventually, it was removed.

* * *

Mitchell First has learned not to write any humorous-false articles on Purim. On the internet, they can easily be erroneously viewed as true. Instead, he incorporates his humor into his articles throughout the year.

8. Biography of Josephus (1st century CE)

Josephus is our main source for much of Jewish history in the last centuries of the Second Temple period. Who was he? Do we have to believe anything he says? I will present a short biography. Admittedly, almost everything we know about Josephus comes from his own statements! One scholar has written that his biography "must be pronounced the least trustworthy portion of his writings."

He was born in 37 CE into a priestly family in Jerusalem. He could trace his lineage on his mother's side to the Hasmoneans. He had an excellent memory and understanding; at age fourteen, the chief priests used to come to him with questions about ritual laws. At age sixteen, he experimented with the three main sects (Pharisees, Sadducees and Essenes) and a fourth. At age nineteen, he decided to join the Pharisees.

At age 27, he was sufficiently prominent to be sent to an embassy to Rome to plead for the release of some priests who had been sent there as prisoners on some slight charge. He was successful.

When he returned to Jerusalem, he found that many Jews were elated at the prospect of revolt from Rome. He attempted to dissuade them, without success.[48]

He was present in the Temple in 66 CE when a faction of priests

48. His visit to Rome probably impressed upon him its strength.

marked the start of the rebellion from Rome by ending the ancient custom of offering a sacrifice for the well-being of the emperor.

The initial attempts by Rome to impose order were unsuccessful. In October of that year, the government of the self-declared independent Jewish state appointed him to oversee the defense of the Galilee. The Roman assault came and the end result was that, in early 67 CE, the general Vespasian subdued the Jews in the Galilee.

As the Romans destroyed the city of Jotapata (Yodefat), Josephus and 40 others were able to take refuge in a deep pit. When they were discovered by the Romans and were shortly to be taken, the others wanted to kill themselves. But Josephus did not want to die and was willing to turn himself in to the Romans. The Romans had conveyed a message to him that they wanted to capture him alive. This was not to punish him, but due to admiration of his valor.[49]

He told his fellow Jews that he was willing to kill himself but he came up with a lottery idea: "Let us leave the lot to decide the order in which we are to kill ourselves; let him who draws the first lot fall by the hand of him who comes next."[50] The others agreed. But at the end of this process, "by fortune or by the providence of God,"[51] he was left alone with one other and then convinced the other to break the suicide pact and surrender with him.[52]

When brought before Vespasian and his son Titus, Josephus writes that "Titus in particular was specially touched by the fortitude of Josephus under misfortunes and by pity for his youth.... [H]is pleading with his father was the main influence in saving [my] life."[53]

When alone with Vespasian and Titus, Josephus said: "I come to you as a messenger of greater destinies.... Vespasian, you will be emperor, you and your son here."[54] Vespasian was not emperor at

---

49. *The Jewish War* III, 346–49. But more probably they wanted to take him to Rome so he could be executed in a triumphant manner there. See *EJ* 10:253.

50. Ibid., 387–90.

51. Ibid., 391.

52. Assuming one believes the story, it has been suggested that it must have been through deceit that Josephus was able to engineer that he and another were the last survivors. See *EJ* 10:253.

53. Ibid., 396–97.

54. Ibid., 400–01. It is interesting that in rabbinic literature, we have a story

the time and the prediction was implausible.[55] In very interesting passages that begin at *The Jewish War* III, 350, Josephus writes that he had nightly dreams in which God had told him the impending fate of the Jews and the destinies of the Roman sovereigns.[56]

As a result of the prediction, Vespasian began to be impressed by Josephus.[57] While he did not release him from custody or chains, Josephus writes that he "continued to treat him with kindness and solicitude, being warmly supported by Titus in these courtesies."[58]

Two years later, in 69 CE, Vespasian became emperor and Josephus was released.[59]

---

of R. Yoḥanan ben Zakkai calling Vespasian a king before Vespasian became king (=emperor). See *Gittin* 56a–b and *Lam. Rabbah* 1:31.

55. Martin Goodman, *Josephus's The Jewish War* (2019), p. 3, calls the prophecy "deeply implausible, since Vespasian came from quite a humble background."

Goodman writes that the "story of the prophecy may be doubted since it was in the interest of both Josephus and Vespasian to claim that Vespasian's rise to power had been divinely predicted." He adds that in Suetonius's biography of Vespasian, written in the early 2nd century, Josephus is remembered for this prophecy.

56. Josephus wrote about the thoughts he had while deciding what to do while in the pit at Jotapata. He wrote that he previously had "nightly dreams, in which God had foretold to him the impending fate of the Jews and the destinies of the Roman sovereigns. He was an interpreter of dreams and skilled in divining the meaning of ambiguous utterances of the Deity;... [R]ecalling the dreadful images of his recent dreams, he offered up a silent prayer to God: 'Since it pleases thee...who didst create the Jewish nation, to break thy work, since fortune has wholly passed to the Romans, and since thou hast made choice of my spirit to announce the things that are to come, I willingly surrender to the Romans and consent to live; but I take thee to witness that I go, not as a traitor, but as thy minister.'" Josephus was a very unusual individual!

57. Josephus also writes that he had correctly foretold to the people of Jotapata that their city would be captured after forty-seven days and that he himself would be taken alive by the Romans. Vespasian questioned the other Jewish prisoners on these statements and found them to be true. This led Vespasian to credit the predictions of Josephus concerning himself.

58. Ibid., 408.

59. In the summer of 69 CE, he was proclaimed emperor by the governor of Egypt. Gradually all the army commanders and their legions accepted his rule. The last opposition was in Rome. But eventually that same year he was recognized as emperor by the Roman Senate. See *EJ* 16:116.

Vespasian entrusted his son Titus with the suppression of the Jewish revolt and Josephus accompanied Titus to the siege of Jerusalem.[60] From the vantage of Roman headquarters, Josephus witnessed the siege of Jerusalem from March of 70 CE until the city's destruction in August.[61] During the months of the siege, he made numerous attempts to persuade his former comrades to surrender, or else the city would be destroyed. But his attempts were unsuccessful. At the end, he was able to save the lives of his brother and fifty friends, and many women and children that he recognized.[62]

After the destruction in 70 CE, Josephus went to Rome. Vespasian gave him lodging in the house which he had occupied before he became emperor and assigned him a pension.[63] Josephus was also given Roman citizenship. Vespasian also presented him with a tract of land in Judea. After Vespasian's death in 79 CE, the subsequent emperors Titus and Domitian showed esteem for him as well.[64]

Scholars have noted that Josephus could have retired into a life of leisure in the Roman court and that it is much to the benefit of later generations that he chose to write books.

The *Jewish War* was written within a decade of the end of the war. Its main subject was the war between the Jews and Romans over the years 66–70 CE. But it begins with some material from Hasmonean times and ends with some material after 70 CE.[65] The writing of the *Jewish War* was prompted, according to the introductory remarks in Josephus, by a desire to set the record straight about the war, in response to various unnamed accounts which made great errors.

As to the causes of the Jewish defeat, Josephus emphasizes divine punishment for the sins of the rebel leaders among the Jews and the wickedness of their fratricidal struggles.

The *Jewish War* and his later works were composed by Josephus

60. *Life*, 416.

61. While he was there, the Jews wanted to kill him for being a traitor, while the Roman soldiers thought he might be spying for the Jews. Ibid., 416–17.

62. Ibid., 419.

63. Ibid., 423.

64. Ibid., 428–29.

65. E.g., the story of Masada. Josephus was not a witness to the events of Masada. I discuss this in the next essay.

in Greek. He mentions an earlier version of the *Jewish War*, in his own language, by which he probably means Aramaic. This has not survived.

In the eighties and nineties, he wrote *Jewish Antiquities*, a twenty-book narrative covering the history of the Jews from Creation down to the outbreak of the war against Rome in 66 CE. He added a biographical work, *Life*, as an appendix to this work.

Most of *Life* focuses on his career as a commander in Galilee in 66–67 CE. *Life* was written in response to those who accused him of misconduct in Galilee. We learn very little about his life from *Life*. Rather, we learn much from *The Jewish War* where he often includes himself as a character in the narrative.

His final work is known today as *Against Apion*.[66] The first part of the work marshals a variety of evidence for the antiquity of the Jews and rebuts the absurd anti-Semitic views of many ancient writers. The second part of the work (starting Part II, section 145) argues for the fundamental wisdom and superiority of the Jewish religion.[67] Josephus goes through the details of many of the laws and shows how they produce ethical and caring people. Josephus here writes as a Jew completely committed to his people and his religion. It is an inspiring read even today![68]

* * *

Mitchell First is a personal injury attorney and Jewish history scholar. Like Josephus, he has two different lives. Unlike Josephus, they are at the same time.

---

66. This was not the original title of the work. The original title was *On the Antiquity of the Jews*. See *EJ* 10:262.

67. This is how he begins (II, 145): "I desire to give, to the best of my ability, a brief account of our constitution as a whole and of its details. From this, I think, it will be apparent that we possess a code excellently designed to promote piety, friendly relations with each other, and humanity towards the world at large..."

68. Goodman writes (pp. 6–8) that "Rome in the last decades of the first century C.E. was not a good place to be a Jew" and that the decision by Josephus "to write so copiously and positively about the Jewish tradition was itself an act of exceptional bravery...."

9. Four Controversial Passages in Josephus

There are surely many controversial passages in Josephus. Here are my favorite four:

1. Persecution of Antiochus

Scholars have debated what motivated Antiochus IV to issue his decrees against the Jews. One view is that he had a grand plan to unify his empire through Hellenism and the Jews resisted his plan. This view has some support in 1 Maccabees 1:41–42. Another view is that the decrees were merely a response by Antiochus IV to what he erroneously perceived as a revolt by the Jews of Judea. This view has support in 2 Maccabees 5:11 ("when the king received the news of the events, he concluded that Judea was in revolt"). But in *Antiquities* 12, 384–85, Josephus writes that it was the Jewish high priest Menelaus who persuaded Antiochus "to compel the Jews to abandon their fathers' religion."

Everyone agrees that there were many Hellenistic Jews at the time. But it is a further step to say that one of these Hellenistic Jews, the high priest Menelaus, was the one who persuaded the king to compel the Jews to abandon their fathers' religion. Even though the author of 2 Maccabees hated Menelaus, he never blames the anti-Jewish decrees on him. No one knows where Josephus got the idea to do so.[69]

2. Destruction of the Temple

In *The Jewish War* (III, 237), Josephus writes that Titus called a meeting of his officers to determine the Temple's fate. After hearing divided opinions, he decided that the Temple should be preserved, as it would serve as an ornament to the Roman empire. The actual setting fire of the Temple began with an unauthorized act of a Roman soldier who ("moved by some supernatural impulse") flung a burning torch at the Temple. The subsequent efforts of Titus, amidst the noise and confusion, to persuade his soldiers to extinguish the flames were in vain.

69. I discussed this in my *Esther Unmasked* (2015), pp. 104–06.

In contrast, an ancient Christian historian[70] maintains that "the destruction of the Temple was the premeditated act of Titus, based on his conviction that its fall would be accompanied by that of the rebellious people, whose fount of strength it was."[71] Probably this writer more closely approximates the truth, as Josephus likely wrote his account in an attempt to clear Titus of blame.

As to the causes of the Jewish defeat by the Romans, Josephus emphasizes divine punishment for the sins of the rebel leaders among the Jews and the wickedness of their fratricidal struggles.[72] But Christians saw the divine punishment as a punishment of the Jews for rejecting Jesus.[73] Accordingly, the works of Josephus were preserved in Christianity.[74]

3. Masada

The Roman campaign at Masada took place in the winter-spring of the year 72–73 (or 73–74). If everyone at Masada killed themselves, how do we know about the two speeches of Eleazar ben Yair and the mass suicide story? Josephus is our only source. He writes:[75] "They had died in the belief that they had left not a soul of them alive to fall into Roman hands; but an old woman and another, a relative of Eleazar, superior in sagacity and training to most of her sex, with five children, escaped by concealing themselves in the subterranean

---

70. Sulpicius Severus, writing around 400 CE.
71. *EJ* 15:1169.
72. Josephus insisted that the Romans won their victory only through the aid of the God of the Jews. It is surprising that he was willing to assert this. The Roman regime encouraged their populace to believe that their victory was the result of Roman military might.
73. Goodman (cited in the previous essay) writes (p. 26) that Josephus "would have been astonished and horrified at the reinterpretation of his narrative as a divine judgment on his people for rejection of [Jesus]."
74. Judaism did not preserve them. Of course, they were composed in Greek (and then translated into Latin).

Eventually in the 10th century, a work called *Sefer Yosippon* was written in Hebrew, based in part on prior adaptations of Josephus into Latin. Rashi and numerous Rishonim were able to learn the history of the last centuries of the Second Temple period through this work.

75. *The Jewish War*, VII, 399–400.

aqueducts, while the rest were absorbed in the slaughter." In the morning when the Romans advanced and saw nothing but solitude and flames, these women and their children emerged and "informed the Romans . . . one of the two lucidly reporting both the speech and how the deed was done." (Presumably, he means the sagacious woman was the reporter.) But one can ask the following questions:

- The whole idea of anyone remembering and recounting two long speeches is hard to believe. Moreover, it seems from Josephus that Eleazar was speaking only to the men (*The Jewish War*, VII, 322). How could that woman, despite her sagacity, have even heard these speeches? Even if she was eavesdropping, she could not have known about the actions of the last ten men. Josephus wrote that these women and children had "escaped by concealing themselves in the subterranean aqueducts, while the rest were absorbed in the slaughter."
- Josephus was writing *The Jewish War* in Rome. He does not claim to have spoken to that sagacious woman. (Was she even brought to Rome?) His only source about the final events would have been what Romans told him about what the woman said to them. This is hardly reliable.

An important article on this topic was written by Shaye Cohen.[76] He makes many of the above arguments. Nevertheless, he is not willing to conclude that the story was entirely an invention of Josephus. He thinks that some of the Jews at Masada did kill themselves and their families, but Josephus turned it into a suicide of all. This helped provide a dramatic ending for *The Jewish War*.

4. The Jesus Passage

In Book 18 of *Antiquities*, we have the following: "About this time there lived Jesus, a wise man, if indeed one ought to call him a man. For he was one who wrought surprising feats and was a teacher of such people as accept the truth gladly. He won over many Jews and many of the Greeks. He was the Messiah. When Pilate, upon hearing him

---

76. "Masada: Literary Tradition, Archaeological Remains, and the Credibility of Josephus," *Journal of Jewish Studies* 33 (1982), pp. 385–405.

accused by men of the highest standing amongst us, had condemned him to be crucified, those who had in the first place come to love him did not give up their affection for him. On the third day he appeared to them restored to life, for the prophets of God had prophesied these and countless other marvelous things about him. And the tribe of the Christians, so called after him, has still to this day not disappeared."

Here the issue is not the credibility of Josephus, but whether this passage was a later interpolation. The church father Eusebius, writing in the early fourth century, quotes the passage. But it seems that the earlier church fathers did not have this passage or at least this version of it. A widespread view is that Josephus did write something about Jesus here, but it was expanded upon by Eusebius or some earlier Christian interpolator. The literature on this topic is voluminous.[77]

Josephus also refers to Jesus briefly in book 20. This reference is considered to be more authentic.

* * *

Because Josephus wrote a lot, he often ends up contradicting himself, damaging his own credibility.[78]

* * *

Mitchell First is a personal injury attorney and a Jewish history scholar. Due to the former, he has credibility problems as a historian as well!

10. Bringing Bar Kokhba Back to Life: Murabba'at and Naḥal Ḥever

What did we really know about Bar Kokhba for two thousand years? The material in rabbinic literature was brief and the passages had a legendary quality (e.g., he had 200,000 soldiers with amputated fingers and another 200,000 who had uprooted cedar trees in Lebanon).

---

77. See, e.g., the article on Wikipedia: "Josephus on Jesus."

78. One scholar has written that Josephus "with all his boasted zeal for truth, shows on occasions, when his statements are subject to control, a lax sense of the meaning of that word."

There were only brief references to him in the writings of the church fathers. The Roman historian Dio Cassius (c. 200 CE) gave important background information about Hadrian's war against the Jews, but did not mention Bar Kokhba.[79] Josephus, whose writings included the events of Masada in 72–73 CE, died before the time of Bar Kokhba.

The only tangible evidence that we had of a Jewish revolt at the time of Bar Kokhba (132–35 CE) were thousands of coins. From these coins, we at least learned that he had a first name, Shimon, and that he titled himself *Nasi Yisrael*. Some of the coins also had another name "Elazar Ha-Kohen."

In his book, *Bar-Kokhba: The rediscovery of the legendary hero of the last Jewish Revolt against Imperial Rome*, archaeologist Yigael Yadin summarizes: "But when all the fragmentary tales and traces of Bar-Kokhba were assembled they amounted to no more than the lineaments of a ghost. He figured in Jewish folklore more as a myth than a man of flesh and blood, as impersonal as a Hercules or a King Arthur."[80]

But then the discoveries at the caves of Murabba'at and Naḥal Ḥever changed all this.

The findings at Qumran in 1947 had motivated Bedouins to look in other caves, and in the fall of 1951 Bedouins discovered four caves at Murabba'at (technically: "Wadi Murabba'at"). This new site was about 11 miles south of Qumran.

In December 1951 and January 1952 the scholar Roland De Vaux was shown by an antiquities dealer a few documents which had the original Hebrew name of Bar Kokhba on them. (I will explain further below). This was a very dramatic find! DeVaux bought what he was shown and was able to be led to the caves, and bring along another scholar. (When the two got there, they found 34 Bedouins fleeing from their illicit exploration!)

Shortly thereafter, a team led by the above two scholars was able to investigate these four caves. A fifth cave in the area was discovered in 1955.

---

79. Of course, there are credibility issues with the material in Dio Cassius and the church fathers.

80. P. 27 (1971). Much of what I have written in this essay is based on this book.

The four caves revealed evidence of occupation from many different periods: (1) the 4th millennium BCE, (2) the period from 2000–1500 BCE, (3) the 8th or 7th centuries BCE, (4) the Hellenistic period, (5) the Roman period, and (6) the Arab period. But the most interesting material came from the Roman period, as these caves were used as outposts by Jewish fighters allied with Bar Kokhba during the Jewish revolt that he led against the Romans.

Among the findings from this period were: (1) fragments from Genesis, Exodus, Deuteronomy and Isaiah, (2) *tefillin* fragments, and (3) contracts and deeds of sale in Hebrew, Aramaic and Greek.

According to the *Encyclopaedia Judaica* (12:528), "the *tefillin* are of the type which became standard from the beginning of the second century CE onward, unlike those found at Qumran, which belong to an earlier type...." Similarly, the texts of the *Tanakh* found at Murabba'at are closely related to our texts today, significantly closer than the *Tanakh* texts found at Qumran. (The Qumran texts are of course earlier, dating from the third century BCE to the first century CE. The Qumran site was destroyed by the Romans in 68 CE)

The fifth cave revealed a scroll of the Twelve Prophets, containing a substantial portion of nine of the twelve books.

But the most important finds in the Murabba'at caves were two letters dictated by Bar Kokhba to the Jewish leader at this site, Yeshua ben Galgoula.

Here is the text of one letter: "From Shimon ben Kosiba to Yeshua ben Galgoula and to the men of the fort, peace. I take heaven to witness against me that unless you – – – [word is illegible] the Galileans who are with you every man, I will put fetters on your feet as I did to ben Aphlul."[81]

The second letter reads: "From Shimon to Yeshua ben Galgoula, greeting! Take cognizance of the fact that you must arrange for five *kors* of wheat to be sent by the [members of] my household. So prepare for each of them his lodging place. Let them stay with you over the Sabbath. See to it that the heart of each is satisfied. Be brave and keep up the courage of the people of the place. Peace! I have

81. Yadin, p. 137.

ordered whosoever delivers his wheat to you to bring it the day after the Sabbath."[82]

According to the *Encyclopaedia Judaica* (12:529), these caves "seem to have been the last redoubt of [Yeshua] and his men and their families. The Romans pursued them there and wiped them out, as they did to their comrades in Naḥal Ḥever. Some of the manuscripts bear signs of having been violently torn up by the invaders."

Naḥal Ḥever is also in the Dead Sea area. The caves at this site were first investigated in 1953 and 1955. They were investigated more thoroughly in 1960 and 1961 by Yadin.[83] In 1955, twenty-four human skeletons were found in one of the caves, leading this cave to be called the "Cave of Horrors." The cave where the letters from Bar Kokhba were found in 1960 (see below) ended up being called the "Cave of Letters." (Evidently, the skeletons found in 1955 were the remains of allies of Bar Kokhba who had taken refuge there with their families.)

At Naḥal Ḥever, a bundle of 15 Bar Kokhba-related letters were found, all tied together.[84] Almost all were dictated by Bar Kokhba himself. Most were in Aramaic, but some in Hebrew. Each has a different handwriting, indicating that they were composed by his assistants. One letter has him using the title *Nasi Yisrael*. (We already knew this title from some Bar Kokhba coins, prior to the discoveries of these letters.)

After reading all the Bar Kokhba letters, Yadin concluded: "Bar-Kokhba seems to have been a strong and tough man.... The letters are written in an abrupt-even telegraphic-style. Most demands and orders are combined with an admonition. Maybe it is unfair to pass the above judgment, since clearly these letters were written towards the end of the revolt, when Bar-Kokhba was already desperate."[85]

---

82. Text based on *EJ* 12:529. See Yadin's briefer description of the letter at p. 139.

83. In 1999 and 2000, the caves were excavated again by an archaeologist from the University of Hartford.

84. Naḥal Ḥever is also famous for the discovery of a scroll of the Twelve Prophets in Greek, and for the discovery of a bundle of 35 legal documents (in Greek, Aramaic, and Nabatean) belonging to a Jewish woman named Babata, from the years prior to the Bar Kokhba rebellion.

85. Yadin, p. 124.

Almost all the letters at Naḥal Ḥever are addressed to one or both of the following individuals: Yehonatan and Masabala. The two were the military commanders of Ein-Gedi. These letters were surely sent by Bar Kokhba to these two at Ein-Gedi, before they escaped with these letters to a cave in Naḥal Ḥever.

Here are some excerpts from the letters dictated by Bar Kokhba:[86]

- "Seize Yeshua bar Tadmoraya and send him to me in safe custody… and do not neglect to take off his sword."
- "Get hold of the young men and come with them; if not – a punishment. And I shall deal with the Romans."
- "Send to the camp four loads of salt…"[87]
- Another letter concerns the cargo of a ship in the port of Ein-Gedi with which Yehonatan and Masabala did not deal properly. Bar Kokhba chides them: "In comfort you sit, eat and drink from the property of the House of Israel, and care nothing for your brothers."
- "Concerning every man of Tekoa who will be found at your place – the houses in which they dwell will be burned and you [too] will be punished."

  "Let all men from Tekoa and other places who are with you, be sent to me without delay. And if you shall not send them, let it be known to you that you will be punished…." [88]

  Yadin explains that those attempting to avoid the mobilization orders of Bar Kokhba had been fleeing from Tekoa to Ein-Gedi, a more remote location.

5. The following letter was not sent by Bar Kokhba to Yehonatan or Masabala but to someone else. But the letter relates to them:

   I have sent to you two donkeys that you shall send with them two men to Yehonatan…and to Masabala in order that they shall pack and send to the camp, towards you, *lulavin* and *etrogin*. And you, from your place, send others who will bring you *hadasin* and *aravin*. See that they are tithed and send them to the camp.

---

86. Yadin, p. 125–132
87. Ein-Gedi was situated on the shores of the Dead Sea, a salt source.
88. This is a different letter than the one "Concerning…"

6. Another letter also relates to Sukkot, although not sent by Bar Kokhba. The name of the sender of the letter is "So...ios," and this letter is in Greek. This individual informs Yehonatan and Masabala that he is sending them a certain Agrippas, so that they should send back with him palm branches and citrons "for the camp of the Jews." He urges them to be "as quick as possible." Then comes the following: "the letter is written in Greek as we have no one who knows Hebrew" and he could not delay writing it "because of the holiday."

   When this letter was first published, it was thought that the sender was Bar Kokhba and that the name "So...ios" was the equivalent of "Shimon" in Greek. That would be very interesting: Bar Kokhba dictating a letter in Greek. But Yadin concludes that the sender was a gentile. The existence of gentiles in Bar Kokhba's ranks is corroborated by the Roman historian Dio Cassius: "Many outside nations, too, were joining them through eagerness for gain."[89]

* * *

Regarding the name of the leader of the Jewish revolt,[90] the rabbinic sources consistently record his name with a middle letter of *zayin*: בן כוזיבא, בן כוזבא, or בן כוזבה.[91] In contrast, from the early Christian sources, it would seem that his name had a middle letter of *caf*. The earliest reference to him in a Christian source is found in the church

89. Yadin, p. 257.

90. The next three paragraphs are based on *EJ* 4:228–29 and Emil Schürer, *The History of the Jewish People*... (Vermes, Millar and Black translation, 1973), vol. 1, pp. 543–44. See also Yadin, pp. 29 and 124.

91. See M. Jastrow, p. 618, and *Seder Olam*, chap. 30, *Sanhed.* 93b, and J. Talmud *Taanit* 4:8. Whether this name represents his father's name or a place name is not known.

The *EJ* entry writes that the rabbinic sources have: "בן כוזיבא, בר כוסבא, בן כוזבה." I am fairly confident that the middle entry here is a mistake (and a very unfortunate one).

father Eusebius (c. 300 CE). Eusebius writes: "The Jews were at that time led by a certain Barchochebas,[92] which means 'star'…"[93]

With the Murabbaat and Naḥal Ḥever letters, we now have, for the first time, letters with the actual spelling of his name. We see that the middle letter is always a *samekh*. The name seems to have been pronounced *Kosiba*.[94]

A widespread suggestion is that the other two versions of his name were based on puns. The one based on the ככב (=star) spelling was probably what his supporters called him (based on Numbers 24:17), and this name must have spread to the gentiles. But in the rabbinic sources, since his Messianic rebellion ended in failure, they always used the root כזב when referring to him.[95] This root has meanings like "false" and "lie."

* * *

Yadin tells the story that there was a custom for the President of Israel to invite archaeologists to his home to report on their latest discoveries. He was invited to one such meeting in 1960 at the home of President Yitzhak Ben-Zvi. It was attended by Prime Minister Ben-Gurion and Cabinet ministers and other distinguished guests. He projected on the screen the photo of one of the documents from Naḥal Ḥever and read aloud the first line: "Shimon Bar Kosiba, President over Israel." He turned to President Ben-Zvi and said, "Your excellency, I am honored to be able to tell you that we have discovered fifteen

---

92. Eusebius was writing in Greek. He wrote: Βαρχοχεβας. Jerome, writing in Latin, also has a middle sound of "ch" in the name. Jerome describes him as "the instigator of the Jewish uprising" and adds that he "kept fanning a lighted blade of straw in his mouth with puffs of breath so as to give the impression that he was spewing out flames…." Yadin, p. 258.

93. Eusebius continues: "A man who was murderous and a bandit, but relied on his name, as if dealing with slaves, and claimed to be a luminary who had come down to them from heaven and was magically enlightening those who were in misery." Yadin, p. 258.

94. The name in the Hebrew and Aramaic documents does not have vowels. But we have his name in one Greek letter, with a vowel: Χωςιβα. This is consistent with the *vav* in the name כוזיבא in the rabbinic sources.

95. See *Lam. Rabbah* 2:4 (regarding the leader of the revolt and Num. 24:17): אל תקרי כוכב אלא כוזב.

dispatches written or dictated by the last President of ancient Israel 1800 years ago." The audience was struck dumb, and then the silence was shattered with spontaneous cries of astonishment and joy. (That evening the radio interrupted its scheduled program to broadcast the news of the discovery, and the next day the newspapers came out with banner headlines.)

Yadin tells another story that when he showed Prime Minister Ben-Gurion some of the documents in Aramaic, Ben-Gurion's reaction was: "Why did they write in Aramaic and not Hebrew!"[96] It was as if Ben-Gurion was expressing anger at the members of his staff for doing this!

* * *

Yadin ends his book on Bar Kokhba poignantly: "Here were we, living in tents erected by the Israel Defence Forces, walking every day through the ruins of a Roman camp which caused the death of our forefathers. Nothing remains here today of the Romans save a heap of stones on the face of the desert, but here the descendants of the besieged were returning to salvage their ancestors' precious belongings."

* * *

Mitchell First is a personal injury attorney and Jewish history scholar. His handwriting is terrible and he suspects that Bar Kosiba may have had the same problem. (He did not write his own letters, only dictated them.) Also, like the name Bar Kosiba, the name First is also useful for punning!

11. When Did Jews First Use *Gematria*?

1 Samuel 13:1 tells us that Saul was one year old when he began to reign: *ben* (בן) *shanah Shaul be-malkho*. If you look at the Soncino, their translation suggests that there is a textual difficulty here and

96. This took place when only the Aramaic letters had been opened, so these were the ones shown to Ben-Gurion. In the time of Bar Kokhba, Aramaic was probably in more widespread use among Jews than Hebrew.

offers: "Saul was __ years old when he began to reign." But one of the suggestions offered in *Daat Mikra* is: בן was a way of writing "52." This raises the issue of whether the ancient Israelites thought in terms of numerical equivalents of letters.

There are many references to *gematria* by Amoraim and some laws seem to be derived from them. For example, when a Nazirite takes a vow for an unspecified period, the period is assumed to be 30 days based on a *gematria.* [97]

But what about derivations from *gematria*, or at least the use of numerical equivalents of letters, earlier than the Talmud?

At *Avot* 3:23 there is a statement that *tekufot ve-gematriot* are only *parperaot* (=peripheral) to wisdom. But the meaning of *gematriot* here may simply be "mathematics." (*Tekufot* means "astronomy.")

The last Mishnah in *Uktzin* uses a *gematria* and states that God will give each righteous person 310 worlds, citing a verse that uses the word יש. But this statement is in the name of R. Joshua b. Levi, an Amora.

Careful examination of the Talmud does reveal scattered statements by Tannaim employing *gematria*. One example is a statement by the Tanna R. Natan at *Shabbat* 70a.[98] He cites a *gematria* based on a verse to explain the source of the concept of 39 forbidden labors on Shabbat. Another example of a *gematria* from the tannaitic period is the *baraita* at *Berakhot* 8a about the word תוצאות.[99]

But what about before the Tannaim? Can we find examples of *gematria* in the period before the Common Era? Even simpler, do we even know that Jews understood their letters as having numerical values in this early period?

---

97. See *Nazir* 5a. But Rav Hershel Schachter writes that *gematria* is "not the actual source for any matter in Halakha or in Jewish thought." See his *Divrei Soferim* (2017), p. 126. He is willing to take this position because there are Rishonim and Acharonim who write, in particular instances, that the *gematria* mentioned in the Talmud is just an allusion to an idea that was derived independently. He cites as examples, Rambam, Ramban and *Pnei Yehoshua*.
98. For other examples, see *EJ* 7:369–70.
99. See also Mishnah *Shekalim* 3:2 which refers to Greek letters used for a numerical purpose on baskets used in the Second Temple. The precise numerical purpose of the Greek letters is not stated.

The earliest source for the use by Jews of letters to reflect numerical values are coins in the Aramaic language issued by King Yannai (=Alexander Janneus). The earliest one uses a כ as a date to indicate the 20th year of his reign.[100] This was the year 83 BCE.

But is it possible that we used letters to reflect numerical values even in the First Temple period and earlier? It is possible, but we have no sources for this practice. (The fact that we have no sources here is not surprising. In the First Temple period and earlier, we barely have sources for anything outside *Tanakh.*)

Already in the 3rd century BCE and probably earlier, the Greeks used letters to reflect numerical values and they too had a system where equations between words were made based on numerical values. Their system was called "isopsephy."[101] The scholar Saul Lieberman took the position that "the use of letters as numerals is apparently a Greek invention which was adopted by the Semites at a much later time."[102] But no one really knows. It is interesting that in the Greek system the value for their 11th letter is 20, the value for their 12th letter is 30, etc., etc., just like in our system. This perhaps implies a common origin for the two systems but it is not telling us which came first.

Now let me address a different issue. There is a system that we call today אתב"ש (=*atbash*). It is a way of writing where you write the last letter ת to mean א, ש to mean ב, etc., etc. The Talmud refers to this system.[103]

At Jeremiah 51:41, a place name ששך is referred to in the same verse

100. See Joseph Naveh, "Dated Coins of Alexander Janneus," *Israel Exploration Journal 18* (1968), pp. 20–26. Naveh writes that "[a]s far as we know, this is the earliest example of Semitic letters used as numerals, not only on coins but in any epigraphical source." Stephen J. Lieberman cites an article which considers the כ to be an engraving error for כה. Janneus issued many other coins with the כה date. See his "A Mesopotamian Background for the So-Called Aggadic 'Measures' of Biblical Hermeneutics?," *Hebrew Union College Annual* 58 (1987), p. 194, n. 179.

101. It means "equal pebbles." The early Greeks used pebbles arranged in patterns to learn arithmetic. The word "calculate" derives from the Latin word "calculus"=pebble. There is an interesting article on Wikipedia on "isopsephy."

102. *Hellenism in Jewish Palestine* (1962), p. 73.

103. It calls this system *gematria.* See *Sanhed.* 22a.

as a reference to בבל and seems to be another way of referring to Bavel.[104] Is it possible that Jeremiah is using *atbash* here? In this system, בבל would be written as שׁשך. Many scholars are willing to accept this approach since we have never found a place with a name similar to *Sheshakh* in or around Babylonia. Also, *atbash* is not dependent on the use of letters to represent numerals.

There is other evidence for the use of *atbash* by Jeremiah. At 51:1, he uses the phrase לב קמי (=the heart of those who stand against me). לב קמי is the equivalent of כשׂדים. The term Kasdim is sometimes used in *Tanakh* as a synonym for the Babylonians.

To sum up, a mainstream (but unproven) view is that Jews did not use *gematria* prior to the Hellenistic period, since we may not have equated letters with numerical values until the Hellenistic period. But *atbash* may have already been in use in the biblical period.[105]

* * *

Regarding the etymology of the word *gematria*, the Greek word ("geometry") originally meant "measuring the earth." Marcus Jastrow and many other scholars observed that the way the Talmud used the word *gematria* did not correspond with this. They suggested that the word *gematria* in the Talmud was a transposition from a Greek word *grammatia* that meant "letters." But more recent scholarship observes that even in Greek we can find the word "geometry" used as a number which results from a numerological calculation.[106] So there is no reason to posit a transposition and connect it with *grammatia*.

* * *

Mitchell First is a personal injury attorney and Jewish history scholar. In his own alternative *gematria* system, the *gematria* of his last name is "1."

---

104. שׁשך is also mentioned at Jer. 25:26.
105. But perhaps mainly to amuse and not to conceal.
106. See Stephen J. Lieberman, pp. 173–74.

12. The Distinction between *Neviim* and *Ketuvim*, and Insights into the Canon

The Talmud (*Bava Batra* 14b) lists 19 books in *Nakh*: 8 in the *Neviim* and 11 in the *Ketuvim*. (Once the five books of the Torah are added, that gives a total of 24 books.) The book of Ezra is mentioned on this list, but the book of Nehemiah is not. This is because these two books were joined together as one book at the time, so the listing for Ezra includes it.

What is the distinction between *Neviim* and *Ketuvim*? For example, why is the book of Joshua in the *Neviim* while the book of Ezra-Nehemiah is in the *Ketuvim*, when these seem to be the same type of work?

If you respond that the various books had different levels of inspiration and sanctity, this is a later idea, not found until the time of the early Rishonim. See Sid Z. Leiman, *The Canonization of Hebrew Scripture* (1976), pp. 64–66. At the time of the Talmud, there was not any distinction between the *Neviim* and the *Ketuvim* in terms of levels of inspiration and sanctity.

A reasonable explanation for our different categories is as follows.[107] There was originally a distinction between books that reflected the history of the nation of Israel and the exhortations of their prophets versus books that were not historical, like the book of Psalms. But at a certain point, probably between 518 BCE and approximately 400 BCE, the *Neviim* section began to be treated as closed. Any book that came to be accepted thereafter was only able to enter the *Ketuvim*. The last specific date mentioned in the *Neviim* is the 4th year of Darius I (see Zech. 7:1). This was 518 BCE So the *Neviim* were presumably open until at least that year. The *Neviim* section must have been closed by approximately 400 BCE. If it were still open, the books of Ezra-Nehemiah and Chronicles, which probably date to around this time, would have been included within it.

Now we understand why there is no common thread among the *Ketuvim*. The section is a catch-all. The *Ketuvim* came to include all types of books once the *Neviim* were closed.

---

107. I am here following the explanation of Leiman, at pp. 27–29.

With regard to when the *Ketuvim* were closed, this is a much-debated issue. A widespread view is that the book of Daniel was one of the last books added to the canon and that it accurately describes events through the persecution of Antiochus IV in 167–164 BCE. Perhaps the Pharisaic/Rabbinic canon was closed around this time. But this is just conjecture.

An important issue is whether the different groups of Jews in the late Second Temple period even viewed the same books as authoritative. A leading canon scholar has written: "[T]here were different collections of authoritative texts used by the various Jewish communities before the Pharisaic canon became the majority canon of Rabbinic Judaism."[108]

There is a section in the book of Ben Sira that perhaps sheds light on the development of the canon. Ben Sira is dated by most scholars to approximately 200 BCE. At the end of this book, there is a long section that includes mentions of Joshua, the Judges, Samuel, Nathan, David, Solomon, Jeroboam, Elijah, Hezekiah, Isaiah, Josiah, Jeremiah, Ezekiel, Job, Twelve Prophets,[109] Zerubabel, and Nehemiah. Since Ben Sira seems to be going through the books of *Tanakh* and its major figures (why else would Job and Twelve Prophets be mentioned!), we would have expected a mention here of Mordechai (or Esther), and Daniel. Yet there is none. Many scholars believe that this is evidence that the books of Daniel and Esther were not yet in *Tanakh* in his time. (With regard to the book of Ezra, he mentions Nehemiah so that suffices, since these seem to have been one book in ancient times.)

With regard to passages such as Mishnah *Yadayim* 3:5, where some Sages of the 2nd century CE argue about the status of Song of Songs and Ecclesiastes, Leiman argues that they are merely arguing about the inspired status of books in a canon that was closed long before. Leiman distinguishes between inspiration and canon. A book can be in the canon, but that does not necessarily mean that it was viewed as being composed with *ruaḥ ha-kodesh.* Whether Song of Songs and Ecclesiastes were composed with *ruaḥ ha-kodesh* is what is being

108. Timothy H. Lim, online article, April 2018, "The Canonical Process Reconsidered."
109. *Shneim Asar Ha-Neviim.*

debated by these 2nd century CE Sages. But Leiman argues that all Sages agreed that they were already in the canon.[110]

It bears stating again that scholars know nothing definitive about the canonization process. Anything that anyone writes is merely conjecture.[111] But at least I can tell you what the word "canon" means. It comes from a Greek word that means "measuring stick." It is related to the English word "cane."

Now I will address some other *Nakh* and canon-related issues:

1. There is a famous statement by Josephus, writing around 100 CE, that the Jews have 22 books in their canon. Based on this, many scholars had speculated that at the time of Josephus, two of our books were not yet canonized. But scholars eventually figured out, based on later statements by church fathers in Palestine (e.g., Origen and Jerome), that counting the books of *Tanakh* as 22 in number was a common way of referring to them. In this enumeration, the book of Ruth was combined with the book of Judges, and the book of Lamentations was combined with the book of Jeremiah.
2. In the list of biblical books at *Bava Batra* 14b, the book of Esther is called "Megillat Esther." The other four books that we include in *Ḥamesh Megillot* volumes today do not have the word "Megillah" prefaced to them.[112]
3. An interesting issue is the order that the 12 small books of The Twelve Prophets should be presented in. The talmudic passage at *Bava Batra* 14b lists these as one book, but does not include an order for the 12 books within it.

---

110. It is also important to distinguish between "authority" and "canon." A book may be viewed as having "authority," but when most scholars today use the word "canon" or "canonical," they understand the implication to be that a decision has already been made to exclude other books.

111. I highly doubt that there was a meeting every few years or decades by some important communal body where new additions were voted upon! Probably, canonization was a gradual evolving process, perhaps even led from the bottom-up, i.e., by the evolving practices of the common people.

112. I have discussed this in a different essay: "The Origin of the Reading of the *Ḥamesh Megillot*."

4. Who is the last king mentioned by name in *Tanakh*? Fortunately or unfortunately, there is more than one correct answer to this question. Nehemiah 12:22 mentions a king named "Daryavesh." Most scholars interpret the reference as being to Darius II (423–404 BCE), in which case he would be the last king mentioned by name in *Tanakh*. But it is also possible that the reference is to Darius III (336–331 BCE).

   On the other hand, others (e.g., *Daat Mikra* commentary) take the position that Nehemiah 12:22 is referring to Darius I (522–486 BCE). If so, the last Persian king mentioned in *Tanakh* would be the Artaḥshasta of the time of Ezra and Nehemiah. This is Artaxerxes I. He reigned from 465–424 BCE. (He was the son of Xerxes=Achashverosh.)

   A separate issue is who is the last king alluded to in *Tanakh*, but not mentioned by name? Daniel 11:4 clearly alludes to the sudden death of Alexander the Great and the division of his empire into four parts. Alexander the Great died in 323 BCE. Even later than this, most scholars believe that the book of Daniel, especially chapters 9 and 11, alludes to Antiochus IV and his persecution of the Jews from 167 BCE to 164 BCE.

* * *

Mitchell First is a personal injury attorney and Jewish history scholar. Because his name is "First," he is fascinated with dating, chronology, and putting things in order.

13. The Earliest Surviving Texts of the Torah

Many of us are aware that the oldest complete Hebrew Bible is the Leningrad Codex which dates to the early 11th century. It is currently stored in the National Library of Russia in the city of St. Petersburg (formerly called Leningrad). Earlier than this, we have the Aleppo Codex which dates to the first half of the 10th century.

In the Aleppo Codex, most of the Pentateuch is now missing, due to anti-Jewish riots that broke out in Aleppo (Syria) on Dec. 1, 1947. This was a few days after the UN voted to partition Palestine. The rioters broke into the synagogue and burned many Torah scrolls. They also broke into the locked iron chest that housed the Codex. After the riots, only 295 of the original 490 pages of the Codex remained. In 1958, what remained was smuggled to Israel. We do not know precisely what happened to the missing pages. Probably most were burned in the riots. Periodically, individual Jews acknowledge possessing fragments.

Another notable early text of the Pentateuch is British Museum Codex Or. 4445. This text dates to the early 9th century and has most of the Pentateuch. We also have other texts of the Pentateuch from the 10th century, aside from the Aleppo Codex.

If we go 1000 years prior to this, we have the Dead Sea Scrolls. Among these scrolls, there are approximately 220 texts that are biblical texts (usually very fragmentary). These texts date from the late third century BCE to the first century CE. We have texts covering a significant percentage of the Torah and the *Nakh*. In the case of the book of Isaiah, we even have a scroll that covers the entire book (66 chapters!), aside from a few small damaged portions. We also have biblical texts from the first to second centuries CE from Masada and a few other sites.

But what about the centuries between the 3rd century and 8th century CE? The following is what we have from the Pentateuch during these intervening centuries (a period referred to as "the silent era" in terms of biblical texts):

1. A chunk of charcoal that was once a scroll was found in 1970 at a synagogue in Ein Gedi. The synagogue burned down around 600 CE. It was too dangerous to the text for anyone to attempt to open the chunk. But in recent years, using the latest advanced imaging techniques, the text inside the chunk of charcoal was finally able to be read, without the chunk being opened. The text dates to approximately 300 C.E. and has verses from Leviticus chapters 1–2.
2. There are texts known as the London sheet, and Ashkar-Gilson sheet 2. In recent years, when the latter was on display in the Shrine of the Book in Israel, it was realized by two Israeli scholars that the London sheet and Ashkar-Gilson sheet 2 derive from the same

scroll. The scroll dates to around 700 CE. The surviving sheets contain Exodus 9:18–13:2 and 13:19–16.1.[113] Where these sheets originated is unknown. Probably, they originated from the Cairo Genizah and then ended up on the antiquities market. (Most of the material from the Cairo Genizah dates from the 10th through 13th centuries.)

The London sheet was in the collection of Jews' College in London for many years. It is now held in a private collection. The Ashkar-Gilson sheet is named for Fuad Ashkar and Albert Gilson, two American doctors who purchased the document along with others from an antiquities dealer in Beirut in 1972. Subsequently, they donated the documents they purchased to Duke University.

3. The Ashkar-Gilson collection includes other old Torah texts as well. For example, a text known as Ashkar-Gilson 14 includes the Decalogue in Deuteronomy chapter 5. Many of the texts are so faded that they can only be read utilizing the latest advanced technology.
4. We have the following early biblical fragments which are known to have come from the Cairo Genizah: T-S NS 3.21: portions of Gen. 13–17, and T-S NS 4.3: portions of Gen. 4–6. They both probably derive from the same scroll and date to between 500 CE to 800 CE.

Now let us ask the same question with regard to texts of the Pentateuch preserved in Greek translation and held by Christians over the centuries. Here we have much more. I am not doing justice to this subject and will leave out a lot, but it is important to mention three famous early Septuagint manuscripts:

- Codex Vaticanus from the 4th century, held in the Vatican Library. It has a complete text of *Tanakh*, although a few sections were added in the 15th century.

113. More recently, a scholar has identified 13 additional fragments (most of them in the Cambridge library) that belong to this same scroll. See Mordechai Veintrob, "More Fragments of Early Torah Scroll Come to Light," *Genizah Fragments* 77 (April 2019), pp. 1–2.

- Codex Sinaiticus from the 4th century. The main body of the manuscript is in the British Museum in London. The text includes much of the *Nakh*. With regard to the Pentateuch, what has survived is only Gen. 23:19–24:46, and Num. 5:26–7:20 (with material missing even in these sections).
- Codex Alexandrinus from the 5th century. It is held in the British Museum in London. For centuries it had been held in a library in Alexandria. It has an almost complete text of the *Tanakh*.

* * *

Regarding Codex Sinaiticus, here is its interesting story. There is a monastery in the Sinai desert called Saint Catherine's Monastery, located adjacent to a mountain that many believed was Mount Sinai. This is Christianity's oldest, continuously inhabited monastery, built around 550 CE. This monastery is still a standard travel destination on tours to the Sinai.

In the middle of the 19th century, a German biblical scholar, Constantin von Tischendorf, went all over the world looking for old texts of the New Testament. After his finds in Europe, he made sure to go to this monastery, since it was the oldest in the world. There he saw pages from this old codex and the monks were initially willing to give him some pages as a gift. Over the course of many years and subsequent visits, he negotiated a payment with the monks and was able to take out many more pages. Only 18 sheets of the codex, out of several hundred, remain in the monastery today.

* * *

A codex is the earliest form of a bound book. The advantages of a codex rather than a scroll are ease of browsing and rapid reference, and use of both sides of the sheet. Christians adopted the codex format for the Bible and other writings as early as the 2nd century CE. It took longer for Jews to adopt this format. We continued to write biblical texts on scrolls. But the codex format was eventually adopted by Jews as well, starting around the 8th or 9th century. Most of the material from the Cairo Genizah are fragments from codices, not scrolls.

* * *

Some of the material in this article is based on: (1) Gary A. Rendsburg:

"The World's Oldest Torah Scrolls," *The Ancient Near East Today* 6:3, March 2018 (available online), (2) a later version of the above article in the Nov.–Dec. 2019 issue of *Biblical Archaeology Review*, and (3) Paul Sanders, "Missing Link in Hebrew Bible Formation," *Biblical Archaeology Review* 41:6, Nov.–Dec. 2015.

A useful work on this topic (although a bit out of date) with many pictures is Ernst Würthwein, *The Text of the Old Testament* (translated by Erroll F. Rhodes) (1979).

* * *

Mitchell First is a personal injury attorney and Jewish history scholar. When he was taken on a tour of Saint Catherine's Monastery in the 1970's, before Israel returned the Sinai to Egypt, he had no idea that it was an important place in the history of the text of the Bible.

14. Rashi: Insights into his Life and Works

The scholar Avraham Grossman, a professor of Jewish History at Hebrew University for many years, came out with an important book on Rashi in 2006. It was translated into English in 2012 with the simple title "Rashi." I would like to share some of the things I learned from it.

1. As to the name "Rashi," Grossman suggests that it may have originally been applied to him by his students as an abbreviation of *Rabbeinu She-Yiḥyeh* (="our Rabbi, may he live"). Only later did it come to be understood as an abbreviation for "Rabbi Shlomo Yitzḥaki" (=son of Yitzḥak).

2. Rashi (1041–1105) was born and died in Troyes, a city in northern France. He lived most of his life there, except that at about age 18, he went to the yeshiva in Mainz and later switched to the yeshiva in Worms. Without his approximately ten years of study in Germany, and the traditions and manuscripts he saw there, he could never have written the works that he did. Grossman writes that "he returned to Troyes as a mature scholar and began to engage in literary production and community activity," and "assumed a central position in the leadership of the small Troyes community." Many of Rashi's comments

on the Talmud are derived from his teachers at the German yeshivas. This is true to a lesser extent of his biblical interpretations.

We know very little about Rashi's father and mother and wife. (At least, with respect to his father, we know his name!)

Rashi had three daughters. Yocheved married Rabbi Meir ben Samuel, and they had four sons, including Rashbam and Rabbeinu Tam. Miriam married Rabbi Judah ben Nathan (Rivan). Rachel married a Rabbi Eliezer of whom nothing else is known and they divorced after a brief period. There was perhaps a fourth daughter who died in childhood

In Germany and France, Sages were not paid for teaching in yeshivas. So how did Rashi earn a living? Various scholars maintained that Rashi made his living from the wine business. But Haym Soloveitchik disagreed, arguing that the agricultural conditions where Rashi lived were not suited to growing grapes. Grossman agrees with Soloveitchik. Grossman concludes that Rashi earned his living in commerce with non-Jews, as did most Jews in France and Germany.

Rashi is famous for a wine leniency he gave. Rashi held that non-Jews in his time were not well-versed in the nature of idolatry. Therefore they should be considered like new-born infants whose touch does not make wine forbidden. Accordingly, he permitted drinking wine that had been touched by non-Jews. This view was contrary to the ruling of his teachers and colleagues in Germany. Rashi's leniency made it much easier for Jews in his area to acquire wine from elsewhere, as it facilitated the shipping by non-Jews. Travel on the roads outside the cities was dangerous.

3. The comments that appear in the name of Rashi in the books of Ezra, Nehemiah, Chronicles, and the end of Job (starting with 40:25) are not his.

4. Regarding the text of Rashi's Torah commentary, there are dozens of manuscripts and early printed editions. This makes the task of ascertaining the original text a very difficult one. An important attempt was made by the scholar Abraham Berliner. He published a critical edition in 1866 based on more than one hundred manuscripts and numerous printed editions.

The earliest manuscripts that we have are from the second quarter of the 13th century. This is over 100 years after Rashi's death. Sages and teachers who worked with Rashi's Torah commentary often made marginal notes, and what was originally in the margins was placed by later copyists into the text. Accordingly, Grossman (p. 77) estimates that about 10% of what we have today is not from Rashi himself.

Also, Rashi himself made changes in his commentary, so multiple versions already existed in his lifetime. This raises a conceptual issue: what version of the text are we even searching for?

5. Rashi never cites Rabbeinu Ḥananel's commentary on the Talmud, but it is possible that, late in life, he heard some of its ideas and used them.[114]

6. Rashi's biblical commentaries were widely respected in Germany and France already in Rashi's lifetime. But I cannot resist quoting a different view by Ibn Ezra, whose roots are in Spain: "He thinks he is on the path of plain meaning, but his books lack even one plain meaning [interpretation] out of a thousand; yet the sages of our generation glory in these books."[115] (Ibn Ezra is obviously exaggerating in his criticism.)

Rambam (1138–1204, Spain and Egypt) never explicitly refers to Rashi's commentaries. But Grossman adds that "he may well have been influenced by them." Unfortunately, Grossman does not explain further.

7. Hopefully, we are all taught at some point that what motivated Rashi to make a comment in his biblical commentaries was that he saw a question.[116] But Grossman points out that many times Rashi saw a question where most would see no question. For example, when the Torah mentions names of people or places, Rashi would often make a comment because he tried to explain the additional message in the

114. See, e.g., Rashi, *Ketuvot* 46b, s.v. יציאה.

115. See Ibn Ezra's introduction to *Safah Berurah*, quoted at Grossman, p. 46.

116. I think I was first taught this late in elementary school, in the modern Orthodox elementary school I attended. At the time we all used those blue linear translations of Rashi into English. I don't think this work ever mentioned this idea! It just translated, giving us the misleading impression that Rashi was just writing without a question. (But I admit that I should not criticize them. It was probably hard enough to do an accurate linear translation into English, without getting into any analysis. That could be left to the next generation of works of Rashi in English.)

names. See, e.g., his comments on Genesis 38:5 to the place name כזיב. But did place names and names of individuals really warrant a comment? Cannot the Torah mention a place name or the name of a person without it having an underlying message? Grossman writes that Rashi saw significance in every detail mentioned in the Torah.

Conversely, Grossman observes that there are many kinds of questions that Rashi fails to ask. For example, regarding the *Akeidah*, Rashi explains the verses, but does not ask all of the philosophical questions that arise. E.g., did God not know Abraham's thoughts and the profundity of his faith even without the test? Why does God test individuals? Ramban asks these broader questions. but Rashi was content to consider the local problem. Grossman writes that, for the most part, there are two different approaches that biblical exegetes follow: "One considered only the specific words; the other looked at the broader unit and concentrated on the problems that it raised. Rashi fell within the first category. He interpreted individual words or phrases, only rarely examining the structure and characteristics of the unit as a whole...."

I have just discussed Rashi's questions. The more important topic is Rashi's answers. I will address this in the next article.

* * *

Mitchell First is a personal injury attorney and Jewish history scholar. He still does not know what color shirts Rashi wore.

15. Was Rashi Motivated by Non-Exegetical Factors in his Torah Commentary?

As we all know, Rashi generally took his answers from the midrash, instead of offering suggestions of his own. In the view of some, Rashi was strictly an exegete and consistently chose the midrash that best fit with the plain sense of the verses, and adapted it slightly if necessary. No other considerations influenced him.

But the truth is that Rashi did have goals in his commentary other than correct exegesis. Much has been written on this subject. I am going to base my discussion on an article by Rabbi Hayyim Angel, in *Peshat Isn't So Simple* (2014), pp. 36–57, and on a book and article by Avraham Grossman. Grossman discusses this issue in his book *Rashi*, published in Hebrew in 2006 and translated into English in 2012. Earlier he discussed the issue in an article "Religious Polemic and Educational Purpose in Rashi's Commentary on the Torah." It is included in *Pirkei Nehama* (2001), pp. 187–205.

I am going to focus on Rashi's Torah commentary. That is where the battle among the Rashi scholars really occurs. (In his *Nakh* commentaries, there are times that he explicitly states that he prefers to give explanations to answer the heretics rather than give the interpretations of the Sages.)

Grossman writes (*Rashi*, pp. 84–85): "All agree that Rashi devoted much care to selecting the *midrashim* that he incorporated into his commentary. He referred to his method at several points, and though his description is not as lucid as it might be, and he is not fully consistent in applying the method, he clearly imposed certain standards in selecting the *midrashim*. Were those standards solely exegetical, or were they also aesthetic and conceptual? Did Rashi ever cite a *midrash* for which there was no exegetical need, doing so solely for literary or pedagogical purposes?"

One place in which Rashi sets forth his standard for including midrashim is his commentary on Genesis 3:8: "I come only [to deal with] the plain meaning of the text and with *aggadah* that resolves the words of scripture, *davar davur al ofnav* (Prov. 25:11)." The precise idiom intended in those last four words is unclear. The English translation of Grossman's *Rashi* work has: "a word fitly spoken."[117]

Grossman writes that "other statements made by Rashi suggest that the term 'as a word fitly spoken' encompasses two principal components: an interpretation that adheres to the rules of grammar and that corresponds to the subject and compositional context."[118]

But a close examination of Rashi's commentaries shows that he sometimes uses rabbinic midrashim that fail to meet his two criteria of linguistic and substantive compatibility. He sometimes cites

117. See p. 85. The English translation of Grossman's *Rashi* work was made by Joel Linsider.

118. See also Rashi's comm. to Isa. 26:11.

midrashim that are far removed from the plain meaning, linguistically and substantively.

Here is one example that Grossman cites. I am now quoting from his *Rashi*, pp. 86–87:

> The injunction against eating forbidden foods begins as follows: "These are the living things [*haḥayah*] which ye may eat among all the beasts [*habehemah*] that are on the earth" (Lev. 11:2…). The difficulty is obvious: why are "beasts" referred to initially as "living things"? Rashi offers a plain-meaning interpretation, mentioned also in *Ḥulin* 70b, according to which "beasts" are included within the category of "living things," that is, *ḥayah* is a general noun that includes *behemah*. But Rashi is not content solely with the plain-meaning interpretation and first offers a rather remote *midrash*: "'These are the living things' – it refers to life, for Israel is bonded to God and ought to be alive. He therefore separated them from impurity." In other words, the statement "These are the living things which ye may eat' means that the commandment instills life into the Israelites.… Is it conceivable that Rashi did not sense the magnitude of the divide between the *midrash* and the plain meaning of the verse? It is evident that he – like the author of the *midrash* – was motivated by pedagogical considerations whose purpose was to energize the Jews to avoid forbidden foods and to emphasize the advantage they enjoyed over the non-Jews who ate them. That, rather than any linguistic or substantive factor, is what led him to make use of this *midrash*.[119]

Grossman concludes that Rashi had certain goals that exceeded that of linguistic and substantive exegesis and led him to stray from his declaration of intent. These goals were "to educate Jews and to fortify them and equip them for the difficult confrontation with Christian supersessionist propaganda.… When he found a rabbinic

119. In order to truly understand Grossman's point, one has to look up the Rashi and the parable from *Midrash Tanḥuma* that Rashi cites at the end about the physician. Rashi does not summarize the parable, but it is printed in the notes in some editions of Rashi.

midrash that promoted one of these goals, he did not hesitate to cite it, even if it was far removed from the plain meaning of the verse.... It is evident that he felt deep affection for these *midrashim*, and sometimes found it hard to refrain from citing one even if it clashed with his declaration of intent."[120]

Rabbi Angel (p. 41) summarizes the view of Grossman: "Rashi saw assimilation and persecution among French Jews, and therefore used his commentary to inspire them during the grim period surrounding the First Crusade.... Rashi may have selected Midrashim he knew were far from *peshat* in order to convince his community that they are loved by God and should remain faithful to the Torah and *mitzvot*...."

Another scholar Yitzchak Gottlieb adopts a similar conclusion. He concludes that Rashi cited certain midrashim instead of others as part of his desire to provide comfort for persecuted Jews, to affirm God's love of Israel, and to defend Judaism against Christian polemical accusations.[121]

One of the most famous Rashi's in this regard is his reinterpretation of Jacob's statement to Isaac at Gen. 27:19. Rashi offers a change in punctuation so the words should be read: אנכי. עשׂו בכרך. As Rabbi Angel writes (p. 42, summarizing the view of Grossman), "Rashi knew he was deviating from *peshat* in this instance.... He did so, in all likelihood, because Christians regularly accused Jews of being deceitful in business, emulating their ancestor Jacob. By writing that Jacob did not use deceit (even translating '*mirmah*' as 'wisdom' on 27:35), Rashi deflated the Christian indictment at its roots."

Angel continues: "Grossman also demonstrates that Rashi consistently quoted Midrashim that defended the character of Jacob and those that lambasted Esau. Such consistent patterns plausibly can be understood against the background of Jewish-Christian tensions in medieval Europe. Rashi used Jacob as a symbol for the Jews, and Esau represented a combination of Edom, Rome, and Christianity. Although several of Rashi's comments [on Jacob and Esau] also may address textual anomalies, the consistent pattern

120. *Rashi*, pp. 87–88.
121. See Angel, p. 41.

of midrashic selections can be understood more fully against the polemical backdrop."

Angel concludes (summarizing Grossman's conclusion): "[T]he *primary*, overarching goal of his commentary was to provide religious guidance to Jews. If his educational goals coincided with *peshat* – which they usually did – then Rashi could teach biblical text and Judaism simultaneously. If not, Rashi favored religious teaching over a sterile, 'scientific' response to the biblical text."

* * *

Mitchell First is a personal injury attorney and Jewish history scholar. Rashi's repunctuating of Jacob's statement reminds him of a passage in a book by Ezer Weizman, *The Battle for Peace*: "The switch from peace to war could be sharp and swift. Sadat would not have to retract a single word; even his famous declaration in Jerusalem: 'No more war!' only needed repunctuating to read: "No more! War!"

16. Brief Background to the Cairo Genizah[122]

The term "Cairo Genizah" refers to a small windowless room where documents were stored for centuries in the Ben Ezra synagogue in Old Cairo. This synagogue was just a short walk from where Rambam (d. 1204) lived. Most of the documents found there date from the 10th to 13th centuries.[123]

This room was on the second floor of the synagogue, near the area where the women would sit. It was accessible only through a ladder.[124] Joel L. Kraemer, in his excellent and exceptionally thorough biography of Maimonides[125] (published in 2008), writes that the synagogue "still

122. I am basing much of this essay on Adina Hoffman and Peter Cole, *Sacred Trash: The Lost and Found World of the Cairo Geniza* (2011).

123. The synagogue itself was built in the ninth or tenth century, but it was demolished around 1012 and then rebuilt. The room for the documents may have been built only in the new building.

124. It was 8 feet long and 6 ½ feet wide, and had a height of six yards.

125. *Maimonides: The Life and World of One of Civilizations Greatest Minds.*

stands, refurbished and gleaming."[126] The room is still there, "though now forlorn, emptied of its treasures."

As to the importance of the Genizah materials, Kraemer writes (pp. 13–14):

> [The documents are] now in European, Russian, and American libraries. This treasure trove has placed at our disposal many of Moses ben Maimon's private and communal letters, some in his own handwriting, along with documents pertaining to his career and public activities. These papers are an indispensable source for knowledge of the cultural, economic, and social history of Maimonides' era.
>
> The roughly three hundred thousand manuscripts[127] of the entire Genizah take in a broad range of subjects: the Bible, the Apocrypha, sectarian literature, the Talmud, liturgy, philosophy, medicine, personal and business letters, and commercial, legal and communal documents.... The documents give precious details about daily life, economic structure, education, and family life. We find out about material culture (housing, attire, food, furniture, etc.), court records, marriage contracts, wills and deathbed declarations, and business records. Personal letters reveal details about family relationships and friendships. Many letters from and to women in the Genizah are our only record of women's voices in this period.
>
> As Egypt was a hub of Mediterranean trade and a mail-clearing center, the Genizah documents reflect the situation in the entire Mediterranean area. Documents come from Spain, North Africa (Morocco, Algeria, Tunisia, Libya), Sicily, Egypt, Palestine, Syria and Byzantium.[128]

* * *

126. There was a major renovation by a Canadian team in the 1980's.

127. *Sacred Trash*, the later of the two works, gives the count as 193,654. Each fragment is given a number in the cataloging process. Probably *Sacred Trash* is counting the number of fragments catalogued. I am guessing that perhaps two fragments that are easily combined may sometimes be given only one number.

128. Kraemer also points out that letters were often copied in Cairo before

The Genizah owes its existence to the Jewish custom of storing away worn books and manuscripts containing the divine name. But much more than that ended up in the Cairo Genizah. One theory is that people brought both the sacred and the secular there, without bothering to separate. Also, there was a common practice to write "With the help of God" on secular documents. The documents deposited in the Cairo Genizah are typically in Hebrew, Aramaic, or Judeo-Arabic (=Arabic written in Hebrew letters).

Although Solomon Schechter is the one responsible for getting most of the documents out of the Genizah, there were others before him who were able to get some documents out from the Genizah.[129]

Also, around 1889, the Ben Ezra synagogue began to be renovated and workers spread the pages from the storage room out in the courtyard. This also led to pages getting out and being sold.

Now I will explain what Schechter did. In 1896, two adventurous Christian women (twin sisters) returned to England after a trip to Cairo and brought back some Hebrew fragments that they had acquired from a dealer. They were very knowledgeable and could identify some of the fragments. One day in May of 1896, one of them happened to run into Schechter on the street. She had met him previously. She told him that they had some fragments that they could not identify. He went to their home very soon thereafter to inspect what they had. Among them he recognized a fragment from the Hebrew original of the book of Ben Sira. At the time, the book was only known in Greek translation. This got Schechter interested and he realized he had to secretly arrange a trip to Cairo. He was able to have his friend, the scholar Charles Taylor, a Christian Hebraist, fund his trip. Finally, in December of 1896, he was able to travel to Cairo to search for the source of the fragment. He learned that it came from the Ben Ezra synagogue. He had heard about a genizah there even before this trip.

He spent four weeks in Cairo. During this time, he made a variety of payments to those at the synagogue and was able to arrange for the transfer of the entire contents of the room to Cambridge University.

---

being sent on their way.

129. See *Sacred Trash*, chapter 2.

He took some pages home by himself, and shipped the rest. (Today, more than half of the documents remain in the library of Cambridge University where they were shipped initially.)

Schechter was born in Romania in 1847. His father was a Habad Hasid. Solomon's birth name was Shneur Zelman. He studied in Vienna and Berlin. When he came to England in 1882, he could not speak any English.[130] But in 1890, he was able to get a position as a teacher of rabbinic literature at Cambridge University. This was what he was doing in 1896. He later came to New York in 1902, accepting an invitation to become the president of the Jewish Theological Seminary. He remained in this position until his death in 1915.

The field of Jewish history has changed tremendously due to Schechter's trip to Cairo in 1896 and the decades of analysis that took place by scholars thereafter (which continues to this day). Manuscripts of both Talmuds, Geonic responsa, and piyyutim of Yannai and Kallir are some of the treasures discovered. With regard to Rambam, aside from letters he wrote, some in his own handwriting, we now have early versions of the *Moreh Nevukhim*, and an early draft of the *Mishneh Torah*. (The cross-outs in the latter are fascinating because they reveal his thought process. Unfortunately, only a few fragments of this early draft have survived.)

There is an iconic photo of Schechter in the Genizah room in Cambridge, studying a single scrap, with boxes and boxes of fragments surrounding him.[131] But the photo is staged. In the photo he is wearing normal clothing, whereas he regularly wore a big dust-coat and nose-and-mouth protector in the room.

But what did the mass of papers look like when Schechter first saw them in the storeroom in the synagogue? There are no photos of the inside prior to its emptying.[132] Schechter later wrote a piece in the London *Times* about what the jumble of documents in the

130. When he came to England in 1882, one of the first English phrases that Schechter insisted on learning was "weak tea," as he could not stand the strong tea that the English used to drink!

131. It is found at *EJ* 7:405 and is on the cover of *Sacred Trash*.

132. *Sacred Trash*, p. 19, does include a photo the authors took in Dec. 2009 of the opening to the room.

storeroom looked like. The title: "A Hoard of Hebrew Manuscripts." Here is an excerpt:[133]

> One can hardly realise the confusion in a genuine old Genizah until one has seen it. It is a battlefield of books, and the literary productions of many centuries had their share in the battle, and their *disjecta membra* are now strewn over its area. Some of the belligerents have perished outright, and are literally ground to dust in the terrible struggle for space, whilst others, as if overtaken by a general crush, are squeezed into big, unshapely lumps, which even with the aid of chemical appliances can no longer be separated without serious damage to their constituents. In their present condition, these lumps sometimes afford curiously suggestive combinations; as, for instance, when you find a piece of some rationalistic work, in which the very existence of either angels or devils is denied, clinging for its very life to an amulet in which these same beings (mostly the latter) are bound over to be on their good behavior and not interfere with Miss Jair's love for somebody. The development of the romance is obscured by the fact that the last lines of the amulet are mounted on some I.O.U., or lease, and this in turn is squeezed between the sheets of an old moralist, who treats all attention to money affairs with scorn and indignation. Again, all these contradictory matters cleave tightly to some sheets from a very old Bible. This indeed ought, to be the last umpire between them, but it is hardly legible without peeling off from its surface the fragments of some printed work, which clings to old nobility....

(I am sure that Schechter is exaggerating in his battlefield narrative!)

Schechter's labor of several weeks of boxing the fragments from the storeroom was very difficult. Schechter described the room as "a beastly unhealthy place. "It was dark and filled with medieval dust,

133. *Sacred Trash*, p. 70.

which "settles in one's throat and threatens suffocation," and it was "full of all possible insects." [134]

* * *

I mentioned above that there were some who had been to the storeroom in the synagogue before Schechter. There was also a tradition that it was dangerous for anyone to enter the room and that there was a serpent there. In the 1860s a Jerusalem rabbi, Yaakov Safir, was able to coax the synagogue's caretaker and treasurer to let him in. They initially laughed at his request and said: "Why would a man risk his life for nothing? He won't live out the year!" He pleaded with them and showed them that he had a small *mezuzah* for protection and that he knew how to charm snakes. He also promised them a reward if they would bring him a ladder. They finally agreed to let him in. He toiled for two days there, ending up covered with dust and grime, but he did pick out a few pages.

* * *

When Schechter went through the documents, he was looking for fragments of important works and matters about important figures.[135] He was not interested in fragments that involved ordinary figures in their daily lives. Accordingly, many boxes were put aside that he thought of little importance.[136] Like Schechter, the Genizah scholars after him were also focused on major matters: e.g., liturgical fragments, pages of Talmud and Midrash, and rabbinical rulings on important issues. (The fragments in all these areas were typically in Hebrew or Aramaic.)

In 1955, there was a German-born scholar living in Jerusalem named Shelomo Dov Goitein. He had come to Israel in 1923, on the same boat with his friend Gershom Scholem. While in Germany,

134. The authors of *Sacred Trash* add: "Still worse than the bugs were the synagogue beadle and his helpers – whose assistance Schechter realized he needed in order to pack up the stash and whose incessant demands for bakshish Schechter had little choice but to meet."

135. This is similar to the oft-quoted approach to history of the 19th-century British historian Thomas Carlyle: "The history of the world is but the biography of great men."

136. At least one box of such fragments was labeled with the word "Rubbish."

Goitein had studied Arabic and Islam. He later became a professor at Hebrew University and gave lectures on these topics.

In the fall of 1955, he was temporarily in England, looking at Genizah fragments for a book he was working on about Jews who traded with India. One day, the head of the Cambridge library and the head of its Oriental Department mentioned to him that they knew of boxes from the Genizah that had been put away decades before and were not being looked at. They took him upstairs to see them.

He immediately realized how fascinating they would be. These documents were typically in Judeo-Arabic and reflected the daily life of regular individuals, including marriage contracts, wills, business records, court records, and personal letters. Analyzing these documents became Goitein's project for the rest of his life. Goitein referred to himself as an "interpretive sociographer," i.e., one who describes a culture by analysis of its texts. In 1957, he left Israel and took a position at the University of Pennsylvania to continue this work.[137]

Goitein eventually produced a classic work: *A Mediterranean Society: The Jewish Communities of the Arab World as Portrayed in the Documents of the Cairo Geniza (5 vols., 1967–88).*[138]

One of Goitein's major findings was that Jews in this Arab world could enter into close business partnerships with Muslims and Christians and live in any part of town they pleased. It all reminded him of the U.S., "even though we do not wear turbans here." (One of his other notable findings was that he could find no evidence that Jews in this Arab world had a bar-mitzvah ritual.)

The authors of *Sacred Trash* write that if Schechter can loosely be considered the discoverer of the Cairo Genizah, Goitein can be considered its "rediscoverer."

* * *

Mitchell First is a personal injury attorney and Jewish history scholar. He is similar to Schechter and Goitein in that the room where he

137. The funding for his work was better in the U.S. His friend S.Y. Agnon criticized him for leaving.

138. After Goitein died, a colleague completed the work on the India book. It was published in 2008: *India Traders of the Middle Ages.*

works at home is full of piles and piles of documents. These serve as ideas for potential articles!

17. A Letter by Rambam to the Rabbis of Lunel

Rambam wrote a few letters to the Rabbis of the main communities in southern France: the communities of Lunel and Montpellier.[139] I am going to discuss one of them, a letter that was composed in the year 1200, four years before Rambam passed away. Rambam had been living in Egypt since about 1166.

The background to this letter is that, a few years before, a group of Rabbis from one of these communities had written to Rambam for the first time, asking about the status of astrology in Judaism.[140] Rambam replied with a letter that instructed them that thinking that the stars influenced behavior is foolishness. Impressed by his detailed letter, this group of Rabbis and other Rabbis associated with them thereafter sent him a few other letters.[141] For example, they asked him some respectful questions about passages in his *Mishneh Torah*.

The scholar Joel Kraemer writes: "It was uplifting for [Maimonides] to receive letters from scholars who appreciated what he had done and asked friendly and constructive questions.... After Maimonides had worked for ten years on the *Mishneh Torah*, learned colleagues found it wanting, accused him of self-aggrandizement, and tried to

---

139. For some background to all the letters, see Charles H. Sheer, *Maimonides' Grand Epistle to the Scholars of Lunel: Ideology and Rhetoric* (2019). Sheer's work focuses on a different letter than the one I am discussing here. For additional background, see the work of Kraemer.

140. Rambam had addressed the issue of astrology in his *Mishneh Torah*, completed around 1177. But this work had still not reached these communities in southern France at the time they wrote their first letter to him in the 1190's.

141. The first letter to Rambam was sent from Montpellier. A leading Rabbi from this group later moved from Montpellier to Lunel. In this essay, I am not trying to distinguish between these communities. But the letter I am focusing on from 1200 is addressed mainly to the Rabbis of Lunel.

It is important to point out that there were delays of **years** between letters and replies!

destroy his reputation. Now in southern France he found scholars who valued his work, who were sincerely puzzled by some passages, and addressed him with veneration. The Spanish origin of many Provencal scholars surely pleased him. His hopes for a continuation of learning were centered in southern France...."[142]

As further background, Rambam completed his *Guide to the Perplexed* around 1191. But it was composed in Arabic. The Rabbis who wrote to him from this region in France could not read Arabic and asked that Rambam translate it into Hebrew, along with some of his other works.

Here is the main part of the letter that Rambam wrote in the year 1200, addressed to the Rabbis of Lunel:

> ...I am forwarding to you now the third part of the *Guide of the Perplexed* in the Arabic language. However, with regard to your request that I may translate the text into the holy tongue for you – I myself could wish that I were young enough to be able to fulfill your wish concerning this and the other works which I have composed in the language of Ishmael....But I must blame the unfavorable times for preventing me from doing so. I have not even time to work out and to improve my commentaries and other works composed in the rabbinic language, which contain various obscurities, in order to arrange new editions – to say nothing of making translations from one language into another....
>
> But you have in your midst the learned and well instructed R. Samuel ben Judah (Ibn Tibbon), on whom the Lord has bestowed the necessary insight...for performing the translation you have asked for. I have already written to him about this subject.
>
> To you, my honored friends, may you remain confident and strong, I have now to tell the truth: You, members of the congregation of Lunel, and of the neighboring towns, stand alone in raising the banner of Moses. You apply yourselves to the study

142. Kraemer, *Maimonides: The Life and World of One of Civilization's Greatest Minds* (2008), p. 432.

> of the Talmud and also cherish wisdom. The study of Torah in our communities has ceased; most of the bigger congregations are dead to spiritual aims; the remaining communities are facing the end. In the whole of Palestine there are three or four places only, and even these are weak, and in the whole of Syria none but a few in Aleppo occupy themselves with the Torah according to the truth, but they have it not much at heart. In the Babylonian Diaspora there are only two or three groups in Yemen, and in the rest of Arabia they know little of the Talmud and are merely acquainted with aggadic exposition.
>
> Only lately some well-to-do men came forward and purchased three copies of my code which they distributed through messengers in these countries, one copy for each country. Thus the horizon of these Jews was widened and the religious life in all communities as far as India revived. The Jews of India know nothing of the Torah and of the laws, save the Sabbath and circumcision. In the towns of Berbery which belong to the realm of Islam, the Jews read the Torah and observe it according to its literal meaning. What was inflicted upon the Jews of Maghreb as punishment for their sins you know.
>
> Therefore be firm and courageous for the sake of our people and our God; make up your minds to remain brave men. Everything depends on you; the decision is in your hands. Do not rely upon my support, because I am an old man with gray hair. And know that for this not my age but my weak body is responsible...[143]

1. This letter is interesting because of the broad survey of the Jewish communities that Rambam undertakes in the year 1200. He describes Torah learning as dying or deteriorating everywhere and believes that the future of Judaism depends on the study of Torah in Lunel and its neighboring communities.

His failure to mention the communities of northern France and Germany is also interesting, as there was much Torah learning going

143. The above translation of this Hebrew letter is taken from *A Maimonides Reader* by Isadore Twersky (1972), pp. 481–82. A slightly different text is printed in Yitzchak Shailat, *Iggerot Ha-Rambam*, vol. 2 (1995), pp. 557–59.

on there in the year 1200. Today, we can name numerous communities and many learned Rishonim from this broad region from this time.

When I first observed this omission, I thought it reflected some type of implicit criticism by Rambam of the method of learning in northern France and Germany. But it was pointed out to me that I was reading too much into the omission. Rambam had been living in Egypt for about 34 years when he wrote this letter. By that time, the communities of northern France and Germany were probably not on his radar. As noted in the *Encyclopaedia Judaica* (11:757), we have evidence of Rambam corresponding with every part of the Jewish world, except for the area of northern France and Germany.

That what was going on in northern France and Germany was off Rambam's radar is hard for us moderns to imagine. Every Shabbat, I turn the pages of one of the weekly Orthodox Jewish newspapers and without even trying I am informed of the happenings in far-off Jewish communities such as Ireland, Australia and India, just to name a few examples.

The letter did refer to "members of the congregation of Lunel, and of the neighboring towns." Perhaps the latter phrase (*ve-khol he-arim asher sevivoteikhem*) was meant to include the towns of northern France and Germany, but a fair reading of the entire letter makes this interpretation unlikely.

2. The text of the letter printed by Yitzchak Shailat has an additional phrase. Rambam tells the Rabbis of Lunel: *ve-aleikhem mitzvat yibbum, o ḥalotz o yabbem*. Here Rambam is comparing the Torah, now being abandoned in most communities, to a widow. He is encouraging the Rabbis of Lunel and its neighboring communities to do the proper thing and "marry it," rather than let it remain abandoned.

3. I always enjoy Rambam's comment about being proud of one copy of *Mishneh Torah* being sent to each of three countries. In Teaneck, where I live, there are many thousands of copies!

* * *

Mitchell First is a personal injury attorney and Jewish history scholar Like Rambam, he hopes to have his books sent to far away venues to revive Jewish learning. Unlike Rambam, he has not composed any books in Arabic.

18. A Letter by Rambam to a Simple Jew

Here I will present a letter that Rambam wrote to a simple Jew in Baghdad, Joseph Ibn Gabir. Joseph, not knowing any Hebrew, was unable to read the *Mishneh Torah* and asked Rambam to respond in his own hand and give him some encouragement.

The translation is from *A Maimonides Reader* by Isadore Twersky (1972), pp. 478–80:

> I gather from the letter of the esteemed Mar Joseph called Ibn Gabir that he regrets being an am-haaretz because he knows Arabic only but not Hebrew and that he, therefore, while studying our Commentary on the Mishnah with great zeal, is unable to read our code *Mishneh Torah*. He reports further in that letter that some scholars in Baghdad reject some of my decisions…
>
> First of all I must tell you, may the Lord keep and increase your welfare, that you are not justified in regarding yourself as an am ha-aretz. You are our beloved pupil[144]; so is everybody who is desirous of studying even one verse or a single halakhah. It makes also no difference whether you study in the holy language, or in Arabic, or in Aramaic; it matters only whether it is done with understanding. This is the important thing whichever language may be used in the commentaries or in the summaries. But of the man who neglects the development of his spirit it is said: "he has despised the word of the Lord;"[145] this applies also to a man who fails to continue his studies even if he has become a great scholar, for the advancement of learning is the highest command. I say, therefore, in general, that you must not belittle yourself nor give up the intention of improving. There are great scholars who did not begin their studies until an advanced age, and who became scholars of distinction in spite of this.
>
> If you want to study my work [=*Mishneh Torah*], you will

144. Despite this language, there is no reason to think the two ever met.
145. Rambam is citing Num. 15:31.

> have to learn Hebrew little by little. It is not so difficult, as the book is written in an easy style, and if you master one part you will soon be able to understand the whole work. I do not intend, however, to produce an Arabic edition, as you suggest; the work would lose its specific color. How could I do this, when I should like to translate my Arabic writings into the holy language!...
>
> The statement you have heard, namely, that I deny in my work the resurrection of the dead, is nothing more than a malicious calumny. He who asserted this is either a wicked man who mispresents my words, or an ignorant one who does not understand my views on Olam ha-Ba. In order to make impossible any further mistake or doubt, I have composed in the meantime a special treatise on this subject[146]...
>
> I have been informed – although I do not know whether it is true – that there is in your city somebody who speaks evil against me, and tries to gain honor by misrepresentation of my teaching. I have heard also that you protested against this, and reprimanded the slanderer. Do not act in this way! I forgive everybody who is opposed to me because of his lack of intelligence, even when he, by opposing, seeks his personal advantage. He does no harm to me.... While he is pleased, I do not lose anything.... You trouble yourself with useless quarrels, as I do not need the help of other men, and leave it to the people to follow their own will....

Twersky only included about one-third of the letter and I did not print everything that Twersky included. The full letter in Arabic and a Hebrew translation are found in Yitzchak Shailat, *Iggerot Ha-Rambam*, vol. 1 (1995), pp. 402–418.

A few comments:

1. Aside from what I printed above, the letter includes brief discussions on the following topics (and a few others as well): *mitzvot* that were kept by the *Avot* (this section was printed by Twersky), the issue

146. Rambam is referring to his *Treatise on Resurrection*, written in the year 1191.

of traveling on a boat on Shabbat, a certain leniency that Rambam gave in the laws of *niddah*, his forbidding *tzitzit* with verses written on them, and his unwillingness to allow for more than two *aravot* on a *lulav*. There is also a brief discussion about whether we will have bodies in *olam ha-ba*. Rambam advises Joseph not to think too much about this difficult issue.

2. The letter refers to criticism of Rambam's writings in Baghdad. The criticism referred to was by Samuel ben Ali. Ali was the head of the Academy at Baghdad from around 1160 to 1200 and was also the recognized leader of the Jewish communities in the neighboring countries. He was the most outspoken detractor of Rambam during Rambam's lifetime. (Rambam died in 1204.) Rambam had criticized his forceful methods of raising money and opposed the trappings of office of the Geonic Academy. He also rejected the curriculum of the Geonic Academy which left no room for anything except Talmud. There was a struggle between them that was "both personal and political, fought on the battlefield of the law."[147]

* * *

Mitchell First is a personal injury attorney and Jewish history scholar. Unlike Rambam, he does need the help of others and he encourages people to defend the views expressed in his books.

19. A Letter by Rambam About the Death of his Brother David

Aside from our knowledge of his father Maimon, we know very little about the family of Rambam. For example, we know nothing about his mother. As to his wife, we know that he married in Egypt late in life, in 1171 or a bit later, and his son Abraham was born in 1186. We know the name of his wife's father, but not the name of his wife.

Rambam was born in 1138. Since his marriage in 1171 or later was late in life, biographers often surmise that he must have had a first wife. But there is no evidence for this at present.

In one letter Rambam mentions a daughter who died young.

147. Kraemer, *Maimonides*, p. 412.

But it is unclear if the reference is to his own daughter or a friend's daughter. He did have three sisters and there is a bit of information about them.

I am getting all this information from the exhaustive work *Maimonides*, authored by Joel L. Kraemer in 2008.

Aside from having three sisters, Rambam had a younger brother David. The most important thing we know about him is that he died in a shipwreck in the Indian Ocean. A letter from Rambam has survived that describes his reaction to the death of his brother. That is the letter I will focus on here.

This letter was written in the year 1185 to a judge named Yefet in Acre. Rambam had become close to Yefet years earlier when Rambam and his father and brother had first arrived in Eretz Yisrael in around the year 1166, landing in Acre. The four of them later visited Jerusalem and the Temple area together. (A famous letter from Rambam describes this visit.)

This letter from 1185 has a very unusual beginning. In his letter, Yefet had complained that Rambam had not written to him to inquire about his welfare since their meeting in Acre decades earlier. But Rambam then turns the tables on him and points out that it was Yefet who had ignored him! Here is the letter from that point on:

> Moreover, a few months after we departed from [the land of Israel], my father and master died (may the memory of the righteous be a blessing). Letters of condolences arrived from the furthest west and from the land of Edom, a distance of several months, yet you disregarded this.
>
> Furthermore, I suffered many well-known calamities in Egypt, including sickness, financial loss and the attempt by informers to have me killed.
>
> The worst disaster that struck me of late, worse than anything I had ever experienced from the time I was born until this day was the demise of that upright man (may the memory of the righteous be a blessing), who drowned in the Indian Ocean while in possession of much money belonging to me, to him and to others, leaving a young daughter and his widow in my care.

> For about a year from the day the evil tidings reached me, I remained prostrate in bed with a severe inflammation, fever and mental confusion, and well nigh perished.
>
> From then until this day, that is about eight years, I have been in a state of disconsolate mourning. How can I be consoled? For he was my son; he grew up upon my knees; he was my brother, my pupil. It was he who did business in the market place, earning a livelihood, while I dwelled in security.
>
> He had a ready grasp of Talmud and a superb mastery of grammar. My only joy was to see him. "The sun has set on all joy." [Isa. 24:11.] For he has gone on to eternal life, leaving me dismayed in a foreign land. Whenever I see his handwriting or one of his books, my heart is churned inside me and my sorrow is rekindled.... And were it not for the Torah, which is my delight, and for scientific matters, which let me forget my sorrow, "I would have perished in my affliction" [Ps. 119:92].
>
> In spite of this, while I complain not of any sage, disciple, friend, or acquaintance, I should complain about you above all others. For... all four of us walked together in God's house in fear and trepidation. But you did not seek or inquire. I would be justified in not answering your letter that has now arrived pertaining to power of attorney. But my affection is drawn up in full and secured. I shall not forget our wandering together in wastelands and forests after the Lord, and therefore I do not ascribe to you sin and transgression. "Love covers up all faults." [Prov. 10:12].... If you were here with me, I would care for you properly, and I would honor and please you according to my ability....

(My translation is taken from Kraemer, pp. 255–56. This letter was originally written in Hebrew. The Hebrew text is at Yitzchak Shailat, *Iggerot Ha-Rambam*, vol. 1 (1995), pp. 228–230. If the questioner wrote to Rambam in Hebrew, he would typically respond in Hebrew, as occurred here.)

* * *

Rambam's remark that David had on his possession money belonging to Rambam is of interest. Perhaps it indicates that Rambam was a partner in this business venture of David.[148] Very likely, Rambam had been a partner in other business ventures of David as well.

Some biographers have written that David's death caused Rambam to relinquish the life of a scholar and take up medicine as a profession. This is not true. Rambam already attained prominence as a physician in his early days in Egypt. He also seems to have earned money on his own from commerce in precious gems and from teaching sciences (e.g., mathematics, logic and astronomy) to intellectuals.[149] Admittedly David's business trips helped Rambam, as Rambam stated in the letter above: "It was he who did business in the market place, earning a livelihood, while I dwelled in security." See also the letter from David cited by Kraemer, at p. 251. But it is wrong to read these letters as implying that Rambam had not been earning money on his own.

* * *

A letter was found in documents from the Cairo Genizah from David himself, written while he was in the Sudan, talking about his forthcoming journey to India. David wrote that in the locale that he was, in the Sudan, no imports had arrived recently, so he decided to continue his journey and go by sea to India. There is no date on this letter, but for reasons explained below, it almost certainly dates from either 1169, 1170 or 1171.

Kraemer assumes that this letter was referring to David's imminent journey to India that ended with his passing. In the 1185 letter, Rambam wrote that the evil tidings about David came to him eight years earlier. This would mean that David left for India around 1169–71 and Rambam did not find out about his passing until 1177. But this seems like an inordinate amount of time. Shailat (pp. 72–73 and 198) takes a different approach. He believes that the letter that David wrote in 1169–71 concerned an earlier trip to India, and that in 1176–77 he took another trip to India which resulted in his passing.

How were scholars able to estimate the date of David's letter to 1169, 1170 or 1171? David dated his letter to the 22nd of Iyyar, and mentioned that the Muslim month of Ramadan was forthcoming. Many

148. See Shailat, *Iggerot Ha-Rambam,* vol. 1, p. 229.

149. See Kraemer, *Maimonides*, pp. 161 and 258.

of us have learned that the Muslims have a lunar calendar without an adjustment. Thus, the beginning of Ramadan moves continually. In 1172 and for the three decades after that, Ramadan **preceded** the Jewish month of Iyyar.[150]

* * *

Mitchell First is a personal injury attorney and Jewish history scholar. He does not have any sea voyages to India planned.

20. *Mazkeret Batya*: The Inspiring Story of an Early Jewish Settlement in Palestine

The background to the late 19th-century Jewish settlements in Palestine was a wave of pogroms in Russia in 1881, which made most of Russian Jewry realize they had no future there. Of the two million Russian Jews that left Russia over the next few decades, 90% came to America. But a small portion went to Palestine.

Historians characterize the first wave of these Russian Jewish settlements in Palestine as "The First Aliyah." These settlements spanned the years 1882–1903. The settlements from 1904–14 are referred to as "The Second Aliyah."

A tremendous misconception is that all the early settlements were founded by secular Jews. It is true that the Second Aliyah was mainly a secular one, and this Aliyah formed the basis of Israel's early secular and socialist character. But with regard to the First Aliyah, almost all of the settlements were established by Orthodox Jews. A fascinating book came out in 2012, entitled *Rebels in the Holy Land: Mazkeret Batya, An Early Battleground for the Soul of Israel*, by Sam Finkel. This book tells the story of one of these early settlements founded by Orthodox Jews from Russia. As this book stresses, these were Orthodox Jews with beards and *payot*.

This is a must-read book. It is extremely well-documented with extensive photographs.[151] I am now going to summarize its story.

In 1882, a few Orthodox Jews in a small town in Russia were

150. See Kraemer, *Maimonides*, p. 544, notes 36–37.

151. The author came out with a revised edition in 2015. It is important to get the revised edition. See, e.g., the footnote below.

presented with a proposal. Baron Edmond de Rothschild in Paris was willing to support their establishment of a farming colony in Palestine. These Jews were already farmers in Russia. These men agreed to separate from their families for an extended period, and make the arduous trek to Palestine and start from scratch. They ended up establishing the sixth Jewish agricultural settlement in Israel. It was initially named Ekron, but a few years later, Rothschild renamed the settlement *Mazkeret Batya*, in memory of his mother.

Like all books, this book has heroes and villains. The heroes are Rabbi Shmuel Mohilever, Yechiel Brill, and Baron Rothschild.

Rabbi Mohilever was the chief rabbi of Radom (near Warsaw). He was deeply concerned about the mass exodus to America, due to the lack of a Torah environment there. In 1882, he organized a society whose goal was for Jews to take concrete steps to establish a presence in Palestine.

In the summer of 1882, he traveled to Western Europe to garner support for his society. He first visited Vienna and Germany but failed to win over anyone of importance. His next destination was Paris. But being exhausted, he took some time off to relax at a spa in Germany.

Coincidentally, influential journalist Yechiel Brill happened to be at this spa. Brill had established the newspaper *Ha-Levanon* in Jerusalem in 1863. He later relocated to Mainz and was publishing the paper there. After the pogroms of 1881, Brill began writing about the idea of sending professional Jewish farmers to colonize Palestine. Brill urged Rabbi Mohilever to send a group of experienced Jewish farmers to Palestine to build farms and infrastructure, and then send for their families later.

Mohilever continued on to Paris but initially had no success at getting financial support. Coincidentally, he ran into Brill there. Brill then had the idea of meeting with the chief Rabbi of Paris, who was close to Rothschild, and he convinced the chief Rabbi to arrange a meeting between Rothschild and Rabbi Mohilever.

Mohilever wrote a detailed description of the meeting, and the *devar Torah* he gave.[152] Mohilever wrote that the *devar Torah* was able to break down the initial coldness of Rothschild, and Rothschild

152. The *devar Torah* addressed the question of why Moshe had a speech impediment. I summarized it in my *Roots and Rituals*, pp. 60–61.

agreed that if a few farmers would be willing to come to Palestine, he would be willing to help them financially.[153]

The author writes that the Mohilever-Rothschild meeting lasted only 30 minutes, half of which was consumed by the translator. But this meeting changed the course of Jewish history. Over the next several decades, Rothschild ended up providing significant financial support not only to this group, but also to many of the other early Jewish settlements.

The agreed upon plan was for ten Russian farmers to be selected and then trained at the Mikveh Israel agricultural school, which had opened in Palestine in 1870. After the training, Rothschild would help the farmers acquire their own land. The potential historic impact of the venture was obvious to all. If successful, it would serve as a model for future colonies in Palestine for the oppressed Jews of Russia. Shortly thereafter, ten farmers from the town of Pavlovka were selected. On *Parshat Lekh Lekha* in 1882, a contract was signed, outlining everyone's obligations.

Brill agreed to accompany the men to Palestine, temporarily abandoning his family. He felt obligated to ensure that the ten men made their transition safely. When he arrived at the train station, eleven men appeared! The added man was one who had left farming and had become a *melamed*. He was not someone that Brill would have chosen. But the ten needed him along so that they could correspond with their families, as they did not know how to write.

The journey was a long one, and many severe challenges arose along the way. When they finally arrived in Alexandria, Brill was able obtain papers which made it appear that the men were born within

153. The first edition of Finkel's book came out in 2012. There, Finkel wrote that the meeting with Mohilever led to a major shift in Rothschild's thinking, and that prior to this Rothschild had not been supportive of the idea of colonizing Palestine. Finkel came out with a second edition of his book in 2015, which included later research on this issue by a scholar named Ran Aaronsohn. It turns out that Rothschild was planning to build colonies even before he met with Mohilever. Rothschild had met with French Jewish communal leader Carl Netter just a month earlier to discuss this issue. Finkel concludes that Rabbi Mohilever's meeting with Rothschild was a case of the Rabbi being the right man in the right place at the right time.

the Ottoman Empire. The Turkish government had recently issued a ban on Russian Jews settling in Palestine. Brill taught the men how to reply in Arabic when asked their names and city of origin. But when they arrived at the port in Jaffa, the inspectors realized that these were Jews from Russia and refused them entry! The men got back on board and attempted to enter again at the next stop, Haifa. After many complications, they were successful in entering there.

One villain in this book is a man named Shmuel Hirsch. He was the head of the Mikveh Israel agricultural school. He continually made things difficult for the farmers, including feeding them bread that was only fit for animals! He was from Western Europe and was not Orthodox. He could not relate to these Orthodox Jews from Russia and was not interested in the grand plans that Brill, Mohilever and Rothschild had for these men.

Brill eventually received a letter from his family in Mainz. His wife had not been able to pay the rent for six months. His creditors had confiscated his printing press and the housewares. His children had been expelled from school because of failure to pay tuition. His daughter and his wife were in need of medical care. Shortly thereafter, in 1883, he was forced to return to his family.

Meanwhile, the farmers needed a plot of land and Hirsch was not making proper efforts to find one. The men were threatening to return to Russia. Rothschild sent a telegram that he did not want these men to return to Russia under any circumstances. He realized that if these experienced farmers returned to Russia, no Jew from Russia would ever think of doing something like this in Palestine again.

Eventually, Hirsch let the Russians search for their land by themselves and they found a barren piece of land that was suitable for their needs near the Arab village of Aqir. Since they were not Ottoman citizens, the land could not be registered in their names. It was registered in the name of a French citizen and later transferred to Rothschild. In November of 1883, they finally began to plow on this land.

The book continues with the story of what happened in the *Shemitah* year of 1888–1889. The settlers of *Mazkeret Batya* felt obliged to let the land rest. They were relying on the *pesak* of the rabbis from the Old Yishuv in Jerusalem. But Rothschild and his men supervising the settlement had different ideas. They wanted the land to be worked in some way and wanted the settlers to rely on the permissive ruling granted by Rabbi Yitzchak Elchanan Spektor of Lithuania. A large portion of the book deals with the conflict that ensued and the difficulties that the settlers faced when they stood firm.

I have only given a very brief summary, but it is very inspiring to learn about the hard work and struggles of these early Jewish pioneers.

* * *

Mitchell First is a personal injury attorney and Jewish history scholar. He tries to write pioneering works of Jewish scholarship.

21. The "Language Conflict" of 1914 in Palestine

Theodor Herzl had not envisioned Hebrew as the language of the Jewish state. In 1896 he wrote in his *The Jewish State*: "who amongst us has a sufficient acquaintance with Hebrew to ask for a railway ticket in that language?" His plan was that everyone in Palestine would continue to speak the language of their home country. He pointed to Switzerland as a country that existed with a confederation of languages. Thereafter, the official documents of the Zionist Congresses (which began in 1897) were all written in German.

In his *Trial and Error*, p. 142 (1949), Chaim Weizmann explains the situation in the years before World War I: "Every foreign institution in the corrupt and feeble Turkish empire placed itself under the protection of a foreign country, and the European Powers vied with each other for influence and prestige within Turkish territory. The Jews in particular were used as cat-paws in this game of intrigue, and the little community which we were struggling to weld into a creative unit was torn apart by its 'benefactors' and 'protectors.' There was one system of Jewish schools supported by the *Alliance Israélite Universelle* of Paris; there the language of instruction was naturally French. The Germans used the *Hilfsverein der Deutschen Juden* with *its* system of schools as *their* instrument of intrigue in the Near East. There the language of instruction was German. England was very much behind in the general competition, having under its aegis only the Evelina de

Rothschild School in Jerusalem, where the language was English. At school Jewish children in Palestine therefore spoke French, English or German according to their foreign 'protectors.'"

The *Hilfsverein* was a German-Jewish (but not Zionistic) organization founded in 1901 to improve the social and political conditions of the Jews in Eastern Europe and the Orient. By the eve of WWI, it had about fifty schools under its auspices in Palestine. Initially their language of instruction was Hebrew. But during the years immediately preceding WWI, a wave of German patriotism swept through the schools. New teachers from Germany were brought in, some of them Christian. The use of Hebrew as the medium of instruction was discarded, except in the teaching of Hebrew subjects. German songs and literature were being taught. This led to tensions with the Hebrew-minded students.

In his *The Story of Hebrew*, pp. 196–97 (2017), Lewis Glinert writes that on the eve of WWI, "most Jews in the land of Israel, many Zionists included, were skeptical about the future of the new Hebrew, and the majority were still not sending their children to Hebrew-speaking schools. German remained the official language of the international Zionist movement as well as a language spoken by many Jews in many countries. Some Zionists were learning Turkish, feeling that they had to be part of the state in which they lived. Yiddish, French and Arabic also competed for linguistic attention."

The issue of the main language of the Yishuv in Palestine finally was resolved on the eve of WWI with the building of the Technion in Haifa. At the time, it was called by its German name, Technikum.

A considerable sum of money for the Technikum was given by Wolf Wissotzky, the Russian tea magnate. The building was completed in 1913. Arthur Zimmermann, who was the German Undersecretary for Foreign Affairs, had obtained from the Turkish government the permission for the land and building, and the Technikum had been placed under the protection of Germany. The *Hilfsverein* was the sponsor of the institution. But the Board of Governors of the Technikum did have some pro-Hebrew members such as Aḥad Ha-Am (Asher Ginsberg), who worked for Wissotzky.

The decisive meeting took place in Berlin in June 1914. The representatives of the *Hilfsverein* were completely against Hebrew as the language of instruction in the Technikum. They argued that German was the great language of science and technology, in contrast to the limited technical vocabulary in Hebrew. Second, the school was under the German flag. Third, Zimmermann had gone to all this trouble to obtain the concessions for the school on the tacit understanding that German would be the language of instruction. But Weizmann warned these German-Jewish leaders that if German was voted to be the language of instruction, nobody in Palestine would pay attention, since it would be entirely contrary to the spirit of the new Palestine. The *Hilfsverein* representatives ignored Weizmann's warnings, and the Board of Governors voted for German to be the official language.

As one scholar wrote: "If the German language was to be predominant in the one and only Jewish institute for advanced professional studies in the 'spiritual center,' then the prospects of Hebrew as the language of the Jews in Eretz Yisrael and as a unifying bond among the Jews of the world were dim indeed. The elementary and intermediate schools in the *Yishuv* would take the cue from this highest educational institution. . . ."[154]

Weizmann immediately telegraphed the vote to Shemarya Levin who was in Palestine. Within 24 hours, on the day the Technikum was to open, its teachers and the pupils went on strike. "No Hebrew, no Technikum" was their slogan.

In the "Technion" entry (15:890), the *Encyclopaedia Judaica* continues the story: "The decision [adopting German] aroused a storm of controversy, in which the Hebrew Teachers' Association took the lead. Meetings were held throughout the country; resolutions of protest were passed by practically all Jewish institutions and organizations; the Teachers' Association issued a ban against the acceptance of posts or the registration of students in the Technikum; pupils at the Hilfsverein's other schools struck in support of a demand to institute Hebrew as the sole language of instruction and many of the teachers resigned." A strike fund was established and new Hebrew speaking schools were organized to replace the schools on strike. The authorities of the *Hilfsverein* employed all sorts of stratagems to break the strike. But it was to no avail.

154. William Chomsky, *Hebrew: The Eternal Language* (1957), p. 242.

Eventually, the *Hilfsverein* withdrew its support not only from the Technikum, but from all the other schools which it had maintained in Palestine. Levin, who was in Palestine when the strike occurred, left for America to raise funds for the taking over by the Zionist Organization of this section of the Jewish educational system of Palestine. This was the beginning of the Zionist administration of the schools in Palestine, and of the fusion of the divergent linguistic influences into a single Hebrew system. When the cornerstone for the Hebrew University was laid on July 24, 1918, it was taken for granted that its language of instruction would be Hebrew.

As to the Technion building, the above *Encyclopaedia Judaica* entry continues: "The opening of the Technion was delayed, and before the controversy could be settled, World War I broke out. The unoccupied building served as a military hospital, first for the Turkish forces and later for the British. After the war, the Zionist Organization acquired the property from the Hilfsverein and the first classes on a university level were held in December 1924."

P.S. The Zimmermann mentioned above is famous for sending a secret telegram to Mexico in early 1917, asking them to side with Germany and promising them U.S. territory in return. It was deciphered by the British and shown to President Wilson and was one of the factors that led to the U.S. finally declaring war on Germany in April 1917.

* * *

Mitchell First is a personal injury attorney and Jewish history scholar. He knows that today a railway ticket in modern Hebrew is called a כרטיס רכבת.

22. Nehama Leibowitz: The Early Years

Yael Unterman authored a book: *Nehama Leibowitz: Teacher and Bible Scholar* (2009). I am going to provide a summary of Nehama's early life, based on this book.

As Unterman points out, Nehama Leibowitz preferred to be called "Nehama." Using only her first name evokes her humility and warmth. That is how Unterman refers to her and how I will as well.

Nehama hated publicity. She would say: "I'm not worth writing about – go learn Torah instead." But after her death, much has been written about her. There is a motto that people follow in these situations: *aḥarei mot kedoshim, emor* (= after saintly people pass away, speak). So even those who kept silent during her life (pursuant to her request) were willing to speak her praise after her death!

Nehama requested that there be no eulogy at her funeral and her request was honored. The author continues (p. 15): "Nevertheless, Nehama's biography belongs not to her alone, but also to the Jewish people whom she loved so much, and to history, and it is under this premise that the book was written." The author continues: "The only apology owed her is in writing this work in English, for she believed that the Hebrew language is the only proper medium for all Jewish life."

Nehama was born in Latvia in 1905. She was born two years after her brother Yeshayahu.

Her family was religious and broadly educated. The children spoke Hebrew with their father, and German or Yiddish with their mother. Her parents' social circles included many non-observant Jews. Her father created weekly *Tanakh* quizzes for his children. Her mother died early on.

Nehama did not go to the schools in Latvia. She and her brother were taught by hired teachers.

In 1919, due to the creation of the independent republic of Latvia, the family was forced to move to Berlin. Berlin of the 1920s included many Jewish giants. For example, on the street, Nehama may have passed R. Menahem Mendel Schneerson, and R. Yosef Dov Soloveitchik. One Habad Hasid insisted to her: "Everyone knows that you sat drinking coffee with the Rebbe and R. Soloveitchik in the cafés in Berlin!" Nehama replied: "It could be that we sat at the same table for lunch, but if we did, I didn't know it."

Another story (slightly contradictory to the above) is that Nehama was told of the brilliant young Jewish scholar, Rabbi Yosef Dov Soloveitchik who sat in the library "behind the tallest stack of books." With a description like that, she located him easily, but never introduced herself. (But in another version of this story, it was he who was told to look for her, but he could not locate her because **she** was hidden behind **her** tower of books!)

Reportedly, her mother never allowed her into the kitchen! She was treated as the intellectual equal of her brother.

She spent the years 1925–30 in the Universities of Berlin, Heidelberg, and Marburg, studying English and German philology and literature, and Bible studies.

At the same time, she advanced her Jewish studies at the *Hochschule für die Wissenschaft des Judentums*. This was the only institution where she did any formal learning of Jewish studies. The college's doors were open to all, including women and non-Jews, and it was the closest thing to a yeshiva that a woman could attend at the time. Here, as nowhere else at the time, Nehama could interact on an equal footing with Jewish scholars, rabbis, and rabbinical students. One of her classmates was Leo Strauss. Strauss taught Nehama philosophy, reading Plato with her in the original Greek, while she taught him Hebrew, studying Saadia Gaon's *Emunot Ve-Deot* and other Hebrew works with him.

This is the era when Nehama began to teach high school students. She used the *Ivrit be-Ivrit* method, so that Hebrew might be experienced as a living language. This technique was first used by Eliezer Ben-Yehuda in 1883, but it was unheard of in German schools at that time.

She married her father's brother Yedidyah Lipman Leibowitz in Berlin in 1930. (She did not have to change her name!) He was 31 years older than her! He died in 1970. Decades later she said to a friend about marrying her much older uncle: "This was the wisest decision I ever made, and I have been extremely happy my entire life!" The only thing she regretted was never having children. (Of course, her thousands of students were her "children"!)

The couple left Germany at the end of 1930. After they arrived in Israel, her first position was teaching at the Mizrachi Teachers Seminary of Jerusalem. She did this for over 20 years. From 1957, she taught Bible at Tel Aviv University. After she came to Israel in 1930, she only left one time, when she went to meet her parents in Europe and accompany them to settle in Israel.

In Israel, she was known for many years for her weekly *gilyonot* (questions about the *parshah*) which she mailed out to thousands over the years.

* * *

Regarding her brother Yeshayahu: When I accessed Wikipedia, it described him as follows: He was "an Israeli Orthodox Jewish public intellectual and polymath. He was professor of biochemistry, organic chemistry, and neurophysiology at the Hebrew University…, as well as a prolific writer on Jewish thought and western philosophy. He was known for his outspoken views on ethics, religion, and politics."

In the original *Encyclopaedia Judaica* (1972), he has his own entry with a photo, while Nehama's entry is a very small one subsumed within his. (Unterman suggests that in general the original *Encyclopaedia Judaica* was guilty of neglecting women.) The updated *Encyclopaedia Judaica* (2006) grants Nehama her own entry.

P.S. There is a story of two brothers, one a philosophy professor and the other a history professor. They used to argue which was more important, history or philosophy. Eventually, it was the *Encyclopaedia Judaica* (1972 edition) that decided the issue. They both had entries, but only the history professor had his entry with a photo! See the entries for Irving and Jacob Agus![155]

* * *

Mitchell First is a personal injury attorney and Jewish history scholar. Like Nehama, he avoids the kitchen. He is hoping to get into a future edition of the *Encyclopaedia Judaica* (with or without a photo).

23. The Heroism of Kibbutz *Yad Mordechi*

There is a kibbutz just north of the Gaza strip called *Yad Mordechai*. It fought valiantly during the War of Independence and its tenacious fighting for six days was able to significantly delay the Egyptian invasion. The kibbutz was on the main road between Cairo and Tel Aviv. If not for that delay, the Egyptian army could have quickly reached Tel Aviv and the other important cities in the north.

In 1965, Margaret Larkin wrote a book about the kibbutz: *The Six Days of Yad-Mordechai*. I am going to summarize it here.

Two groups of pioneers from Poland (members of *Hashomer*

155. I thank Rabbi Richard Schiffmiller for sharing this story with me.

Hatzair) came together to found this kibbutz in 1936. It was originally in an area near Netanya. They called it *Mitzpeh Ha-Yam*, because by looking out to the sea, they could watch for the coming of the comrades they had left behind.

After several years the membership grew. They were 140 adults and 43 children, and the few acres of land they had were not enough to support them. With the help of the Jewish National Fund, they found a new site five miles north of the Arab town of Gaza. Here there would be 400 acres of land and both grain and oranges could be grown. As Larkin writes (p. 23), "Rarely did the Jews move onto fertile land in Palestine. Nearly always they had to reclaim the soil from years or centuries of neglect. In some places they drained the malarial swamps; here, sand would be the enemy." They moved to this new site in December 1943.

The new name for the kibbutz would be *Yad Mordechai*. It was named for Mordechai Anielewicz, the leader of the Warsaw ghetto uprising. He fell in a battle in May 1943. The meaning of the name: "A Memorial to Mordechai."[156]

A few years later came the November 1947 partition plan. As Larkin writes (p. 51): "The foundation of a Jewish State had been their dream and hope since their youth. For this they had severed their ties with their families and with their native land. For this they had remade themselves, the sons and daughters of shopkeepers, into farmers. With their own sweat and energy they had extracted wealth from ruined soil; with high idealism they had created a unique way of life. And now that their efforts were about to crowned by the establishment of their own state, it seemed that they were not to be a part of it. The new borders, as defined by a Commission of the United Nations, put *Yad Mordechai* in the Arab state."

When independence was declared in May, they rejoiced, but with sorrow. Many of the members thought of Moshe: he saw the Promised Land from afar, but after all his years in the desert, he could not enter it.

The "good news" was that since the Arab leaders announced that

156. As to the meaning of *yad* as "memorial," see essay #13 in the Hebrew Roots section.

they would not respect the U.N. decision anyway, the exact partition plan line did not matter much. The Arabs were going to fight all the Jewish settlements. Everyone understood that the settlements must provide centers of resistance, and must hold out until final borders or armistice lines were established.

Interestingly, there was a widespread belief at the time that the kibbutz would not have to face the Egyptian army. Egypt's opposition to the invasion plans of the other Arab countries was known. It was assumed that the kibbutz would only have to hold out against Arab bands of irregulars. In a meeting of the Arab League on April 30, the Egyptians had refused to commit themselves to the use of their army. Their Minister of Defense had stated: "We shall allow our men and officers to volunteer for service in Palestine and we shall give them weapons but no more." (The reality was that their army was not prepared for war.)

But a few days later his government changed its mind. Larkin writes (p. 83) that "[t]he fears of the politicians that a triumphant Trans-Jordan, engorged with the lands of Palestine, would emerge as the leading power in the Middle East had proved stronger than caution." Egypt was fighting in Palestine mainly to prevent King Abdullah from taking more than his share.

Thereafter, one of the members of the kibbutz was able to get into Gaza while pretending he was a Red Cross driver. He spoke to an Egyptian major. The major told him that the next day there would be an attack on *Yad Mordechai.*

What to do next? Who to evacuate? The kibbutz had not been thinking this way, as they had been assuming that there would be no invasion of the Egyptian army. "Nothing lowers the spirit of a fighter so much as when he sees first steps in evacuation," a Palmaḥ commander once wrote. The kibbutz hastily decided to evacuate the children, the nursing mothers, and the few other women who were more sensitive than most. Some made a point of giving their children their photograph albums (in case the worst happened). The children were evacuated to a nearby settlement ten miles to the east.

On May 19, the Egyptian planes came. Larkin writes (p. 101) that "within fifteen minutes they had destroyed much of what had taken the settlers years to build."

When the battle began, the defenders numbered only 113 men and boys, only slightly over half had guns. They were fighting an Egyptian army of about 2000. What happens during the fighting? The phone lines are cut, the kibbutz members cannot communicate with one another. They have to risk their lives and run amidst gunfire to send messages to one another, as they are scattered in different (barely) fortified places in the kibbutz. They have very little ammunition. (Sometimes they obtain new ammunition by taking it from dead Egyptian soldiers.) They did not have enough mines. Instead they put up signs to scare the Egyptian invaders: "Warning-Mines."

They hoped that the Haganah, recognizing the strategic importance of the kibbutz, would send reinforcements and strike or bomb the Egyptian army from the outside. But the Haganah was too overwhelmed. There were too many other isolated points that needed help.

The end result was that after a few days, after suffering 23 dead and 40 wounded, the defenders had to retreat and abandon the kibbutz. During the following days, they tried to convince the Haganah that with more men they could recapture the kibbutz. But the Haganah had other priorities at the time.

A few months later, on November 5, Israel was finally able to recapture the kibbutz.

In that initial time in May, the Egyptian army had expected to take the kibbutz within a few hours. Instead, they lost their momentum and had to change their battle plans. The Haganah benefited greatly because of the delay and were able to fortify other areas.

Today, there is a memorial statue to Anielewicz next to the destroyed water tower at the kibbutz. He is depicted standing heroically and holding a grenade. There is also a Holocaust museum at the kibbutz: "From Holocaust to Revival Museum." The kibbutz is known for producing honey and olive oil, and supplies a major portion of the honey consumed in Israel.

I have left out so many details and I highly recommend that you read this book!

* * *

Mitchell First is a personal injury attorney and Jewish history scholar. (He has no jokes to make about Israel's War of Independence.)

24. The Story of the Initial Dead Sea Scroll Finds

I thought it would be interesting to tell the story of how the first Dead Sea scrolls came to light. I am basing this on a summary in a book by Hershel Shanks, *The Mystery and Meaning of the Dead Sea Scrolls* (1998). (There are surely accounts by others with slightly different details.)

Shanks writes: "Probably in late 1946 or early 1947, a shepherd boy of the Ta'amireh tribe [of Bedouins]... was searching for a lost sheep. He tossed a stone into a cave, hoping to scare the sheep out. But instead of the bleating of a sheep, he heard the sound of cracking pottery. When he and a friend explored the cave, they discovered two large jars. Inside, wrapped in linen, they found some ancient scrolls." This occurred in a cave near the northwestern shore of the Dead Sea. The closest settlement to the cave was the ancient settlement of Qumran.

In April 1947, the two finders brought the scrolls to Bethlehem, the principal market town of the Ta'amireh tribe. There they contacted two antiquities dealers: Faidi Salahi and someone known as Kando. It is possible that Kando went back with one or both of the finders to locate more scrolls. In any event, the total number of intact scrolls numbered seven, either because the two finders originally recovered that many or because Kando's excavation added to the original number.

The seven scrolls were then divided into lots: three in one lot and four in the other. The first lot was sold to Salahi and the second to Kando. First, I will discuss what happened to Salahi's scrolls.

Salahi contacted an Armenian friend named Levon Ohan. Ohan contacted Eleazar Sukenik, who was a professor of archaeology at Hebrew University. Sukenik was the father of Yigael Sukenik, later to be known as Yigael Yadin. Yadin later became famous as an archaeologist, but at the time, he was chief of operations for the Haganah.

The time was the final days of the British Mandate. Shanks writes:

> Violence was rife. The British security forces had divided Jerusalem into military zones separating Jewish and Arab sections of the city; barbed wire marked the boundaries. To move from

> zone to zone required a military pass. Neither Sukenik nor his friend Ohan had a pass, so they agreed to meet at the gateway to Military Zone B. On the other side of the barricade from Sukenik, Ohan removed a scrap of parchment from his brief-case and showed it to Sukenik through the barbed wire. Sukenik noticed that the form of the Hebrew letters resembled that of letters… [from] some two thousand years ago…. [Sukenik] asked [Ohan] to show him more samples. Sukenik obtained a pass to enter Zone B, and after looking at more fragments, he resolved to go to Bethlehem to negotiate a purchase price.

Shanks continues: "It was a dangerous journey at the time and his wife objected to his going…. Tension was especially high because… the United Nations was about to vote on the partition of Palestine into a Jewish state and an Arab state. If the vote was affirmative… the Arabs might declare war to prevent the formation of the Jewish state, and full-fledged fighting could breakout, replacing the sporadic violence that preceded the vote." Sukenik then consulted his son.

Yadin describes his reaction: "What was I to tell him? As a student of archaeology myself, I felt that an opportunity of acquiring such priceless documents could not be missed. On the other hand, as Chief of Operations of Haganah, I knew perfectly well the dangers my father would be taking in traveling to Arab Bethlehem…. I told him not to go."

Sukenik did not listen to his wife or his son, and decided to go. On Nov. 29, 1947, he and Ohan boarded an Arab bus for Bethlehem. Sukenik was the only Jew on the bus. In Bethlehem, they met Salahi who was willing to loan him two of the three scrolls so he could take them back to Jerusalem and examine then more carefully. Sukenik boarded the bus for the short ride back to the city. He was carrying in his hands the two scrolls that would later become known as the Scroll of Thanksgiving Psalms and the War Scroll. (The third scroll was a partial copy of the book of Isaiah, later known as "Isaiah B," to distinguish it from another Dead Sea Isaiah scroll, "Isaiah A," which is a complete text of Isaiah.)

Within hours of Sukenik's return from Bethlehem, the United Nations passed the partition resolution. Sukenik went outside to share the joy of the vote with the Jews of Jerusalem and he found two friends to share his own discovery with. The next day the Arabs attacked.

A few days later Sukenik was shown the third scroll. He purchased all three scrolls and paid only several hundred dollars for all three.

Yadin later wrote: "I cannot avoid the feeling that there is something symbolic in the discovery of the scrolls and their acquisition at the moment of the creation of the State of Israel. It is as if these manuscripts had been waiting in caves for two thousand years, ever since the destruction of Israel's independence until the people of Israel had returned to their home and regained their freedom."

What happened to the four scrolls in the hands of the other antiquities dealer, Kando? In Jan. 1948, Sukenik received a call about these four scrolls. Kando had sold them to the Syrian Orthodox archbishop of Jerusalem, Mar Athanasius Yeshue Samuel. A friend of Samuel's brought them to Sukenik, so he was able to see them. But Samuel decided that the time was not yet ripe for them to be sold and that he would prefer to wait until the political situation settled and he could get a fair price in the international market.

These four scrolls turned out to be: (1) a complete copy of the book of Isaiah (Isaiah A); (2) a sectarian text that came to be known as the "Manual of Discipline," (3) a commentary on the book of Habakkuk, and (4) a text that came to be known as "Genesis Apocryphon."

Samuel and those he knew had the scrolls photographed and the photos were sent to William Albright, a biblical archaeologist at Johns Hopkins University in Baltimore. Albright's reply arrived on May 15, 1948: "My heartiest congratulations on the greatest manuscript discovery of modern times! There is no doubt in my mind that the script is more archaic than that of the Nash papyrus.... I should prefer a date around 100 BC!... What an absolutely incredible find!"

In January 1949 Samuel arrived in the U.S. with the scrolls. He needed money for his church and was looking for a buyer. To generate interest in the scrolls, he arranged to exhibit them publicly. In October 1949, they were exhibited at the Library of Congress. Thereafter, they were exhibited at other museums and art galleries in Baltimore, Chicago, Worcester, and Durham. Shanks writes: "Interest was high, but strangely, no institution was ready to make an offer to buy the scrolls."

Years passed. In the meantime, Samuel settled permanently in New Jersey. On June 1, 1954, he placed a classified ad offering the scrolls for sale in the *Wall Street Journal*. The ad read: "The Four Dead Sea Scrolls. Biblical manuscripts dating back to at least 200 B.C.E. are for sale. This would be an ideal gift to an educational or religious institution by an individual or group. Box F 206, The Wall Street Journal."

By chance, Yigael Yadin was in the U.S. on a lecture tour at the time, and someone called his attention to the ad. He decided to buy the scrolls for Israel and arranged for an intermediary to reply to the ad and negotiate for their purchase. Yadin kept himself and Israel out of the deal for fear that Samuel would not consent. The nominal buyer was a New York businessman named Sydney Estridge and the agreed upon purchase price was $250,000. But before turning over the money, a scholar needed to examine the scrolls. Yadin did not want to be the one doing the examination as this would make Samuel suspicious.

Yadin called a biblical scholar he knew named Harry Orlinsky at Johns Hopkins University. Orlinsky was literally out the door about to go on vacation. He writes: "My wife was already seated in the car and I was locking the [house] door when the telephone rang." Yadin asked Orlinsky, without telling him why, to postpone his vacation and immediately come to New York on a matter of importance to Israel. Orlinksy wrote: "I asked for a minute or two to talk it over with my wife. Together we decided that if Israel needed me, we had no choice."

Orlinsky arrived in New York. He was told to take on the name "Mr. Green" and state that he was an expert for his client. He went with Mr. Estridge to the vault of a bank at the Waldorf-Astoria Hotel. There a representative of Mar Samuel would let him examine the scrolls. After examining the scrolls, he went to a payphone and uttered the code word: *le-ḥayim*! His mission had been successful!

The four scrolls were flown to Israel, one at a time. (This was 1954. It was too risky to fly them all at once!)

Sukenik had died the previous year, so he did not see this part of the story. In 1948, after failing to obtain the four scrolls, he had written in his diary: "Thus the Jewish people have lost a precious heritage."

On Feb. 13, 1955, Prime Minister Sharett called a press conference to announce that all seven scrolls were now in Israel. Presumably Mar

Samuel now learned for the first time that he had sold the scrolls to the government of Israel![157]

Shanks speculates that the reason people and institutions were not interested in the scrolls, despite the extensive publicity, was that they feared that Jordan would later sue them for possession of the scrolls. He also observes that Israel did Samuel a favor by hiding its identity as the purchaser. Samuel benefited from this subterfuge.

Shanks points out a final irony: Samuel was selling the scrolls on behalf of his church. But the sale papers were badly drawn and the IRS contended that the proceeds were personal income to Samuel. He resisted the claim, but ended up losing. The result was that much of the proceeds of the sale were paid in taxes to the US government.

* * *

Mitchell First is a personal injury attorney and Jewish history scholar. His scholarly work is not that dangerous or exciting. Nor does it have significant tax implications.

25. The Original Logo of the Israel Postal Company and Genesis 49:21

I once wrote a column about Jacob's blessing to Naftali. At Genesis 49:21, we read: *Naftali* ***ayalah*** *sheluḥah, ha-noten imrei shefer*= Naftali is a hind that is sent out, and delivers beautiful sayings. A "hind" is a female deer. *Ayal* would be the word for a male deer.[158]

After I wrote the column, I received emails from two friends[159]

---

157. Aside from the four scrolls that he sold, Samuel also owned three smaller fragments. Those he kept. Periodically, these were loaned out to exhibitions. Samuel died in 1995. I moved to Teaneck, New Jersey in 1988. I only learned recently that he was the head of a church in Teaneck that was not far from me. After he passed away, his congregation remained in Teaneck for many years, but it is no longer there. I am not sure where those original fragments are today. But they have already been photographed by scholars.

158. *Noten* suggests that the subject of the second part of the sentence is Naftali. But the meaning could be: "Naftali, as a female deer, delivers...."

159. Abby Leichman and Myron Chaitovsky.

advising me that the original logo of the Israel Postal Company, which featured a deer, was based on this verse. One of these two friends also sent me an article by Sharona Margolin Halickman from December 2014 which explained that the postal logo was based on this verse.

The original Israel Postal Company logo first appeared in 1950 and continued in use for decades. It was designed by the Shamir brothers who had already won the design contest for Israel's *menorah* emblem.

But another friend[160] reminded me that it is only male deer that have antlers. The logo of the Israel Postal Company was a deer with long antlers! I looked online and learned that it is very rare for female deer to have antlers. (This occurs only if they have excess testosterone!)

I emailed Sharona and she was kind enough to send me some material put out by the Israel Postal Company. Indeed, the official explanation stated there does state that the logo was based on our verse. (Somewhere else on that same site one can find a statement that the logo symbolizes a *tzvi*, an entirely different animal. But that statement was just made as a side statement, and not as an official explanation.)

My wife found me a site, Shamir-brothers.com, which enables one to contact the deceased Shamir brothers and ask questions. Well, not exactly. Both Shamir brothers died in the 1990's. But Yoram Shamir, a son of one of them, runs the site. He responded: "I don't think that the Shamir brothers were inspired by the Bible in designing the emblem of the Israeli Post."

Several solutions present themselves:

One choice is to accept the approach of Yoram Shamir and move on with my life. But children do not really know the intentions of their parents on all matters. In English, we have a saying "as swift as a deer." But is a deer the only animal that symbolizes swiftness? I don't think so. Why precisely was a deer chosen? The end of our verse in Genesis was: "delivers beautiful sayings." Surely this ending, together with the swiftness image, is what motivated the Shamir brothers to

---

160. Mollie Fisch.

use the deer design! (OK, bills are not beautiful, but hopefully most mail is not bills.)

We have to allow for the possibility that the designers were unaware that it is only male deer that have antlers. After all, they did not have the internet and Wikipedia as we do today, which makes us all experts on any topic.

But I think that the most likely solution is that they were aware that it is rare for female deer to have antlers, but took some artistic license by depicting a male deer instead. After all, without antlers, how will anyone know that the logo represented a deer?[161]

In recent years, the logo has been modified, and unless you knew, you cannot tell that a deer, or any animal, was even intended originally.

As I mentioned earlier, the Shamir brothers are the same individuals who won the design contest for the State of Israel's *menorah* emblem. There is a fascinating article online by Yoram Shamir and Daniella Gardosh-Santo on this topic.[162]

Here is a summary of the article: In 1948, shortly after Israel's establishment, the government invited the citizens of Israel to propose a design for the national flag and emblem. The guidelines specified the colors "sky-blue and white" "and any other color as per the artist's taste." Also, the emblem had to feature a seven-lamp candelabrum and seven stars. Hundreds of proposals were submitted. The Shamir brothers' proposal won the contest. The *menorah* and the stars appeared as required. But the Shamir brothers added the olive branches and the shield image. After the design was approved, they were asked to make some changes. They were asked by the committee in charge to add the name "Israel" and to replace their modern *menorah* with the one carved into the Arch of Titus. The committee also decided to drop the stars. The final proposal was submitted and approved in 1949. The

---

161. A friend who understandably wishes to remain anonymous suggested to me another choice: it was too immodest to have a female deer as a logo!

162. It is dated Dec. 11, 2017 and titled "The Initial Proposals That Fell Short: How The Israeli National Emblem Was Chosen." Gardosh-Santo is the daughter of the famous Israeli cartoonist "Dosh."

lengthy delay in the process was criticized, but Ben-Gurion replied: "Choosing a flag and emblem for the state is not done every day."

* * *

Here is some more information on the Shamir brothers which I found at Shamir-brothers.com:

Gabriel (1909–1992) and Maxim (1910–1990) were born in Latvia. Their original last name was "Scheftelowitsch." They came to Tel Aviv in 1934/5 and chose a location on Rothschild Boulevard. This location served as their graphics studio and as residence of the two brothers' families.

They were among the founders of the "Graphic Designers Association of Israel." They focused mainly on designing posters, newspaper ads and labels for consumer products in modern language and styles. They often included in their works images of Israeli landscapes, pioneering stereotypes and images of soldiers. Aside from the 1949 *menorah* competition win, they also won a competition a few years later to design several of the banknotes issued by the Bank of Israel. The brothers were also commissioned to distribute institutional messages expressing the needs of the time such as fundraising for the National Bond, war on the black market, the law of compulsory education, and the like.

In 1974 the brothers began to work separately. Maxim focused on designing stamps mainly for African, Central American, and Asian countries while Gabriel worked in graphic design as a volunteer for institutions such as the University of Tel Aviv, hospitals, and other non-profit organizations.

* * *

Mitchell First is a personal injury attorney and Jewish history scholar. He tries to complete his lawsuits swiftly and produce his scholarly articles expeditiously as well.

Liturgy

1. What is the Meaning of שׂכוי in the Morning Blessing?

The phrase מי נתן לשכוי בינה (=who gave the *sekhvi* understanding?) is found at Job 38:36. The entire verse has two parallel parts: who put wisdom in טחות and who gave understanding to the שׂכוי? (*Le-havḥin bein*... is not in the verse.)

With regard to the word טחות (=*tuḥot*), it also appears at Psalms 51:8. These are the only two times the word appears in *Tanakh*. It is evident from there that its meaning is a "covered/hidden part of the body" (from the root טוח = covered). It is usually interpreted as "kidneys." ArtScroll's *Tehillim* commentary there remarks: "The kidneys are considered to be the seat of human intellect, as in Job 38:36, and Psalms 7:10, 16:7."[1]

Since the word *sekhvi* at Job 38:36 is parallel to the word *tuḥot*, *sekhvi* almost certainly refers to a body part. The root of *sekhvi* is שׂכה which means "to see."[2] Most of the traditional commentaries interpret it as "heart." Another reasonable interpretation is "mind." This is the only time that the word *sekhvi* appears in *Tanakh*, which makes its proper interpretation difficult. But even though its precise

1. Slightly different is the Soncino commentary to Psalms 7:10: "In the Bible, *heart* is the seat of the intellect and *reins* (kidneys) of the emotions."

2. We see this root elsewhere in *Tanakh* in the word משׂכית which appears six times and likely means "image."

In Rabbinic Hebrew, the biblical שׂ often evolved into a ס (see, e.g., the Rabbinic word ארוסין.) In the song *Barukh Kel Elyon*, we refer to God as כל סוכה. The meaning is "the One Who sees all."

meaning is hard to discern, there is no reason from the context to suggest that it is an animal.

Several centuries later, at *Berakhot* 60b, there is a statement that when one hears the sound of the *tarnegola* (=rooster), one should recite the blessing "***asher natan la-sekhvi vinah*** *le-havḥin bein yom u-vein laylah*." The statement utilizes the text of our verse in Job for the beginning of the blessing, but we saw above that *sekhvi* did not mean any kind of animal there! How can we understand this passage in the Talmud?

The Talmud, at *Rosh Hashanah* 26a, gives us two clues: (1) we are told that in a city in Syria, *sekhvi* meant *tarnegol*, [3] and (2) a statement is reported in the name of either Rav or R. Yehoshua b. Levi that the *sekhvi* of Job 38:36 is a *tarnegol*.

So a possible scenario is that Rav or R. Yehoshua b. Levi (or Sages prior to them) picked up the *sekhvi=tarnegol* interpretation from another region and language, such as Aramaic.

We have to remind ourselves that our Tannaim and Amoraim did not have our standard *Tanakh* commentaries to assist them. They were faced with a vague one-time word in *sekhvi* at Job 38:36. They may have learned a possible meaning from another region and this became the widespread way to understand the word's meaning. OK, the meaning was not a good fit for the verse in context. But it was not egregiously inconsistent with the context and at least now they had a meaning for this vague word. Once *sekhvi* in this verse was understood as *tarnegol*, it became reasonable to utilize this verse when it was decided to enact a blessing upon man's hearing the sound of the *tarnegol*.

Or in an alternative scenario, once it was decided to enact such a blessing, it was decided to use this verse, even though it was widely understood that the *sekhvi* reference in the verse was not to a *tarnegol*.

---

3. At *Lev. Rabbah* 25:5, we are told that this was the meaning of the word in Arabia. At Jerusalem Talmud, *Berkahot*, chap. 9, we are told that this was the meaning of the word in Rome. (It is possible that *sekhvi* did not mean *tarnegol* in all these regions, and that what we have here are merely different variants of one tradition.) The exact city name recorded at *Rosh Hashanah* 26a is *Kan-Nishraya*. According to M. Jastrow, p. 1387, this is Kennesrin, a city in northern Syria.

The authors of blessings enjoyed using verses from *Tanakh* where they could. Here perhaps they added *le-havḥin bein yom u-vein laylah* so that *sekhvi* in the meaning of the blessing would be seen to have a new meaning, the *tarnegol* meaning.

The reason I am elaborating on this is to avoid the "heart" meaning or "double meaning" interpretation of our morning blessing. All *siddur* translations and commentaries are faced with a dilemma here. They know (from *Berakhot* 60b) that the blessing is a response to the sound of a *tarnegol*, but at the same time they also most likely believe that the verse is about a body part like the heart. So how should they translate *sekhvi* in the blessing? *The Complete ArtScroll Siddur*, in its text of the blessing, translates *sekhvi* as "heart." But then the commentary below writes: "In the context of this blessing, both meanings are implied." Indeed, many of the commentaries on this blessing write that both meanings are implied.

But do you think the Sages would have enacted for us, in this early morning context,[4] a blessing with a double meaning? Wordplays with double meanings are features that authors of *piyyutim* use, not enactors of preliminary morning blessings.

I am here reminded of an article I read about paradoxes. One "paradox" mentioned was that there are people in the world who cannot do anything in the morning until they drink their coffee. The problem is, if this were literally true, these people would not be able to function ever, as they are unable to make their coffee in the morning! In my view, our blessing authors were sensitive enough not to make us think too much with this early morning blessing! (By the way, the suggestion for those dysfunctional coffee drinkers is for them to do most of the steps of making the coffee the night before, and only leave a minimal amount of coffee preparation for the morning!)

* * *

4. At the time these blessings were enacted, they were recited at the time of the activity mentioned (and most likely without *shem* and *malkhut*). *Sekhvi* was not the first in a long list of blessings in a row the way we recite the blessings today. In fact, in the *Siddur of R. Saadia* (p. 93), it is not even mentioned in the same context as the "opening your eyes and dressing" blessings. It is in an entirely different section that records blessings regarding man's senses.

1. The *Daat Mikra* commentary to Job. 38:36 has a long discussion of *sekhvi* and *tuḥot*. Among their many points, they mention that some interpret both of these words with meanings related to "cloud."[5] There is support for such interpretations in the context of the surrounding verses. The Soncino commentary also prefers this approach.

2. I mentioned above that there was an interpretation reported in the name of either Rav or R. Yehoshua b. Levi that the *sekhvi* of Job. 38:36 was a *tarnegol*. Perhaps this interpretation did not arise from a foreign region and language as I suggested earlier. Rather, one of our Sages saw the root שׂכה in the word שׂכוי and knew that the root meant "see," and then decided that the word was an allusion to the rooster who sees the dawn. But this is still farfetched, as there is little reason to have read an allusion to an animal into this verse.

The only possible justification for an animal-type interpretation of *sekhvi* in Job. 38:36 would be if *tuḥot* there could also be interpreted as an animal. *Daat Mikra* on our verse, at note 44, mentions such an interpretation of an ambiguous passage in *Leviticus Rabbah*. But the interpretation is unlikely.[6]

3. I never realized until I wrote this article that the simple Hebrew word בין (= between) is likely connected to the word בינה. Probably, the original meaning of בינה was "understanding the difference between things."[7]

* * *

5. See, e.g., Brown-Driver-Briggs, which mentions this as a possibility on both words.

Regarding *sekhvi,* Koehler-Baumgartner does something very surprising. This is a work designed to give readers the meaning of the word in the Bible. Yet here their entry translates the word as: "cock, rooster." I.e., they took the later meaning and just pretended that was the biblical meaning! This will mislead an entire generation! All they had to say was "biblical meaning uncertain."

6. *Daat Mikra* notes that the 16th-century commentator *Matanot Kehunah* interprets the word בטויא, given as an interpretation of *be-tuḥot* at *Lev. Rabbah* 25:5, as a kind of bird. But it is hard to imagine that any of our Sages would have given such an interpretation to the *tuḥot* of Job 38:36, since it is clearly not an animal at Ps. 51:8. M. Jastrow, p. 156, does not accept the interpretation of *Matanot Kehunah* and interprets בטויא, as "column-like receptacles (of water)."

7. See S. Mandelkern, p. 187, M. Jastrow, pp. 162–63, and *TDOT*, vol. 2, p. 99.

Mitchell First is a personal injury attorney and Jewish history scholar. When he recites his morning blessings, he tries to block out the biblical meaning of *sekhvi* and have only the *tarnegol* meaning in mind.

2. The Morning Blessing הנותן ליעף כח

At the beginning of our daily prayers there is a section with fourteen blessings, beginning with the *sekhvi* blessing. Where do these blessings come from?

Ten appear at *Berakhot* 60b. The three identity blessings, which we insert as numbers 2, 3, and 4, appear at *Menaḥot* 43b (and elsewhere). But that last blessing, *ha-noten la-yaef koaḥ*, is not in the Talmud. Where did it come from? (Admittedly, the phrasing derives from Isaiah 40:29, which describes God as: נתן ליעף כח.)

One work on the *siddur* speculated that the blessing was authored by the post-talmudic Savoraim and that while the simple meaning of the blessing refers to the feeling of refreshment upon awakening, its deeper meaning is the acknowledgement that God gave the Jewish nation the strength to endure the centuries of exile. (The Savoraim preceded the Geonim, and a rough estimate for the beginning of the Geonic period is the latter half of the 6th century.[8])

The idea that the post-talmudic Savoraim instituted the *ha-noten la-yaef koaḥ* blessing is an interesting one. But is there any basis for it? A scholar named Moshe Chalamish researched the above blessing extensively and would not agree. His article is at pp. 446–463 of his *Ha-Kabbalah be-Tefillah be-Halakha u-be-Minhag* (2000). I will summarize his findings.

The earliest source we have for this blessing is not any Savoraic or Geonic source.[9] It is a poem by Abraham Ibn Ezra (d. 1167). The

8. See Robert Brody, *The Geonim of Babylonia and the Shaping of Medieval Jewish Culture* (1998), pp. 8–9.

9. But there is found in a work from the time of the Babylonian Geonim a prayer designed to weaken the strength of *sheidim*. This prayer includes a description of God as: "*zokef kefufim, ha-meraḥem segufim, ha-noten koaḥ la-ya'efim, ha-pokeaḥ ivrim*." A possible implication is that our blessing was recited as a morning blessing in the era of this work. See Chalamish, p. 446.

poem includes a brief allusion to each of the morning blessings. It is evident from the poem that *ha-noten la-yaef koaḥ* was included in the morning blessings of Ibn Ezra.[10] A bit later, *ha-noten la-yaef koaḥ* is found among the morning blessings in a manuscript known as Corpus Christie College #133. The estimated date for this manuscript is the last quarter of the 12th century.[11]

Our blessing is not in the *Siddur* of R. Saadia (d. 942). Nor is it in the *Seder* of R. Amram. It is also absent from *Rokeaḥ* (c. 1160–1238) and early Sephardic sources such as Rambam (*Tefillah*, chap. 7). It is also absent from the earliest manuscript of *Maḥzor Vitry* (early 12th century).

The *Tur*, writing in the first quarter of the 14th century, refers to the blessing as one found *be-siddurei Ashkenaz*[12] and gives a beautiful explanation for it. See his *OH* 46 and the midrash he cites there. When the *Tur* uses the term "Ashkenaz," perhaps he means both Germany and France. By the time the *Tur* is writing, the blessing is found in manuscripts of *Maḥzor Vitry* (in France).

There is a widespread (but not universal) view that blessings not found in the Talmud should not be said at all, or at least can only be recited without *shem* and *malkhut* (i.e., what is permitted is: *barukh ha-noten la-yaef koaḥ*). Therefore, R. Yosef Caro writes in his *Beit Yosef*: "Since [this blessing] is not found in the Talmud, I do not know how anyone had permission to enact it." In his *Shulḥan Arukh*, he writes: *yesh nohagin le-varekh ha-noten la-yaef koaḥ, ve-ein divreihem nir'im* (=some have the custom to recite the blessing..., but their opinion does not make sense).[13]

---

10. The poem is found in Yisrael Levin, *Shirei Ha-Kodesh shel Avraham Ibn Ezra* (1975–80), vol. 1, pp. 459–462.

11. See next article.

12. Ibn Ezra spent much of the latter part of his life living among Ashkenazic Jewry, so the reference to the blessing in the poem of Ibn Ezra is not inconsistent with the blessing having originated in an Ashkenazic region.

13. It is interesting that R. Caro is more lenient regarding a different blessing not found in the Talmud that he mentions at *EH* 63. I am referring here to *birkat betulim*. See his *Beit Yosef* and *Shulḥan Arukh*. For more on this interesting blessing, see Israel Ta-Shema, *Ha-Tefillah Ha-Ashkenazit Ha-Kedumah* (2003), pp. 181–87.

So how did *ha-noten la-yaef koaḥ* become an almost universally accepted blessing today, even in non-Ashkenazic communities? With regard to Ashkenazic communities, the Rema had glossed in *OH* 46: "The widespread custom in Ashkenaz is to recite it."[14]

Chalamish documents that R. Isaac Luria (=the ARI) recited the blessing. This helped the blessing spread among Sephardic Jewry, and among the Kabbalists, despite the earlier objection of R. Yosef Caro.[15] (There is also a tradition that R. Yosef Caro withdrew his objection, once he heard that the ARI supported the blessing!)

It is interesting that some authorities, such as R. Joel Sirkes (17th cent.), opine that our blessing must have been in the text of the Talmud of those who initially authorized the blessing.[16]

P.S. Chalamish admits that he did not check the material that was discovered in the Cairo Genizah. (It was not as accessible then as it is now). I encourage anyone interested in the earliest source for our blessing to continue this research at genizah.org. If a fragment with our morning blessing is identified, it can be dated and its place of origin estimated on paleographic grounds. (Most of the material from the Genizah dates to the 10th to 13th centuries.)

* * *

Immediately following Chalamish's article about the morning blessing *ha-noten la-yaef koaḥ*, he included another article about another such blessing: *magbiah shefalim* (=who raises the lowly ones).[17] Never heard of this blessing? Neither did I until this article. Although this blessing is not found in the Talmud, it is already mentioned in Geonic sources from the 9th century such as R. Natronai, R. Amram, and *Baal Halakhot Gedolot*. (There are also traditions that report that R. Amram eliminated the blessing. This at least shows that the blessing existed in his time.) This blessing is also found in the *Siddur* of

---

14. Note that the blessing does not seem to have taken root in Yemenite communities.

15. R. Isaac Luria recited the blessing earlier, after the blessing of *malbish arumim*. This different location was picked up by some Kabbalistic and Hasidic *siddurim*.

16. See his *Bayit Ḥadash*, comm. to *OH* 46.

17. PP. 464–73.

Rav Saadia (d. 942), and in the poem of Ibn Ezra mentioned above. Chalamish collects dozens of other sources in the centuries thereafter that included the blessing.

Admittedly many were opposed to it as well, including eventually R. Yosef Caro. The main reasons for the opposition were: it is not found in Talmud and it is somewhat duplicative of *zokef kefufim*.

But this blessing did not survive (except in the Italian rite). Why not? Chalamish suggests that it did not survive because it did not receive the support of the ARI and his followers. It was not included in their *siddurim*.

* * *

Mitchell First is a personal injury attorney and Jewish history scholar. The former saps his strength, but writing weekly articles for the *Jewish Link of New Jersey* restores it.

3. Two Interesting Old Siddurim with *Aleinu*

Aleinu was part of the Rosh Hashanah *Musaf Amidah* for centuries before it began making its way into the end of the daily *Shaḥarit* service in France, England, and Germany in the 12th and 13th centuries.[18] One of the interesting questions in *Aleinu* research is when and why it first entered the end of the daily *Shaḥarit*.[19]

We have documentation that in 1171 the martyrs of Blois (a town in northern France) chanted *Aleinu* with their last breaths as they were being burned to death. Many scholars have theorized that this is what led *Aleinu* to penetrate the hearts of the people and be incorporated into the daily *Shaḥarit*.

But is this theory true? The earliest source that we have that records *Aleinu* at the end of daily *Shaḥarit* is a manuscript of *Maḥzor Vitry*

---

18. Regarding the migration of *Aleinu* into the Yom Kippur service, see Ezra Fleischer, *Eretz-Israel Prayer and Prayer Rituals as Portrayed in the Geniza Documents* (1988), pp. 126–128. (This work is in Hebrew.) See also the forthcoming work by Reuven Kimelman (see below).

19. I discussed this in *Roots and Rituals* (2018), pp. 32–37 ("*Aleinu*: A Rosh Hashanah Prayer that Migrated into the Daily Service").

which had been estimated to date to the 12th century. (*Maḥzor Vitry* is a work usually attributed to R. Simcha of Vitry, a town in northern France. R. Simcha was a student of Rashi.)

But can this manuscript be more precisely dated? After all, handwriting analysis is not that precise. Fortunately, this manuscript had some calendars attached to it. Two scholars, Sacha Stern and Justine Isserles, did a detailed study of this manuscript. Based on the calendars found in the manuscript, they were able to narrow down the date of the manuscript to between 1123/4 and 1154/5.[20]

This enables us to disprove the theory that *Aleinu* entered into the daily *Shaḥarit* as a result of the events in Blois in 1171. (Of course, the events of 1171 may have contributed to the **spread** of the custom to recite *Aleinu* in *Shaḥarit* daily.)

Once we reject the Blois-origin theory, what are we left with? Most likely, *Aleinu* was introduced into the daily *Shaḥarit* as a prayer meant to express a rejection of Christianity. Its introduction probably came as a response to the Crusades of 1096 or due to the general feeling of downtroddenness that the Jews of France felt while living as second-class citizens in a Christian land.[21]

Interestingly, there is an instruction given in *Maḥzor Vitry* that the daily *Aleinu* is to be recited silently. The reason for this instruction may be that the Jews understood that the Christians would view the prayer as an anti-Christian one.[22]

---

20. See their "The Astrological and Calendar Section of the Earliest *Maḥzor Vitry* Manuscript (MS ex-Sassoon 535)," *Aleph* 15.2 (2015), pp. 199–318.

21. See, e.g., *EJ* entry for *Aleinu*, last sentence, 2:559, my own article (see earlier footnote) and Reuven Kimelman: *The Rhetoric of Jewish Prayer: A Literary and Historical Commentary on the Prayerbook* (forthcoming).

22. But it can also be argued that the instruction merely reflects that the prayer was viewed as a new non-mandatory prayer at this time.

Whether *Aleinu* was originally composed as an anti-Christian prayer is a separate issue, and depends on when and where *Aleinu* was composed. Certain statements in the Jerusalem Talmud imply that *Aleinu* was composed by Rav, early 3rd century CE. See my *Esther Unmasked*, pp. 18, and 26–27. (See also the forthcoming work by Kimelman for further discussion on the date and authorship of *Aleinu*. He estimates a date in the 5th century CE.) As to Rav, although he gained prominence in Babylonia, he had been a student of R. Judah Ha-Nasi in Israel.

The scholar Israel Ta-Shema has a different theory to explain the entry of *Aleinu* into the daily *Shaḥarit*. See his *Ha-Tefillah Ha-Ashkenazit Ha-Kedumah* (2003), pp. 139–53.

An interesting sidelight on the *Maḥzor Vitry* manuscript I just discussed is that the manuscript was formerly known as "MS Sassoon 535," named for the previous owner David Sassoon. Since 1975, it has been owned by a private collector who wishes to remain anonymous. Thus Stern and Isserles refer to the manuscript as "MS ex-Sassoon 535"!

* * *

Now I am going to focus on a different old *siddur* with *Aleinu*, a manuscript known as Corpus Christie College 133, preserved in a library in England.

Today, if any of us went on a trip to collect business loans and took along a *siddur* that had blank pages at the end, we would feel intuitively that it would not be appropriate to use these blank pages to record the business loan payments that we collected. Fortunately, a Sephardic Jew who traveled to England with a *siddur* at the end of the 12th century did not share this view. Now I am going to tell the story of this fascinating *siddur.*

Based on the method of binding of the *siddur*, it can be guessed that it was produced in England. Its texts reflect the *nusaḥ* of northern France, which probably spread from there to England. This *siddur* includes *Aleinu* three times: once at the end of the daily *Shaharit,* once in the *Musaf Amidah* for Rosh Hashanah, and once in a different section.[23]

The *siddur* is undated, but the individual who acquired the *siddur* used the blank pages at its end to record the payments he received from his money-lending business while in England. He recorded

23. This section was a special prayer service conducted after the daily prayer service, modeled after the *maamadot* of mishnaic times. Ta-Shema believes that *Aleinu* first entered the daily *maamadot* service and from there entered into the regular daily *Shaḥarit*. I disagree because there is insufficient evidence to support this. His earliest evidence for *Aleinu* being in the daily *maamadot* service is this Corpus Christie College manuscript, which dates only to around the last quarter of the 12th century. See my next discussion.

these payments in Arabic. This suggests that he was a Sephardic Jew. The Arabic was written in Hebrew characters, as was their custom.

Scholars can give a rough estimate of a 12th-century date to the *siddur* based on the texts of the prayers, the paleography, and the method of binding. But can they be more precise?

Here is a translation of the first lines of what is written on the blank pages at the end:

> The year commencing first of July...
> all that I have since being here in England:
> from the Bishop of Exeter one mark, twice;
> also from the Bishop of Bath half a mark;
> also from the Count two and a half marks, twice;
> also from William Chemillé, three times four and a half marks;
> from the Bishop of Winchester five marks, twice;
> from Sir Walter Aud Luna half a mark, twice...
> from Rau Bruyerre five paid...

A certain scholar did the research on the individuals listed and was able to estimate a date for the *siddur*.[24] Not all of the individuals could be identified and dated. But regarding William de Chemillé, he served as the arch-deacon of Richmond and in other positions, and is known to have died in 1202. Since the payment seems to have been taken from him while he was alive, this *siddur* must have been composed in 1202 or earlier.

I mentioned at the outset that we have early evidence for *Aleinu* in daily *shaḥarit* in France, England and Germany. The evidence from France is Ms. ex-Sasson 535 that I discussed above, from the 2nd quarter of the 12th century. The recital of *Aleinu* at the end of daily

---

24. See Appendix 2, pp. 36–48 by Zefira Entin Rokéaḥ, in Malachi Beit-Arié, *The Only Dated Medieval Hebrew Manuscript Written in England* (1189 CE). (The title of this book is **not** describing manuscript Corpus Christie College 133, but a different manuscript. This has misled many into believing that the undated Corpus Christie College manuscript was dated to 1189 CE!) The main discussion of manuscript Corpus Christie College 133 is by Beit-Arié and is at Appendix 2, pp. 33–35. There is also discussion of the manuscript in various places in the earlier part of the work.

shaḥarit in England (evidenced by Ms. Corpus Christie College #133) was almost certainly an outgrowth of its recital in France. Its recital in Germany may simply have been an outgrowth of its recital in neighboring France, or its recital may have developed independently in Germany for other reasons. The earliest source for *Aleinu* in daily *Shaḥarit* in Germany is *Siddur Ḥasidei Ashkenaz*, a work which reflects the order of prayers of R. Judah he-Ḥasid (d. 1217).[25] The work was compiled by his students.

Up until now, I have been addressing *Aleinu*'s recital at the end of the daily *Shaḥarit* in Europe. But what was going on in Palestine and its surrounding areas? One of the most interesting finds from the Cairo Genizah is a Palestinian *siddur* which includes *Aleinu* in the middle of the daily *Pesukei De-Zimra*. (Genizah texts generally date from the 10th–13th centuries.) Almost certainly, *Aleinu* was introduced into their daily *Pesukei De-Zimra* because a prayer that begins with the theme of *shevaḥ* (*Aleinu le-shabeaḥ*) was thought of as appropriate for *Pesukei De-Zimra*, a section whose purpose is one of *shevaḥ* and which begins and ends with blessings which focus on the theme of *shevaḥ*. [26]

Finally, regarding the entry of *Aleinu* into the daily *Minḥah* and *Maariv* services in Europe, these are later developments.[27]

* * *

Mitchell First is a personal injury attorney and Jewish history scholar. He tries not to write notes on the meanings of words in the blank pages at the end of his *siddurim*. But you never know what might happen centuries later if he would!

25. Ed. Moshe Hirschler (1972), p. 124.

26. For all the references, see the article in my *Roots and Rituals*.

27. *Aleinu* entered the daily *Maariv* service not long after it entered the daily *Shaḥarit* service. This was several centuries before it entered the daily *Minḥhah* service. For all the earliest references to *Aleinu* in the daily *Maariv* and *Minḥah* services, see the forthcoming work by Kimelman.

4. The Origin of the Reading of the *Ḥamesh Megillot*

Today we are all familiar with the term *Ḥamesh Megillot*. We also probably imagine that there were once five books that were each called a *megillah* and that the custom or enactment to read each arose at the same time. But these are all misconceptions. The term *Ḥamesh Megillot* and our five readings are only the end result of a long evolutionary process.

The origin of the reading of Esther on Purim is an obligation set forth in Mishnah *Megillah*, and repeated in the Talmud. (The yearly ritual reading may even have long preceded the time of the Mishnah.)

In contrast, there is no mishnaic or talmudic obligation to read *Eikhah* on the 9th of Av. Rather, the Talmud (*Taanit* 30a) lists *Kinot* (=*Eikhah*) as one of the texts that we are **permitted** to read on the 9th of Av, despite the general prohibition of study on this day. (See also Jerusalem Talmud, *Shabbat* 16:1, referring to Amoraim who were studying *megillat Kinot* on the eve of the 9th of Av, after *Minḥah*.)

So at least with respect to Esther and *Eikhah*, a connection between the texts and the holiday is found in talmudic sources or earlier.

This is not the case with regard to the other three readings. For two of these, our earliest source is a post-talmudic work, *Soferim*. The *Encyclopaedia Judaica* entry on *Soferim* in the 1972 edition (15:81) viewed it as a compilation of Palestinian origin, dating from the middle of the 8th century. But according to more recent scholarship, the work was not completed until the ninth or tenth century.[28]

---

28. Admittedly, the material in the first nine of its twenty-one chapters is older, but the Babylonian Geonim never refer to the material in chapters 10–21. Scholars have also begun to regard it as a work compiled outside of Palestine, in an area under Palestinian influence such as Italy or Byzantium. See M.B. Lerner, "The External Tractates," in *The Literature of the Sages*, ed. Shmuel Safrai (1987), pp. 399–400, and Debra Reed Blank, "It's Time to Take Another Look at 'Our Little Sister' Soferim: A Bibliographical Essay," *Jewish Quarterly Review* 90 (1999), p. 4, n. 10.

The 2006 edition of the *Encyclopaedia Judaica* did not revise its entry to reflect the latest scholarship, and merely reprinted the 1972 entry. Unfortunately, this is typical of how this edition often proceeded.

There are three relevant passages in *Soferim*. 14:3 states briefly that for Ruth, *Shir Ha-Shirim*, *Eikah* and Megillat Esther one recites the blessing *al mikra megillah*. 14:18 refers to a practice of reading *Shir Ha-Shirim* on Pesaḥ and Ruth on Shavuot. The custom referred to was to read these at night on separate evenings, breaking the reading into two. Finally, 18:4 tells us that some read *sefer Kinot* (=*Eikhah*) in the evening and others read it in the morning. (Nowhere does *Soferim* provide the reason for the Ruth and *Shir Ha-Shirim* readings.)

Critically, *Soferim* does not refer to any practice of reading Kohelet on Sukkot.[29]

So even though we have a concept of *Ḥamesh Megillot* today, the origin of each ritual reading differs widely.

What is our earliest source for the practice of reading Kohelet on Sukkot? The introduction to Kohelet in the *Daat Mikra* edition (p. 5) is very vague on this issue, and I wondered for decades about it. Only in writing this article did I discover the answer. I will now explain.

The tannaitic *baraita* found at *Bava Batra* 14b lists the order of the *Ketuvim* as follows: **Ruth**, Sefer Tehillim, Iyyov, Mishlei, **Kohelet, Shir HaShirim**, **Kinot**, Daniel, **Megillat Esther**, Ezra, and Divrei Ha-Yamim. ("Ezra" included Nehemiah. They were joined as one book in this period.) As you can see, the books that we read today as *megillot* are scattered in this list.[30]

Now let us turn to the Aleppo Codex. This codex was composed in Tiberias in the early 10th century. After some periods in Jerusalem and Egypt, it made its way to Aleppo, Syria, and it was stored there from the 14th century until recent times. Large sections of the Aleppo Codex are now missing, due to anti-Jewish riots that broke out in Aleppo on Dec. 1, 1947 after the UN voted to partition Palestine. In 1958, what remained was smuggled to Israel.

In the Aleppo Codex, *Kohelet*, *Eikhah* and Esther are all missing

29. There are Rishonim who quote the passage at 14:3 with the word "Kohelet." But most likely the word "Kohelet" was not in the original passage.

30. Even though Jews were not yet using codices in this early period, they still needed guidance for an order in the event that they chose to pursue the economical practice of writing multiple books on one scroll. See Sid Leiman, *The Canonization of Hebrew Scripture* (1976), p. 162, n. 258.

now. But over the centuries, the Aleppo Codex was much studied, so we know how it presented the order of its books. Its order in Ketuvim was: Divrei Ha-Yamim, Tehillim, Iyyov, Mishlei, **Ruth, Shir HaShirim, Kohelet, Eikhah, Esther**, Daniel, Ezra-Nehemiah. All of our five ritual reading texts are grouped together! This strongly suggests that they were **all** read on our five holidays in the early 10th century in the locale where the Aleppo Codex was written, Tiberias.[31] So this 10th century source from Palestine is our earliest source documenting or at least strongly implying a Kohelet reading on Sukkot.

I mentioned earlier that *Soferim* itself was not compiled until the 9th or 10th century. So our implied reference to the reading of Kohelet on Sukkot is not much later than the estimated date of the compilation of *Soferim*. (I am willing to conjecture that after readings originated for Pesaḥ and Shavuot, it was decided that the third *regel*, Sukkot, needed a reading as well. Kohelet was perhaps the obvious choice from the remaining books of the Ketuvim.)

There is no reference at all to the Ruth, *Shir Ha-Shirim* and Kohelet readings in the Babylonian Geonim. The origin of all these readings seems to be Palestine.

With regard to the order of the five in the Aleppo Codex, they are presented in chronological order. Ruth, from the time of the Judges is listed first, followed by two works attributed to Shelomoh. *Eikhah* and Esther are listed last. Later, a different order is found in biblical manuscripts, the order the books were read in the calendar year. This order is *Shir Ha-Shirim*, Ruth, *Eikhah*, Kohelet, Esther. In modern times, the former is the order in the *Daat Mikra*. The latter is the order in the Soncino.

What about the term *megillah*? In the passage at *Bava Batra* 14b (a *baraita* which probably dates from the 2nd century CE), the term is only used in connection with Esther. Later, we find the term *megillah* used in connection with *Eikhah* in the Jerusalem Talmud: *megillat Kinot* (*Shabbat* 16:1).

I was going to suggest that the term *megillah* only came to be used with the three others **after** the custom to read them ritually developed.

---

31. See Roger Beckwith, *The Old Testament Canon of the New Testament Church* (1985), pp. 202–203.

But the book of Ruth is referred to as a *megillah* by an Amora named R. Zeira at *Ruth Rabbah* 2:14, and this reference would seem to precede the practice of reading Ruth on Shavuot. (But note that the term used here is not "Megillat Ruth." Rather, the statement is *megillah zo ein bah lo tumah ve-lo taharah...*)

Soferim 14:3 is very interesting. The passage states that for Ruth, *Shir Ha-Shirim*, *Eikah*, and Megillat Esther one recites the blessing *al mikra* ***megillah***. Yet the passage itself only used the term *megillah* for Esther!

I also want to mention a responsum of R. Moses Isserles (Rama). He explains that in his time (16th century), the practice was for *Shir Ha-Shirim*, Ruth, and Kohelet to be read by each individual. There was no public reading for these three.[32]

* * *

With regard to the word *megillah*, its root is גלל, which means "to roll." This root has always interested me because of the word בגלל. This word is found ten times in *Tanakh*. It always means something like "because of." I always thought it derived from גלל and this "roll" meaning, i.e., "as a result of the way things rolled." I have seen this idea in Solomon Mandelkern (p. 265). See also Rav S.R. Hirsch (comm. to Gen. 39:5). But it seems that this view is not accepted today and another approach, based on an Arabic cognate, is widely accepted. (I remain unconvinced.) I do wish to point out that it is widely accepted that סבה=reason derives from סבב=turn. Even in English, we explain a result by saying "turn of events" and "this is how things turned out."

* * *

Mitchell First is a personal injury attorney and Jewish history scholar. There are Jews all over the world who have fragments of the Aleppo Codex. He does not (yet) have one.

32. This and more is discussed by Rabbi Shlomo Yosef Zevin, *in Festivals in Halachah* [ArtScroll translation, Shavuos section], pp. 284–286.

5. The Meaning of אשרי העם ידעי תרועה (Psalms 89:16)

Right after the shofar is blown, we recite a set of verses. The first of these is *Ashrei ha-am yodei teruah*... from Psalms 89:16. Based on the time of the recital, we get the impression that the first four words mean: "Happy is the nation that knows how to blow the shofar on Rosh Hashanah."

A deeper interpretation of this phrase is found at *Leviticus Rabbah* 29:4. There it is explained that, unlike other nations, we are the nation that knows how to influence the Creator with a *teruah* on Rosh Hashanah and change Him from judging with *middat ha-din* to *middat ha-raḥamim*. This interpretation is followed by Rashi to Psalms 89:16 and cited in the ArtScroll Maḥzor.

But the context of the phrase in Psalms is not Rosh Hashanah. What is the plain sense of the phrase in Psalms?

The full verse is: *Ashrei ha-am yodei teruah, Hashem be-or panekha yehaleikhun.*

In order to get a handle on our phrase, we first have to address the meaning of the word תרועה. This word, in its various forms, appears over thirty times in *Tanakh*.

Almost all the time in *Tanakh*, it is used as a word derived from the root רוע, which means a "loud sound." But there is still a large ambiguity. The word can sometimes refer to a loud sound of war or threats. But other times, it can refer to a loud sound of joy or praise. (For the former, see, e.g., Josh. 6:5, Zeph. 1:16, Amos 1:14, and Jer. 4:19. For the latter, see, e.g., 1 Sam. 4:5, Job 8:21, Ezra 3:11, and Ps. 150:5.)

There is also at least one time in *Tanakh*, at Job 33:26, where the word derives from a different root: רעה. There it means something like "friendship, closeness."

So we have three possible understandings of our word תרועה: (1) loud sound of war or threats, (2) loud sound of joy or praise, and (3) friendship.

Let us see how some of our commentators have understood our phrase at Psalms 89:16.

The translation in the Soncino edition is: "Happy is the people that know the joyful shout."[33] The commentary explains by mentioning

33. This is taken from the 1917 Jewish Publication Society of America

various joyful sounds that occurred in our religion in ancient times: the sounding of trumpets, the sound of the shofar that acclaims a king, and the happy cries of pilgrims on festivals. It explains that "Israel has been privileged to know them all as God's people."

Daat Mikra views the word *teruah* as a symbol for the initial acceptance (=inauguration) of a king. See, e.g., Psalms chapter 47, and particularly verses 2–3. It suggests that the meaning of the verse is "How fortunate is the nation that knows how to inaugurate Hashem as a king." (The commentary does not mention Rosh Hashanah, and does not seem to be referring to the yearly *teruah*/symbolic acceptance of God as king that occurs on Rosh Hashanah.)

Radak focuses on the "war/threat" meaning of the word *teruah*. He believes the import of the phrase is something like: "Fortunate is the nation Israel who have God on their side and who can sound the *teruah* which symbolizes military victory over their enemies."

But a few of our commentators understand the verse as using the "friendship, closeness" meaning of the word *teruah*. They suggest a meaning like "Fortunate is the nation that knows how to be close to God." See, e.g., *Metzudat Tziyyon*, *Metzudat David*, and Malbim.

How do we decide which view to prefer? Often it helps to look at the parallel in the balance of the verse. Here the balance of the verse is: "They walk in the light of your face." But this phrase can be parallel to all of the suggestions above.

As mentioned earlier, the "closeness, friendship" meaning of the word *teruah* is a rare one. It is certainly the meaning of the word at Job 33:26. It also may be the meaning of the word at Numbers 23:21, a verse like ours, where the meaning of the word *teruah* is ambiguous. There we have a statement by Bilam: *Hashem elokav immo, u-teruat melekh bo*. Rashi and many other commentaries give *teruah* the rare "friendship, closeness" meaning there. (Note the first part of the verse: Hashem his God is **with him**.") But others disagree. [34]

So we may have two instances in *Tanakh* of *teruah* meaning "friendship, closeness" to balance out over thirty times where it means "a loud sound."

---

translation which the Soncino edition of the Prophets and Writings used for their translation.

34. This phrase is very ambiguous and deserves its own article.

So what should we conclude about the meaning of our phrase at Psalms 89:16? The problem with all the "loud sound" suggestions is that our phrase is too short. It does not give any clues as to what kind of loud sound the *teruah* is referring to. Perhaps the shortness of the phrase is evidence in support of the "friendship, closeness" meaning! In this meaning, the phrase did make its point in those four brief words.

On the other hand, *teruah* with the meaning "friendship, closeness" is the rarer meaning. Moreover the next verse, 89:17, begins with the following phrase: *be-shimkha* ***yegilun*** *kol ha-yom* (=in your name they rejoice all day). This also points in favor of the "loud sound of joy" meaning at 89:16.

So unfortunately I cannot leave you with a clear conclusion.

It bears repeating that the biblical terms for Rosh Hashanah are *yom teruah* and *zikhron teruah*. (See Num. 29:1 and Lev. 23:24.) The various possible meanings of *teruah* raises the same issue of meaning there. (In that case, because of the presence of the word *zikhron*, a word that often has a sound-related meaning, the "friendship/closeness" meaning is less likely.) I addressed the meanings of *yom teruah* and *zikhron teruah* in my *Roots and Rituals* (2018), pp. 197–200. As I wrote there, one reasonable interpretation of *yom teruah* interprets it as a day of a loud, ominous sound (made by the shofar) that introduces a preparatory period of ten days before Yom Kippur. Something like this is stated by Rambam in his *Moreh Nevukhim*, part III, ch. 43, p. 353 (Friedlander edition).

* * *

I mentioned earlier that there is a root רעה that means "friendship, closeness" (i.e., to be a friend to, be close to). These three-root letters also have the meaning "to pasture/tend to animals." A fundamental issue is whether these two meanings have a common origin. Perhaps the verb originally meant "tending to animals" and then expanded to "befriending humans," or perhaps vice versa. Over the centuries, many believed one or the other of these scenarios. But nowadays the majority view rejects any common origin.[35]

When I think about this issue, I am always reminded of a humorous scene from a movie made by a famous comedian in 1972. (I do not

35. Arabic lacks the "friendship, closeness" meaning.

wish to mention his name.) This section of the movie was a brief story of a man who fell in love with a sheep. After they surprisingly broke up (I don't recall the reason offered in the movie!), the man was sitting forlornly on the outside steps of his building. Usually rejected lovers are portrayed as sitting on outside steps while consoling themselves by drinking from a bottle of alcohol. But in this comedy, the man was depicted sitting on outside steps and consoling himself by drinking from a bottle of "Woolite"!

* * *

Mitchell First is a personal injury attorney and Jewish history scholar. He keeps himself busy writing articles for the *Jewish Link* and books for Kodesh Press, and has not been to a movie in 20 years. That's why he can only refer to movies from decades ago!

6. Who Authored the Prayer ונתנה תקף?

We have all heard the story of this prayer and R. Amnon of Mainz in the 10th century. The story is found in the *Or Zarua* (=R. Isaac of Vienna, c. 1180–1250), "Laws of Rosh Hashanah," sec. 276. He tells us that he found it in the writings of R. Ephraim of Bonn. The latter lived in the 12th century. The story is not found in any other early source.

R. Ephraim tells us that R. Amnon of Mainz was a *gadol ha-dor, ashir u-meyuḥas*, *yefeh to'ar* and *yefeh mareh*. After repeated attempts by a הגמון (=high-ranking Christian general? bishop?) to persuade R. Amnon to accept Christianity, R. Amnon finally asked for three days to consider the matter. He did this just to put him off, but he immediately regretted doing it. R. Amnon failed to appear at the appointed time three days later and was brought in by force. Asked why he had failed to keep his promise, R. Amnon pleaded guilty and requested that his tongue be cut out for not refusing at once and giving the impression that he was considering the conversion. The *hegmon* replied: "Not your tongue, but your legs, which did not bring you at the agreed time." R. Amnon's legs were amputated and he was tortured further and then sent home. Soon it was Rosh Hashanah and he asked to be brought to the synagogue and placed next to the *hazzan*. When it was time for the *Kedushah* prayer, he recited *U-Netanneh Tokef*. When he finished, he expired. Three days later he appeared in a dream to R. Kalonymus b. Meshullam (c. 1000) and taught him the prayer, and asked him to circulate it throughout the Diaspora.

Do we know anything else about this R. Amnon? Did he really author this prayer, as the story implies?

Jewish scholarship can now contribute something on the second of these issues.[36] In the Cairo Genizah, a manuscript was discovered that included *U-Netanneh Tokef* next to a set of other *piyyutim* by Yannai. Yannai was a *paytan* in Palestine who was earlier than R. Eleazar Kallir. There are traditions (not necessarily reliable) that he was the teacher of Kallir. In recent decades, scholarship has been able to estimate Kallir's lifespan as 570–640 CE. If Yannai was the teacher of Kallir, he would have lived a generation before this. But perhaps he lived a few generations earlier. In any event, most scholars today believe that Yannai was the author of *U-Netanneh Tokef*.

Thereafter, there was another important find in the Genizah related to our question: a *piyyut* by Kallir that took the words of *U-Netanneh Tokef* and enlarged upon each line. *Piyyut* expert Shulamit Elitzur has concluded, "This clearly shows that while [Kallir] was not the composer of *U-Netanneh Tokef*, he was familiar with it and it was significant enough in his lifetime that he felt it worthy of being adapted and enlarged upon."[37]

So it turns out that our *piyyut* was authored in Palestine several hundred years before R. Amnon! Based on this, some scholars disbelieve the R. Amnon story in its entirety. Others suggest that the lesson of the story is only that R. Amnon introduced the *piyyut* into the Ashkenazic world.

What do we know about this R. Amnon of Mainz? Actually, nothing

36. The *EJ* entry "Amnon of Mainz," 2:861, published in 1972, had already included the following about *U-Netanneh Tokef*: "it is found in old liturgical manuscripts and in *genizah* fragments. It apparently derives from a very early Palestinian prayer which was later attributed to Amnon."

37. See the post on seforimblog.com of Nov. 20, 2017, reprinted with permission from *Ami Magazine* #337, Oct. 4, 2017. See also her 2014 book with Michael Rand on the Rosh Hashanah *piyyutim* of Kallir, pp. 155–60 and 271–89.

aside from this story! Scholars have observed that "Amnon" is not a name from Germany but a name from Italy. So perhaps he came from Italy (where he may have learned the *piyyut*, due to the influence of Palestinian practices there) and then taught it to German Jewry.

It is also important to point out that the *piyyut* preceding Kedushah has four sections. It seems that what was originally recited, for several hundred years, were these four sections, all composed by Kallir. But the last section, the one that ultimately leads into the Kedushah (the *siluk*), was one in which the angels criticized the Jewish people. It has been suggested that after the First Crusade at the end of the 11th century, *U-Netanneh Tokef* replaced this last section, as it fit better with the mood of the post-crusade Rhineland communities. (As we all know, it includes language such as: "who shall live?" and "who shall die?") As Rabbi Kenneth Brander writes: "It did not seem appropriate to introduce *Kedushah* with a critique of the Jewish people by the angels when Jews were actively sacrificing their lives and the lives of their families.... "[38]

One grammatical point: I always thought that the word נתנה came from the root נתן=give. But instead the root of the word נתנה is תנה=tell. The initial נ just indicates: let **us** tell.

What is most interesting is that one thousand years later Menachem Begin cited the R. Amnon story in his negotiations at Camp David with President Carter. Carter wanted Begin to discuss the issue of dividing Jerusalem, but when Carter broached the topic, Begin related our story to him. The lesson of the story was that R. Amnon regretted having done anything at all that might be interpreted as considering the unthinkable. Carter understood that Begin was making it clear that he would not make R. Amnon's mistake. Carter shared the story with Sadat and the issue of Jerusalem was dropped.[39]

* * *

Mitchell First is a personal injury attorney and Jewish history scholar.

---

38. See his article in *Mitokh Ha-Ohel*: *Tefillot Yom Tov* (2017) pp. 75–86, at p. 82. For further reading on this entire topic, see the article by Avraham Frankel in *Tziyyon* 67 (2002), pp. 125–138.
39. See Daniel Gordis, *Menachem Begin: The Battle for Israel's Soul* (2014), pp. 173–74.

He was thinking that if we allow for the possibility that the R. Amnon story never happened, perhaps the story arose just so that Begin could cite it to Carter and keep Jerusalem off the table!

7. "If I Forget You Jerusalem..." (Psalms 137:5)

Psalms 137:5 reads: אם אשכחך ירושלם תשכח ימיני. But what do the last two words mean? Note that that second to last word is תשכח, not אשכח.

On the simplest level, *tishkaḥ yemini* means "**my right [hand] shall forget**." But forget what? It seems like the *ikar ḥaser min ha-sefer* here!

Many take the approach that the meaning is: "**My right hand shall forget its musical skills.**" One who adopts this approach is the Radak. Note that for most people it would be the right hand that strums the strings of the harp.

To understand the rationale for this approach, let us look at the preceding verses. Verse 2 reads: "On the willows there [in Babylon], we hung up our harps." In verse 3, those that led them captive ask them to "sing us one of the songs of Zion." In verse 4, the Israelite (or Levite) response is: "How can we sing a song of God on foreign lands?" Then comes our verse 5.

But let us look at verse 6 that begins *tidbak leshoni...*: "Let my tongue adhere to my palate if I fail to recall you." This implies that verse 5 may not be limiting itself to loss of musical skills. A loss of speaking ability may be implied here as well. (A response might be that verse 6 is only alluding, in an exaggerated manner, to a singing problem.)

A different approach to our verse is: "**My right hand shall forget its skills in general**." Many understand the verse this way. See, for example, the *Daat Mikra*: *tishkaḥ et pe'uloteha*, and Rav S.R. Hirsch: "all the skills which my hand had known heretofore."

A common English translation of our verse is "let my right hand forget its cunning." Those who translate in this way are merely adopting the King James version of the early 17th century. At that time, "cunning" just meant "ability." So this common English translation is agreeing with the approach just suggested.

What other ways are there to understand our verse?

- Some understand *tishkaḥ* as "become paralyzed," or "cease to function." In this way, there is nothing missing from the end of the verse. But these are not the simplest understandings of *tishkaḥ*.
- There is a Hebrew root כחש that has the meaning "become lean, wither." Some have suggested that this is the meaning of our word here, as perhaps כחש developed the variant שכח.[40] But this seems very farfetched.[41]
- "Let my right hand be forgotten." See, e.g., Pseudo-Rashbam on the site mg.alhatorah. [42]

  Tishakhaḥ would be the passive (*nifal*) form. Our verse has *tishkaḥ*? Well, that is pretty close. We can understand how the former might have evolved into the latter by the time of the Masoretes. If one goes through the entire *Tanakh*, there are often times when the Masoretes use a grammatical form that does not seem to be correct. In these instances, they were perhaps trying to vocalize the word to reflect common speech.

  But contextually does the passive stem make sense here? "If I forget Jerusalem, let my right hand be forgotten." Forgotten by me? Perhaps forgotten by God is better, the implication being that God will not help my hand do its normal activities. (For the latter, see the view of Ḥakhmei Tzarfat at mg.alhatorah.) But the fact that *tidbak* is not in the passive militates against *tishkaḥ* being an evolution from *tishakhaḥ*. *Tishkaḥ*... and *tidbak*... are parallel phrases here.

Our verse has the style of an oath, as it begins with אם.[43] Oaths are often elliptical in style, i.e., they don't finish their sentences and

40. This approach is mentioned as a possibility in the *Daat Mikra*. It is adopted by Robert Alter in his *The Book of Psalms: A Translation with Commentary* (2007).

41. This is not a *keves* versus *kesev* variant, but a more unusual one.

Regarding the root כחש, this is an unusual root. It has two different meanings "become lean" and "deceive, deny." I have seen it suggested that the latter is a sense enlargement of the former, but the connection seems farfetched.

42. This is the online *Mikraot Gedolot* of the site alhatorah.org.

43. This is pointed out by many. See, e.g., Rav S.R. Hirsch and *Daat Mikra*.

they leave out key elements.[44] With this in mind, we should be able to accept the "forget its musical skills" and "forget its skills" approaches expressed above. We should simply imagine that the text has three dots at the end of the verse.

* * *

A separate issue is who is speaking in verse 5. Normally we would understand the speaker as the Israelites or Levites. But the Targum understands God as speaking here, and responding to the Israelite/Levite affirmation of verse 4 that they could not sing a song of God on foreign soil. As ArtScroll Tehillim (ArtScroll *Tanakh* Series) explains the Targum: "God's Holy Spirit responded to Israel's proclamation of faith and declared: 'If I forget Jerusalem, I will forget my right hand.'" (But as I mentioned at the outset, the verse does not use the word אשכח.)

With regard to Rashi, he writes only briefly on our verse: *knesset Yisrael omeret ken*. He is writing this to disagree with the Targum. But he does not explain how he himself understood the verse.

* * *

In Aramaic, the root שכח means "common," "everyday." This is almost the opposite of the Hebrew meaning. This is probably just coincidence. But over the centuries the Aramaic meaning has worked its way into Hebrew. For example, in modern Hebrew שכיח means "common" and שכיחות means "frequency."

* * *

In his book *Power and Principle*,[45] Zbigniew Brzezinski (National Security Adviser to President Carter) writes that Menachem Begin said the following to him while they were talking a walk together at Camp David: "My right eye will fall out, my right hand will fall off before I ever agree to the dismantling of a single Jewish settlement." From Brzezinski's account, it does not appear that he understood what Begin was alluding to![46]

* * *

44. See, e.g., 2 Sam. 3:35.
45. (1983), p. 263.
46. See Gordis, *Menachem Begin*, p. 173.

Mitchell First is a personal injury attorney and Jewish history scholar. He recalls a writer from the 1970s joking about Brzezinsky's first name: If someone says "Zbig," the proper response is "Something caught in your throat?"

Abbreviations of Frequently Cited Sources

Menaḥem Zevi Kaddari, *Millon Ha-Ivrit Ha-Mikrait* (2006). Cited as "M.Z. Kaddari."

Ernest Klein, *A Comprehensive Etymological Dictionary of the Hebrew Language for Readers of English* (1987). Cited as "E. Klein."

Ludwig Koehler and Walter Baumgartner, *The Hebrew & Aramaic Lexicon of the Old Testament* (1995, revised edition). Cited as "Koehler-Baumgartner."

Marcus Jastrow, *A Dictionary of the Targumim, the Talmud Babli and Yerushalmi, and the Midrashic Literature* (1903). Cited as "M. Jastrow."

Hayim ben Yosef Tawil, *An Akkadian Lexical Companion For Biblical Hebrew* (2009). Cited as "H. Tawil."

Solomon Mandelkern, *Heikhal Ha-Kodesh* (1896). Cited as "S. Mandelkern."

Francis Brown, S.R. Driver, and Charles A. Briggs, *A Hebrew and English Lexicon of the Old Testament* (1906). Cited as "Brown-Driver-Briggs."

I also frequently cited to *Theological Dictionary of the Old Testament.* This is a 15-volume work which spanned the years 1974–2006. Each article is by a separate author. Cited as "*TDOT.*"

* * *

All citations to *The Complete ArtScroll Siddur* are to the third edition (1990).

All citations to the *Encylopaedia Judaica* are to the 1972 edition.

All translations from Josephus are from the Loeb Classical Library edition.

I also frequently cited to balashon.com, an excellent site on the etymology of Hebrew words, ancient and modern, by David Curwin of Efrat.

Corrections to *Roots and Rituals*

P. 35: *old* should be *od*

P. 42: Here I wrote that an origin of for the prayer *Ha-Noten Teshuah* in pre-expulsion Spain was unlikely. It turns out that the prayer did have its origin in pre-expulsion Spain. In fact, the earliest reference we have for it is a prayer for King Ferdinand v, the king who later expelled the Jews. See Aharon Arend, *Pirkei Meḥkar Le-Yom Ha-Atzma'ut* (1998), p. 182.

P. 76: The reference to the Letter of Aristeas should be removed. The passage should read: "Also, the Septuagint is preferable because of the tradition about the miracle that occurred: the translators translated separately, but...." I thank Michoel Chalk for pointing out my error to me.

P. 100: In discussing the root חלם, I stated that there are two times in *Tanakh* that there are words from this root that mean something like "healthy" and "strong." I would like to add that the word חלמיש, found five times in *Tanakh*, also perhaps derives from this root. It means "hard stone." Other examples of nouns in *Tanakh* that have *shin* added as a suffix include: חרמש, עכביש and רטפש. See S. Mandelkern, pp. 398 and 1090.

P. 144: Here I implied that שאול with its "netherworld" meaning was not found in other ancient languages unless they were derived from Hebrew. I was basing myself in part on *EJ* 2:996 which has: "The term does not occur in other Semitic languages, except as a loan word from the Hebrew *She'ol*...."

But in 1967, at Deir Alla (= probably the biblical "Succot," about eight kilometers east of the Jordan River), archaeologists found an inscription describing visions of a "Bilam son of Beor," who is described as a *ḥozeh* (seer) of the gods. Its language is a dialect with a mix of Aramaic and Hebrew. The text can be dated to around 800 BCE. Here the reading שאול has been conjectured two times. In one, we have part of the word. The other is a conjecture based on its proximity to the other.

P. 160: "Yet in other ancient sources they are called "Chaldeans." This should be: "In Akkadian, these people are called *kaldu*."

P. 202: "Esau" should be "Jacob." I thank Jonathan Tavin for pointing this out to me.

P. 227: Here I erroneously assumed that *matzah* in early biblical times was flat and dry. But before we can determine the etymology of the word, we must determine, to the best of our ability, what *matzah* would have looked like in its earliest form when the name for it would have arisen. I thank Michoel Chalk for pointing out my error.

P. 243, n. 385: I retract what I wrote that התאוה meant "continually desire." I have given a much better explanation for the *hitpael* in the article on the root חמד in this book.

Corrections to *Links to Our Legacy*

Page 6: (*Berakhot* 1:1) should be: (*Berakhot* 1:1 and *Yoma* 3:2)

Page 8: I listed four approaches that Rashi mentioned. Based on the manuscript evidence at AlHatorah.org, most likely the last was not in the original comment of Rashi and was added by others.

Pages 23–24: Here I wrote that in the *Mekhilta* there was a suggestion that *taavah* is *be-lev* while *ḥimud* is *be-maaseh*. I wrote this because the English translation of the work of Nehama Leibowitz cited such a passage in the name of the "Mekhilta." When I could not find the passage in the standard *Mekhilta* (*Mekhilta of R. Yishmael*), I found that the Hebrew edition of this article by Leibowitz assigned the passage to *Mekhilta of R. Shimon Bar Yoḥai* and that Rabbi D.Z. Hoffmann included this passage in his edition of *Mekhilta of R. Shimon Bar Yoḥai*, published in 1905.

But *Mekhilta of R. Shimon Bar Yoḥai* is an ancient work that was lost and had to be reconstructed from citations elsewhere. Scholars now realize that Hoffmann was overly reliant on *Midrash Ha-Gadol* in his reconstruction. The later and more conservative reconstruction by J.N. Epstein and E.Z. Melamed (1955) did not include the above passage.

Page 58: I wrote regarding Lamentations 1:1 that the import of this verse is that the former "princess of the provinces" is now being humiliated by forced labor of its people. (Also, at note 171, I commented that there is no evidence of forced labor of the Jews exiled to Babylonia.) But more likely, the import of the verse is only that the former "princess of the provinces" was now as low and humiliated as a forced laborer. I thank Michael Alweis for pointing this out to me.

Page 65, item 6: I discussed the story of Moses' raised hands more fully in *Words for the Wise* (2022), pp. 83–86.

Pages 87–91: There are a few mistakes in this article and a few statements that need to be improved. Rather than itemize them, I point out that the mistakes have been corrected and the article has been improved and expanded. It will be published in *Ḥakirah* volume

33 (forthcoming): "Did the Israelites Eat Matzah While They Were Slaves?"

Page 215: The instruction that the *Aleinu* in *shaḥarit* is to be recited silently (בלחש) is not in the earliest manuscript of *Maḥzor Vitry.* It is in some of the later manuscripts. (Here I was misled by a statement by I. Ta-Shema at p. 140.)

Page 223: I wrote that at Job 33:26 *teruah* means something like "friendship, closeness." But the meaning of *teruah* here is much disputed. See *Daat Mikra* for various views. Many view it as parallel to יעתר (a synonym for prayer) earlier in the verse. But *Daat Mikra* does mention ברצון as one possible interpretation, parallel to the וירצהו in the earlier part of the verse. See also the interpretation of Malbim.

Mitchell First,
January 2023

www.ingramcontent.com/pod-product-compliance
Lightning Source LLC
Chambersburg PA
CBHW021356090426
42742CB00009B/878

9781947857667